Archaeological Concepts
for the Study of the Cultural Past

Foundations of Archaeological Inquiry

James M. Skibo, series editor

Archaeological Concepts for the Study of the Cultural Past

Edited by Alan P. Sullivan III

The University of Utah Press
Salt Lake City

FOUNDATIONS OF ARCHAEOLOGICAL INQUIRY
James M. Skibo, editor

 The Defiance House Man colophon is a registered trademark
of the University of Utah Press. It is based on a four-foot-tall,
Ancient Puebloan pictograph (late PIII) near Glen Canyon, Utah.

12 11 10 09 08   1 2 3 4 5

LIBRARY OF CONGRESS CATALOGING-IN-PUBLICATION DATA

Sullivan, Alan P.
   Archaeological concepts for the study of the cultural past / edited by
Alan P. Sullivan, III.
      p. cm.
   Includes bibliographical references and index.
   ISBN 978-0-87480-922-0 (cloth : alk. paper) — ISBN 978-0-87480-916-9
(pbk. : alk. paper)   1. Archaeology—Philosophy.   2. Archaeology—
Methodology.   3. Ethnology—Philosophy.   4. Ethnology—Methodology.
5. Archaeology—United States.   6. United States—Antiquities.   7. Indians
of North America—Antiquities.   8. Prehistoric peoples.   9. Antiquities,
Prehistoric.   I. Title.
   CC72.S85 2008
   930.1—dc22   2007049771

Contents

Figures

Tables

1

Forward to the Cultural Past

ALAN P. SULLIVAN III

American archaeology tends to follow the interests of anthropology.
CLEMENT W. MEIGHAN

REVISITING ARCHAEOLOGICAL EPISTEMOLOGY

Clement W. Meighan's simple declarative sentence succinctly captures a century-old institutionalized relationship whose epistemological, methodological, and pedagogical consequences have managed to elude serious and sustained scrutiny. Seizing this unexploited opportunity, the contributors to this volume explore ways to approach the study of the cultural past that are built on concepts, methods, or problems that did not originate in cultural anthropology. This purpose may seem a little odd at first until one stops to consider why it might be not only interesting but also necessary to inquire about how archaeologists acquire knowledge about ancient behavior, organization, and technology. Such an exercise might prove interesting because it stands a chance of revealing inadequacies in archaeological practice that inhibit the discovery of aspects of the cultural past that are ethnographically unprecedented (Binford 2006; Wobst 1978). This sort of epistemological rethinking is necessary because we now have learned enough to realize that the phenomena archaeologists study (e.g., piles of fire-cracked rock) have little in common with the phenomena that other sorts of anthropologists investigate (e.g., kinship; Aberle 1987; Leach 1973; Melt-

zer 1979:654; Murray 1999:12). Hence, compelling reasons have emerged to warrant the development of lexicons, methods, and theories that are appropriate for the archaeological study of the cultural past (Clarke 1973).

Historically, students in North American anthropology departments who are fortunate enough to have the opportunity to enroll in an autonomous course in archaeological theory likewise have, with few exceptions, invariably taken a swarm of ethnography courses beforehand (McVicker 1989:113). Consequently, those students, particularly those who ultimately become practicing archaeologists, have been instilled (some would say indoctrinated) with at least three notions regarding the relation of archaeology to cultural anthropology. First, far from being simply a subfield of anthropology, archaeology is a subfield of cultural anthropology (Plog and Plog 1997:218; Woodbury 1963:225) or, even more narrowly, a type of prehistoric ethnography (Spaulding 1988). Second, archaeological theory is dependent upon or, at the least, heavily informed by anthropological theory (Schoenwetter 1981; see especially Spaulding 1968:37–39), which itself has a weighty ethnographic component (Wobst 1978:303). And third, ethnographic analogy is indispensable for the interpretation of archaeological data (Chang 1967:229;

David and Kramer 2001:43–54; Gould and Watson 1982:359), an assertion that is responsible in large measure for the invocation that "New World archaeology is anthropology or it is nothing" (Phillips 1955:246–247; cf. Willey and Phillips 1958:2).[1]

Furthermore, under the paradigm of American anthropological archaeology, which is the strain that is most dependent on cultural anthropology, it is widely regarded that, to enhance the reliability of their interpretations of archaeological data, archaeologists should be exposed to a broad range of ethnographic and ethnological studies (Boas 1902; Meskell 2002:199; Woodbury 1973:313). The logic of this position was unassailable to William D. Strong, who in his article "Anthropological Theory and Archaeological Fact" (1936:363) argued that archaeology can "never be fully perceptible to one not thoroughly familiar with the major results and techniques of ethnology"—a position reaffirmed by Elman R. Service (1964) a generation later in "Archaeological Theory and Ethnological Fact" (see also Bullen 1947:133).

These developments, which are entwined with the establishment of anthropology departments at American universities (Pinsky 1992), clearly distinguish the training of New World archaeologists from their Old World counterparts (Gosden 1999; Killick, this volume). They have produced, as well, a tension that affects the practice of archaeology (McVicker 1992). Inter-subfield tension (see VanPool and VanPool 2003 on paradigmatic tensions *within* archaeology) has arisen because the phenomena that archaeologists typically examine—such as variation in anthropogenic sediments (Goldberg, this volume), depositional contexts and their contents (Stein, this volume), lithic artifact form and assemblage diversity (Dibble, this volume), and artifact density (Sullivan, this volume)—are alien to cultural anthropologists (Yengoyan 1985). Hence, as Geoffrey A. Clark (1987:31) cogently summarized the situation two decades ago, "What we have now, and have always had in place of archaeological theory, is a partial and eclectic, at times even idiosyncratic, dependence upon selected aspects of social anthropology." Because of its theoretical dependence upon cultural anthropology, archaeologists have, until recently, rarely given much thought to how variation arises and is expressed in the archaeological record (e.g., Binford 1983; Schiffer 1987; Sullivan, this volume). In addition, interpretations are constrained by units of observation and analysis that have been imported from cultural anthropology (e.g., Kolb and Snead 1997), which is a situation that clouds the thoughtful consideration of ethnographically unprecedented social formations (Dunnell 1982; Gibbon 1984:311–325). Finally, the most deleterious, long-term effect of this dependence has been the stultification of archaeological theory. Consequently, archaeologists have been slow to develop effective methodological tools to assess the effects of equifinality on the origins of archaeological phenomena (Trigger 2006:440; see chapters by Enloe and by Deal, this volume), among other problems (Sullivan 2007). In essence, anthropological archaeology is an exemplification of what Manfred Eggert (1976:57) boldly calls the "fallacy of prehistoric archaeology as cultural anthropology."

CONCEPTS FOR INVESTIGATING THE CULTURAL PAST

The chapters in this volume represent a range of thinking regarding how the tension between archaeology and cultural anthropology might be profitably engaged (cf. Gillespie and Nichols 2003). For instance, James Enloe (an Old World Paleolithic archaeologist) and Michael Deal (a New World archaeologist and ethnoarchaeologist) analyze disparate phenomena —Late Paleolithic alluviated occupation surfaces and recently abandoned Mayan settlements, respectively—to evaluate whether archaeological interpretation can indeed be amplified by incorporating the findings of reference bodies of knowledge (e.g., mammalian anatomy and ethology) and archaeological ethnography (ethnoarchaeology). As they effectively demonstrate, learning about the cultural past often is a consequence of examining the degree to which the content of the archaeological record differs from the ethnographic and cross-cultural records (cf. Strong 1936: 363), and often necessitates the development of "in house" methods, such as spatial analysis of faunal-element refitting patterns (Enloe, this volume), or concepts, such as catastrophic vs. gradual modes of settlement abandonment (Deal, this volume).

The chapters by Kenneth L. Kvamme (a New World archaeologist), Harold L. Dibble (an Old World Paleolithic archaeologist), and Julie K. Stein (a New World geoarchaeologist) approach the study of phenomena—remotely sensed anomalies in and on the Earth's surface, lithic artifacts and assemblages, and archaeological stratigraphy, respectively—that have no counterparts in cultural anthropological research. In these cases, the units of analysis (e.g., spatial distributions of remanent magnetism), the methods (e.g., controlled experimentation), and the concepts (e.g., provenience) they promote represent autochthonous developments or applications within archaeology. Still, these authors are confident that the results of their research can contribute to the study of the cultural past because they are framed in terms of understanding ancient anthropogenic phenomena—their identification, origins, time relations, and sources of variation.

The chapters by me (a New World archaeologist), Paul Goldberg (a global geoscientist), and David Killick (an archaeological scientist who works in Africa) chart some contentious conceptual territory for anthropological archaeologists, particularly those trained in North America. These three chapters, in turn, contend that the historic dependence of archaeology on cultural anthropology has restrained theoretical development (e.g., considerations of what constitutes the archaeological record), perpetuated ignorance of the inferential significance of material routinely discarded in archaeological research (e.g., sediments), and placed American archaeologists at a strategic disadvantage with respect to the global archaeological community (e.g., funding for archaeological science). With compelling data, as well as personal experiences, these chapters illustrate the interpretive possibilities and pedagogical opportunities of an archaeology that is based on premises quite different than those that have shaped traditional American anthropological archaeology (Gumerman and Phillips 1978; Kohl 1981; Wiseman 2001).

FORWARD TO THE CULTURAL PAST

Alfred V. Kidder (1931:289) remarked, good-naturedly but nonetheless quite accurately, that "no archaeologist can ever bear to contemplate the magnitude of [their] probable error." Kidder's remark is not disingenuous because we have been operating for too long under the erroneous assumption that attributes of archaeological phenomena can somehow be rectified or corrected into strong inferences about the cultural past by engaging the ethnographic or cross-cultural records and employing analogical reasoning (Shelley 1999: 598–601). To the contrary, each of the subsequent eight chapters in this volume invites the reader to consider the advances in theory and method that arise from an independent archaeology, or at least an archaeology that is not dependent on cultural anthropology (cf. Embree 1987). More basically, these chapters showcase concepts, many inspired by the field's own internal problems (Chapman and Gaydarska 2007), that do not have to be referred to cultural anthropology for legitimacy or validation (Lyman 2007). With these understandings, the orthodox suggestion that "American archaeology must revisit its roots in the parent discipline of cultural anthropology" (Allison 1999:277) seems profoundly anachronistic. Looking forward instead, the contributors to this volume are committed to the alternative proposition that archaeology is conceptually poised to stake its claim as a science that, once released from the harness of cultural anthropology, has an enormous capacity to reveal aspects of the cultural past that are now unthinkable.

NOTE

1. Gordon R. Willey (1974:321) made this remarkable statement 16 years after the publication of *Method and Theory in American Archaeology* (Willey and Phillips 1958): "I once said that 'archaeology is anthropology or it is nothing.' I find this too restrictive now. Obviously, the anthropological approach has much to offer in archaeology, and it is the one I know best; but it is not the only road to everything worth knowing about the past."

REFERENCES CITED

Aberle, David F.
1987 What Kind of Science Is Anthropology? *American Anthropologist* 89:551–566.

Allison, John
1999 Self-Determination in Cultural Resource Management: Indigenous Peoples' Interpretation of History and of Places and Landscapes. In *The Archaeology and Anthropology of Landscape*, edited by Peter J. Ucko and Robert Layton, pp. 264–283. Routledge, London.

Binford, Lewis R.
1983 *In Pursuit of the Past: Decoding the Archaeological Record.* Thames and Hudson, New York.
2006 Bands as Characteristic of "Mobile Hunter-Gatherers" May Exist Only in the History of Anthropology. In *Archaeology and Ethnoarchaeology of Mobility*, edited by Frederic Sellet, Russell Greaves, and Pei-Lin Yu, pp. 3–22. University Press of Florida, Gainesville.

Boas, Franz
1902 Some Problems in North American Archaeology. *American Journal of Archaeology* 6:1–6.

Bullen, Adelaide K.
1947 Archaeological Theory and Anthropological Fact. *American Antiquity* 13:128–134.

Chang, K. C.
1967 Major Aspects of the Interrelationship of Archaeology and Ethnology. *Current Anthropology* 8:227–243.

Chapman, John, and Bisserka Gaydarska
2007 *Parts and Wholes: Fragmentation in Prehistoric Context.* Oxbow Books, Oxford.

Clark, Geoffrey A.
1987 Paradigms and Paradoxes in Contemporary Archaeology. In *Quantitative Research in Archaeology*, edited by Mark S. Aldenderfer, pp. 30–60. Sage Publications, New York.

Clarke, David L.
1973 Archaeology: The Loss of Innocence. *Antiquity* XLVII:6–18.

David, Nicholas, and Carol Kramer
2001 *Ethnoarchaeology in Action.* Cambridge University Press, Cambridge.

Dunnell, Robert C.
1982 Science, Social Science, and Common Sense: The Agonizing Dilemma of Modern Archaeology. *Journal of Anthropological Research* 38:1–25.

Eggert, Manfred H. K.
1976 On the Interrelationship of Prehistoric Archaeology and Cultural Anthropology. *Praehistorische Zeitschrift* 1: 56–60.

Embree, Lester
1987 Archaeology: The Most Basic Science of All. *Antiquity* 61:75–78.

Gibbon, Guy
1984 *Anthropological Archaeology.* Columbia University Press, New York.

Gillespie, Susan, and Deborah L. Nichols (eds.)
2003 *Archaeology Is Anthropology.* Archeological Papers No. 13. American Anthropological Association, Arlington, Virginia.

Gosden, Chris
1999 *Anthropology and Archaeology: A Changing Relationship.* Routledge, New York.

Gould, Richard A., and Patty Jo Watson
1982 A Dialogue on the Meaning and Use of Analogy in Ethnoarchaeological Reasoning. *Journal of Anthropological Archaeology* 1:355–381.

Gumerman, George J., and David A. Phillips, Jr.
1978 Archaeology beyond Anthropology. *American Antiquity* 43:184–191.

Kidder, Alfred V.
1931 The Future of Man in the Light of His Past: The View-Point of an Archeologist. *The Scientific Monthly* 32:289–293.

Kohl, Philip L.
1981 Materialist Approaches in Prehistory. *Annual Review of Anthropology* 10:89–118. Annual Reviews, Inc., Palo Alto, California.

Kolb, Michael J., and James E. Snead
1997 It's a Small World After All: Comparative Analyses of Community Organization in Archaeology. *American Antiquity* 62:609–628.

Leach, Edmund
1973 Concluding Address. In *The Explanation of Culture Change: Models in Prehistory,* edited by Colin Renfrew, pp. 761–771. University of Pittsburgh Press, Pittsburgh.

Lyman, R. Lee
2007   Archaeology's Quest for a Seat at the High Table of Anthropology. *Journal of Anthropological Archaeology* 26:133–149.

McVicker, Donald E.
1989   Prejudice and Context: The Anthropological Archaeologist as Historian. In *Tracing Archaeology's Past: The Historiography of Archaeology*, edited by Andrew L. Christenson, pp. 113–126. Southern Illinois University Press, Carbondale.

1992   The Matter of Saville: Franz Boas and the Anthropological Definition of Archaeology. In *Rediscovering Our Past: Essays on the History of American Archaeology*, edited by Jonathan E. Reyman, pp. 145–159. Avebury, Aldershot.

Meighan, Clement W.
1982   Environment and Explanation in Archeology. In *Culture and Ecology: Eclectic Perspectives*, edited by John G. Kennedy and Robert B. Edgerton. Special Publication No. 15. American Anthropological Association, Washington, D.C.

Meltzer, David J.
1979   Paradigms and the Nature of Change in American Archaeology. *American Antiquity* 44:644–657.

Meskell, Lynn
2002   Archaeologies of Identity. In *Archaeological Theory Today*, edited by Ian Hodder, pp. 187–213. Polity Press, Cambridge.

Murray, Tim
1999   A Return to the "Pompeii Premise." In *Time and Archaeology*, edited by Tim Murray, pp. 8–27. Routledge, New York.

Phillips, Philip
1955   American Archaeology and General Anthropological Theory. *Southwestern Journal of Anthropology* 11:246–250.

Pinsky, Valerie
1992   Archaeology, Politics, and Boundary-Formation: The Boas Censure (1919) and the Development of American Archaeology during the Inter-War Years. In *Rediscovering Our Past: Essays on the History of American Archaeology*, edited by Jonathan E. Reyman, pp. 161–189. Aldershot, Avebury.

Plog, Fred, and Stephen Plog
1997   Central Themes in Archaeology. In *The Teaching of Anthropology: Problems, Issues, and Decisions*, edited by Conrad P. Kottak, Jane J. White, Richard H. Furlow, and Patricia C. Rice, pp. 218–253. Mayfield Publishing Co., Mountain View, California.

Schiffer, Michael B.
1987   *Formation Processes of the Archaeological Record*. University of New Mexico Press, Albuquerque.

Schoenwetter, James
1981   Prologue to a Contextual Archaeology. *Journal of Archaeological Science* 8:367–379.

Service, Elman R.
1964   Archaeological Theory and Ethnological Fact. In *Process and Pattern in Culture: Essays in Honor of Julian H. Steward*, edited by Robert A. Manners, pp. 364–375. Aldine, Chicago.

Shelley, Cameron
1999   Multiple Analogies in Archaeology. *Philosophy of Science* 66:579–605.

Spaulding, Albert C.
1968   Explanation in Archeology. In *New Perspectives in Archeology*, edited by Sally R. Binford and Lewis R. Binford, pp. 33–39. Aldine, Chicago.

1988   Archaeology and Anthropology. *American Anthropologist* 90:263–271.

Strong, William Duncan
1936   Anthropological Theory and Archaeological Fact. In *Essays in Anthropology Presented to A.L. Kroeber*, edited by Robert H. Lowie, pp. 359–370. University of California Press, Berkeley.

Sullivan, Alan P., III
2007   Archaeological Anthropology and Strategies of Knowledge Formation in American Archaeology. In *Archaeological Anthropology: Perspectives on Method and Theory*, edited by James M. Skibo, Michael W. Graves, and Miriam Stark, pp. 40–56. University of Arizona Press, Tucson.

Trigger, Bruce G.
2006   *A History of Archaeological Thought*. 2nd ed. Cambridge University Press, Cambridge.

VanPool, Christine S., and Todd L. VanPool
2003   Introduction: Method, Theory, and the Essential Tension. In *Essential Tensions in Archaeological Method and Theory*, edited by Todd L. VanPool and Christine S. VanPool, pp. 1–4. University of Utah Press, Salk Lake City.

Willey, Gordon R.
1974   New World Prehistory: 1974. *American Journal of Archaeology* 78:321–331.

Willey, Gordon R., and Philip Phillips
1958   *Method and Theory in American Archaeology*. University of Chicago Press, Chicago.

Wiseman, James A.
2001   Declaration of Independence: The Case for Autonomous Archaeology Departments at American Colleges and Universities. *Archaeology* 54:10–12.

Wobst, Martin H.
1978   The Archaeo-Ethnology of Hunter-Gatherers or the Tyranny of the Ethnographic Record in Archaeology. *American Antiquity* 43:303–307.

Woodbury, Richard B.
1963   Purposes and Concepts. In *The Teaching of Anthropology*, edited by David G. Mandelbaum, Gabriel W. Lasker, and Ethel M. Albert, pp. 223–232. American Anthropological Association, Washington, D.C.

1973   Getting Round Archaeologists Out of Square Holes. In *Research and Theory in Current Archeology*, edited by Charles L. Redman, pp. 311–317. John Wiley and Sons, New York.

Yengoyan, Aram A.
1985   Digging for Symbols: The Archaeology of Everyday Material Life. *Proceedings of the Prehistoric Society* 51:329–334.

2

An Archaeological View of the Archaeological Record

ALAN P. SULLIVAN III

Almost infallibly the numerous potsherds that lie strewn superficially over the slopes of such mounds before any digging is done, give evidence of all the periods represented by the accumulated debris below. When the whole country has thus been methodically and thoroughly explored and the results have been properly tabulated and made available, we shall know infinitely more than we now do regarding the extent of occupation and the movements and distribution of population from period to period.

CARL W. BLEGEN

Of the many achievements of Carl W. Blegen, the towering figure of mid-twentieth century classical archaeology, one of the most enduring was his persuasive demonstration, to his excavation-addicted colleagues, that the interpretive potential of the Ancient World's surface archaeological record was substantial but largely unappreciated. Although Blegen was theorizing then without what some would consider the benefit of an anthropological framework (Renfrew 1980:289), contemporary archaeologists often ruminate about approaches for interpreting the archaeological record in terms of problems that cultural anthropologists typically study (e.g., contributions in Hodder 2002). Despite these and other efforts, the archaeological record, which arguably is the principal phenomenon that archaeologists worldwide employ to investigate the cultural past, has not received the protracted epistemological attention that many think it deserves (e.g., Clarke 1973; Pinsky 1992; Tainter 1998). In contributing to this ongoing but discontinuous dialogue (see be-

low), I focus on developing an internal view of the archaeological record—that is, one that is unrelated to or unconstrained by the conceptual frameworks that cultural anthropologists use to execute their research agendas (cf. Peregrine 2001). By examining a sample of relevant accounts, I show how perceptions of the cultural past can shift, often dramatically, when an archaeological view of the archaeological record, rather than an ethnographic or an ethnological view, guides research.[1]

CONCEPTUALIZING THE ARCHAEOLOGICAL RECORD: FIVE VIEWS

In one of the most original and explicit explorations of the concept of the archaeological record, Robert Ascher (1968) imagined that it represents the ever-increasing disorganization of information about a once-living human community. In Ascher's view, the archaeological record is a "cube below ground" that is a consequence of the actions of natural and cultural "agents" (1968:47). His is a dynamic view of the archaeological record's eternal formation—"change continues in the absence of people" (1968:44)—and one that requires archaeologists to understand and differentiate the historical effects of various causal factors. Ascher suggests that archaeologists focus on developing "descriptions of behavior and its products" (1962:360; cf. the "correlates" component of behavioral archaeology [LaMotta and Schiffer 2002]) that occur in those circumstances when communities are being transformed into or becoming "archaeological data" (Ascher 1961:324). These descriptions, according to Ascher, serve as the basis for advancing analogical arguments about aspects of the "ethnographic past" (Ascher 1968:52).

In a wide-ranging article that initiated the "Pompeii Premise" debate (Murray 1999), Lewis R. Binford (1981) discussed the goals of archaeology and the nature of the archaeological record (see also Binford 1977, 1987). Binford (1981:197) argued that "the time frame of ethnography is largely inappropriate for archaeological research" and that, consequently, archaeologists should focus instead on understanding the dynamics of past "cultural systems." Furthermore, in criticizing the research program of behavioral archaeology (Schiffer 1976) specifically, Binford (1981:197–198) asserted that the archaeological record is "most likely a structured consequence of the operation of a level of organization difficult, if not impossible, for an ethnographer to observe directly" but that is, nonetheless, disorganized —"a massive palimpsest of derivatives from many separate episodes." These remarks set up his view that the archaeological record, far from being (what Michael B. Schiffer considers) a distortion, consists of "matter transformed and organized during the process of energy use and entropy production" (Binford 1981:200; also Binford 1983:19)—a theoretical proposition that is not too dissimilar from Robert Ascher's. Methodologically, this middle-range strategy (Kosso 2001:52; Enloe, this volume) calls for inferring past and unobservable causes of contemporary statics by making "painstaking analogies between the record and the kinds of behaviors that might have generated it" (Sabloff et al. 1987:204).

According to this model, understandings of the formation of the archaeological record and interpretations of its variability are dependent on analyses of ethnographic or ethnological data (Binford 2001a, 2006; Johnson 2004:279–285; see also Speth 1990).

In 1983, Warren R. DeBoer attempted to resolve what he regarded as inadequate portrayals of the complexities regarding how "past behavioral systems" are transformed into "recovered residues" (1983:20–21). Concerned with how the archaeological record forms, DeBoer was dissatisfied with Schiffer's (1972: 157) distinction between *systemic context*, which refers to "the condition of an element [e.g., artifacts, energy] which is participating in a behavioral system," and *archaeological context*, which "describes materials which have passed through a cultural system, and which are now the objects of investigation of archaeologists," because he thought it was too general to be analytically useful. With the idea that the archaeological record is "a static and contemporary by-product of past behavior" consisting of "objects and distributions" (DeBoer 1983:30), DeBoer distinguished four types of assemblages—behavioral, discard, archaeological, and sample—and modeled in each instance how information about the composition of the antecedent assemblage is lost with the passage of time (see also Aberle 1987:556; Deal 1985:250–251). In a coincidental amalgam of Ascher's model (which he does not mention) and Binford's strategy, the implications of DeBoer's view of the archaeological record are that inferences about the cultural past are invariably weak as a result of entropy, artifact loss, and distribution smearing, and that, consequently, they must be justified by employing bridging arguments that incorporate relevant "expectations" drawn from ethnography and ethnoarchaeology (DeBoer 1983:27–30).

In 1985, Linda E. Patrik evaluated two conceptions of the archaeological record. Distinguishing a physical (or, passive) model from a textual (or, active [reactive]) model, Patrik (1985:36) enumerated sets of assumptions, properties, processes, meanings, and problems that are specific to each conceptualization. As a sign of the times, Patrik took great pains to ensure that the role of scientific laws is properly situated in the research agendas of processual and post-processual archaeologies, achieving in the end no grand resolution but concluding reasonably that each model is useful for depicting the intricacies of the inferential process in archaeology: the *physical model* for portraying how remains, principally artifacts, got to where they are found today, and the *textual model* for hypothesizing what they might have meant (symbolically) in the past (see also Jones 2002:17–22).

In his encyclopedic *Formation Processes of the Archaeological Record*, Michael B. Schiffer (1987:3) stated that the archaeological record "contains culturally deposited objects that are no longer part of an ongoing society." This view, like DeBoer's, is somewhat narrowly conceived because the archaeological record, by any reasonable account, is much more than a by-product of behavior. In addition to culturally deposited objects, the archaeological record contains objects that were not culturally deposited (e.g., Nash 1993), as well as non-objects, such as surfaces (Goldberg, this volume) and geophysical anomalies (Kvamme, this volume), that may be indicative of humans and their activities (Holliday 2004). Interestingly, a close reading of Schiffer's definitions of refuse types and abandonment processes (Deal, this volume) discloses that they are based on generalizations about contemporary human behavior, which serve as models of undistorted systemic-context phenomena (LaMotta and Schiffer 2002).

Discussion

These opinions about what constitutes the archaeological record resulted in controversies as to whether it is a fossilized representation or a distortion of past cultural systems or human behavior, disagreements over how to characterize the origins of and changes in assemblages of artifacts, assertions as to whether it is inert or dynamic, and debates over what kind of "evidence model" it represents (Wylie 2002). Paradoxically, since these deliberations and exchanges ended, somewhat abruptly 20 years ago, little attention has been directed to the concept of the archaeological record itself (for exceptions, see Bailey 2007; Murray 1999:15–22), which has promoted the perception that the aforementioned issues have somehow been resolved or no longer matter (Tainter and Bagley 2005).

Nonetheless, the five views are unified by a commitment to engaging the ethnographic and ethnological records, either directly through cross-cultural studies or by ethnoarchaeology, or indirectly by meta-analyses (Binford 2001b). That such a solution somehow would sanitize the archaeological record of its imperfections, thereby elevating its interpretive potential to that of the ethnographic record, is compromised by several factors (Simms 1992). First, it promotes a commitment to *presentism*, which assumes that the sources of archaeological variation do not differ in any profound or demonstrable way from the origins of contemporary cultural variation (Ingold 1992; Trigger 2006:26), thereby stifling consideration of ethnographically undocumented (unprecedented) aspects of the cultural past (Binford 1968:13; Jochim 1991; Wobst 1978). Second, it ensures an allegiance to *uniformitarianism* (Bailey 1983; see especially Moore 1994:931) and to argument by analogy, thereby increasing the likelihood of affirming the consequent (Gould and Watson 1982:372; Patrik 1985:46–47). Third, it provides no methods for assessing the effects of *equifinality* (Minnis 1992:121; Sullivan 1992), which only serves to perpetuate our ignorance about the causes of ambiguous archaeological variability (cf. Binford 1968:24; 2001b:675). Fourth, it enhances the likelihood that *Type II errors*, whereby false hypotheses about the origins of archaeological phenomenon fail to be rejected (or even considered), will continue to propagate (Sullivan 2007: 44; Goldberg, this volume). Fifth, it assumes that the results of cultural anthropological research are unassailable benchmarks to check or calibrate archaeological findings, despite emerging evidence that challenges the veracity of some ethnographic accounts (David and Kramer 2001:101; Porter and Marlowe 2007; Whitley 2007). Finally, archaeology is denied the opportunity to conceptualize the archaeological record in its own terms (Pinsky 1992: 177), which perpetuates the discipline's dependence on cultural anthropology (Dunnell 1982; Schoenwetter 1981; Willey and Phillips 1958:1).

BEYOND ETHNOGRAPHIC AND ETHNOLOGICAL VIEWS OF THE ARCHAEOLOGICAL RECORD

Encouragingly, disparate discourse about the nature of the archaeological record (e.g., Bailey 2007; Binford 1983; Clarke 1968:15; Dunnell 1989:43; Schiffer 1985) coheres in some fairly profound respects. The archaeological record is a contemporary phenomenon that is inconstant with respect to its content (composition), extent (the space it occupies), and exposures. In addition, the archaeological record is ambiguous with respect to its origins and, importantly, exists independently of archaeologists and their problem-led research designs. Despite these understandings, it is irrefutable, paradoxically, that the "archaeological record is an active construct of our assumptions and biases" (Tainter and Bagley 2005:69), which means that its properties and their interpretive potential are neither intrinsic nor evident (Andrews et al. 2000). Hence, even what might be considered the largely uncomplicated matter of encountering the archaeological record and documenting its variability is far from straightforward (Sullivan et al. 2007).

To make some headway with regard to these problems, I explore the usefulness of the following concepts. The concept of the *trace* refers to the introduction or concentration of matter onto surfaces, the modification or rearrangement of matter on surfaces, or the modification of surfaces themselves (Sullivan 1978). Anthropogenic traces are attributable to a variety of relatively well-known causes, such as differences in activities (functional variability), differences in identity (sometimes broadly glossed as "cultural" variability), differences in the duration and intensity of place-use (occupational variability), and differences in decisions related to the design of technology and the allocation of labor (organizational

variability). It is well established, further, that non-anthropogenic sources of variability affect the quantity and character of anthropogenic traces, as well as produce their own effects (Goldberg, this volume; Simmons 1998). Interaction among these independent trace-production contexts produces an astonishing degree of archaeological variability (Goldberg and Macphail 2006) that is constantly changing—hence, the archaeological record is anything but static.

In these terms, the *archaeological record* is the contemporary expression of the aggregate accumulation of traces, some of which are attributable to humans and their actions and some that are not (e.g., de la Torre and Mora 2004; Dibble, this volume). *Archaeological phenomena* are problem-specific (or problem-defined) traces that are encountered as anomalies in ecosystems, such as discontinuous densities of material across a surface (Ebert 1992) or elevated frequencies of wild plant pollen (Dincauze 2000), whose origins cannot be attributed to natural causes (Kvamme, this volume). The challenge for archaeologists is to parse traces according to their causal sources of variability in order to understand their origins and formation histories and, therefore, their suitability for addressing different problems. The following examples illustrate how these understandings affect the archaeological investigation of the cultural past.

COMPETING ACCOUNTS OF GRAND CANYON'S CULTURAL PAST

Beginning with Major John Wesley Powell's speculations regarding the origins of antiquities that were observed during his dramatic rowboat trips down the Colorado River in 1869 and 1872 (Dolnick 2001), the archaeology of the Grand Canyon has been interpreted principally in terms of Hopi ethnography (Euler 1969; Judd 1926:149; Powell 1875). Consequently, architectural remains in and around the canyon were thought to have been built and used by largely peaceful, energetic farmers who periodically engaged in "puebloan" ceremonies and other practices (Coder 2000; Haury 1931; Taylor 1958).

Douglas W. Schwartz's meticulous excavations during the late 1960s in the Inner Canyon and on the North Rim (Schwartz et al. 1979, 1980, 1981) did little to alter this picture, nor did Robert C. Euler's extensive surveys (Euler and Chandler 1978). In addition, results of a one-percent sample survey of the Upper Basin (Rice et al. 1980:24), which is located along the Grand Canyon's eastern South Rim (Figure 2.1), implied that abundant one-room and two-room masonry ruins there were related to extensive agricultural production (see also Effland et al. 1981:41) because of their resemblance to agricultural "field houses" that have been documented among the Southwest's puebloan societies (Mindeleff 1891; see also Kohler 1992; Moore 1978).

However, recent excavations of several one-room structures (Becher 1992; Whittlesey 1992), multiroom structures (Fugate 2003; Sullivan 1986), fire-cracked-rock piles (Sullivan et al. 2003), and other types of archaeological phenomena (Sullivan 1995, 2000a) in the Upper Basin have disclosed inconsequential archaeo-botanical and pollen evidence in support of the maize-dependency model (Sullivan and Ruter 2006). Paleoenvironmental studies, moreover, indicate that persistent manipulation of vegetation, principally by fire (Roos et al. in press; Sullivan 1996), increased the stability of a subsistence economy that was based primarily on the propagation and consumption of wild plants. Thus, the ancient occupants of the Grand Canyon were engaged in provisioning strategies and landscape-management practices that are not featured in nineteenth and twentieth century ethnographic accounts of the Hopi (Bradfield 1995).

BLEGEN OPERATIONALIZED

In order to appreciate the settlement dynamics that would have accompanied the efforts of these small-scale social formations (Gaines and Gaines 2000) to secure a livelihood by extensive wild plant husbandry and active landscape management, intensive survey (i.e., inter-surveyor interval = 10 m) of the Upper Basin was initiated in 1989 (Sullivan

et al. 2002). Because one objective was to record and measure the extent of ancient anthropogenic impacts to this upland ecosystem with interpretation-neutral taxa, the concept of the Mapping Unit (MU) was developed to designate relevant archaeological phenomena (Sullivan et al. 2007). The *site* taxon was eschewed because of its strong ethnographic connotations as well as its inappropriateness for documenting archaeological phenomena in metachronous landscapes (Dunnell 1992) such as the Upper Basin. MU, therefore, refers to a cluster of traces whose origins cannot be attributed to natural processes (Sullivan 2000b). In addition, to quantify variation among Upper Basin masonry structures, which were built, used, and abandoned between AD 900 and 1200 (Uphus 2003), information was secured on several autochthonous archaeological variables, such as artifact density (number of artifacts per 5 m diameter circle), number of room spaces, and room-block area (m²) because it has long been assumed that such measures register differences in occupational variability (e.g., perennial or seasonal [Preucel 1990]), functional variability (e.g., habitation or field house [Pilles 1978]), or organizational variability (e.g., center or satellite community [Varien 1999]).

Examination of Figures 2.2 and 2.3 reveals that one-room or two-room structures commonly disclose artifact densities that are greater than those of larger structures, and multiroom (> two rooms) structures may be smaller than single-room or two-room structures. Unsurprisingly, therefore, neither strong nor significant correlations occur among these variables (range of Kendall's tau b = .081–.144). These results imply that prehistoric Upper Basin settlements were characterized by dramatically inconstant occupation durations, a pattern that is attributable to highly variable relations between occupation mode (e.g., continuous vs. discontinuous) and abandonment mode (e.g., unplanned vs. gradual; Deal, this volume). Consequently, a few comparatively larger structures (i.e., three to five rooms, which are considered "small" by Southwest archaeological standards [e.g., Wilcox 2005])

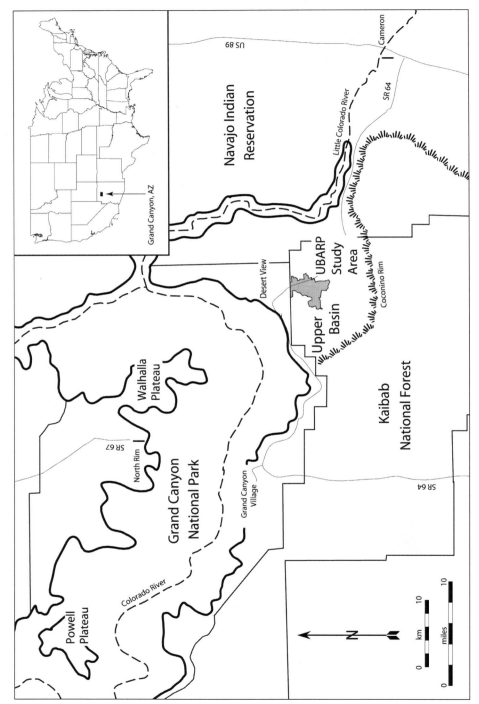

FIGURE 2.1. Location of the Upper Basin Archaeological Research Project (UBARP) study area in northern Arizona.

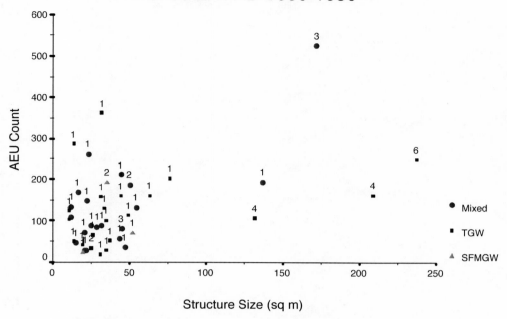

FIGURE 2.2. Scattergram of variation in Period 2.1 (AD 1000–1050) masonry ruin size and standardized artifact density (AEU count) showing number of rooms broken down by primary ceramic ware (TGW = Tusayan Gray Ware, SFMGW = San Francisco Mountain Gray Ware).

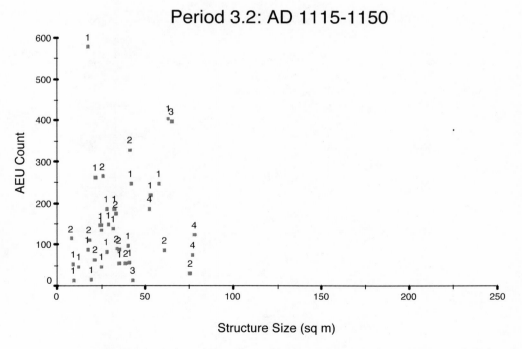

FIGURE 2.3. Scattergram of variation in Period 3.2 (AD 1115–1150) masonry ruin size and standardized artifact density (AEU count) showing number of rooms (by this period, assemblages consist of Tusayan Gray Ware types only).

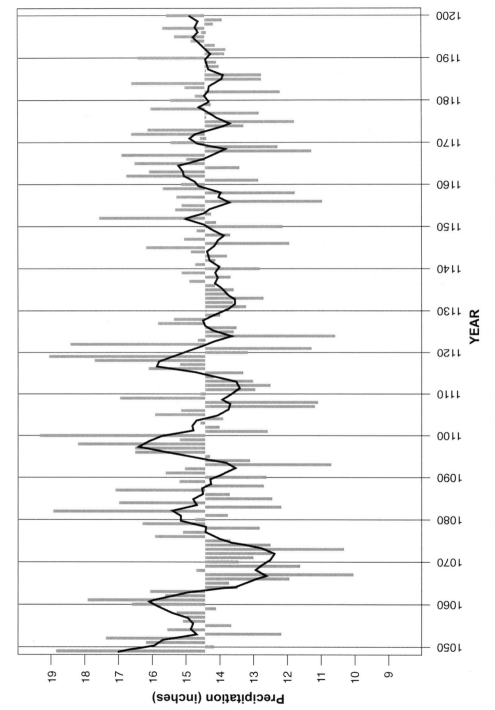

FIGURE 2.4. Variation in annual precipitation (in inches) for the period AD 1049–1200. Solid line is a three-year running average.

appear to have been overbuilt and underused, whereas numerous smaller structures were overused. If correct, these inferences challenge ethnographically based models of small-scale settlement design and land use, which stipulate that short, seasonal durations of occupation would invariably produce "scanty and thinly distributed" scatters of debris (Ellis 1978:65; see also Skinner 1965).

In addition, it has long been supposed that ecological factors are prime settlement determinants for largely autonomous, small-scale socioeconomic groups (Chang 1958; Trigger 1968), such as those of the ancient American Southwest (Gumerman 1988; SARG 1974; Schoenwetter and Dittert 1968). A reasonable hypothesis is that the high degree of variability among Upper Basin masonry ruins is related to variation in paleo-precipitation patterns and the effects it has on decision-making and the organization of activities (Dean 1996; Kohler et al. 2005; Van West 1996). Figure 2.4 shows annual amounts of precipitation, reconstructed from dendrochronological data[2] (Dean 1988:135–137), for the period AD 1049–1200 (Sullivan and Ruter 2006:187); the solid line is a three-year running average. In AD 1053, for example, 12.18 inches of precipitation accumulated, whereas the average for the preceding three years was 15.90 inches (for the preceding year it was 17.36 inches, and for the preceding two years it was 16.77 inches). Because there is a low correlation between the amount of precipitation that actually amassed during a specific year with the amount of the prior year (r = .027), the prior two years (r = .025), or the prior three years (r = .037), it is reasonable to postulate that expected outcomes of decisions based on near-term (i.e., one to three years) memory of precipitation did not materialize as anticipated. Moreover, differences between past ("remembered") and present ("perceived") precipitation amounts would have promoted the premature abandonment of previously built structures, especially those that had been constructed in anticipation of the continuation of near-term conditions, which helps account for the poor association between structure size and artifact density (Uphus 2003).

THE BURDEN OF THE ANCESTORS

Surface archaeological data from the Upper Basin provide some provocative indications as to how the emergence of an "ancestral landscape" may have affected the decision-making of these small-scale social formations (Thomas 2002). Figure 2.5 depicts extrapolated artifact density data for structures that had been abandoned between AD 900 and 1115. This countryside of abandoned structures, plus other types of remains (e.g., such as hundreds of artifact scatters that are difficult to date from their surface properties), may have presented some "planning" challenges to those Upper Basin occupants who were considering building new structures after AD 1115. Notice that for the succeeding period of occupation, AD 1115–1150 (Figure 2.6), a few new and lightly occupied structures (i.e., those with low artifact density values) were established in the density zone of abandoned heavily occupied structures (those with high ranges of artifact density), many new and heavily occupied structures were established on the fringes of moderately occupied or in lightly occupied density zones, and many heavily occupied areas sustained no new settlements. These patterns imply that as a greater percentage of the landscape became "ancestral," as it transformed from profane and ahistorical to sacred and rich with history (Knapp and Ashmore 2000), the mere presence of abandoned settlements, which themselves are often sources of myth (Gosden and Lock 1998), influenced decisions about where new ones could be established (Barrett 2002).[3] In this model, the archaeological record is far from an inert or powerless element of ancient peoples' worlds.

THE ARCHAEOLOGICAL RECORD AND THE STUDY OF THE CULTURAL PAST

Long gone are the innocent, halcyon days when patterning in the archaeological record was thought to represent a "fossil" remnant of patterning in extinct cultural systems (Binford 1964). As the fossil view was cast aside (Schiffer 1972), archaeologists began to consider the epistemology of just what it is they study (Binford 1983; Clarke 1973). At some

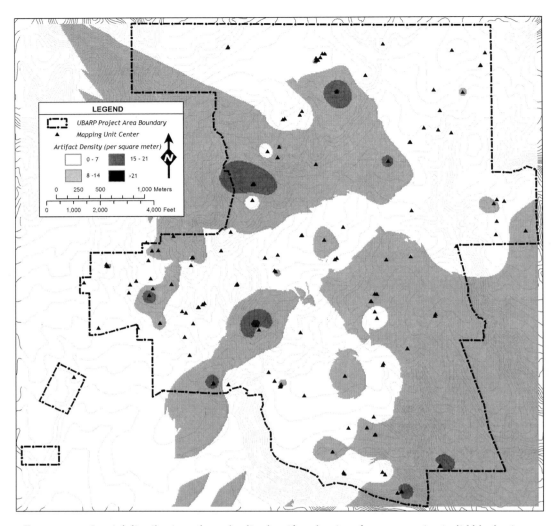

FIGURE 2.5. Spatial distribution of standardized artifact density of masonry ruins (solid black triangles) that were occupied and abandoned between AD 900 and 1115. Shading intensity measures variation in artifact density from low (unshaded) to high (dark gray).

level, I would venture that, among archaeologists of all persuasions, there is an emerging consensus that the archaeological record materializes as humans create traces by transforming matter and modifying surfaces and that consequently, through time, the trace load of the archaeological record changes endlessly by virtue of the actions of human and nonhuman agents (Lucas 2005).

With this view of the archaeological record, archaeological phenomena can be defined, analyzed, and interpreted within a framework that is not informed by or otherwise dependent upon cultural anthropology (cf. Hill 2003:147). It is somewhat liberating to realize, therefore, that in order to conduct archaeological research one does not have to accept the unassailability of ethnographic research or subscribe to presentism, uniformitarianism, or the necessity of analogical arguments. Such freedom carries responsibilities, however, because archaeologists are obligated to design research that routinely considers the effects of equifinality and avoids Type II methodological errors (Roos et al. in press). By embracing an archaeological view of the archae-

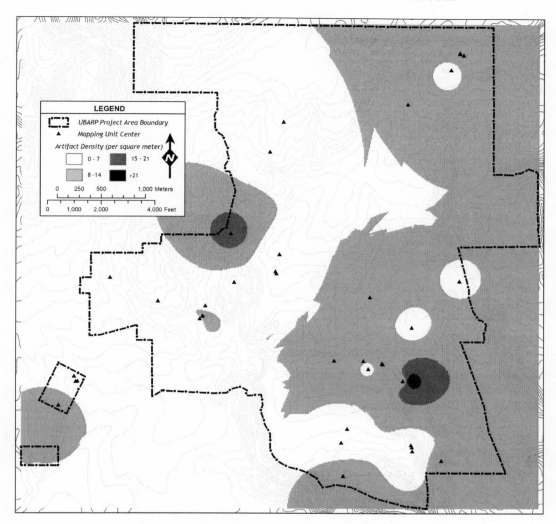

FIGURE 2.6. Spatial distribution of standardized artifact density of masonry ruins (solid black triangles) that were occupied and abandoned between AD 1115 and 1150. Shading intensity measures variation in artifact density from low (unshaded) to high (dark gray).

ological record, we are positioned to develop discipline-specific theory and method (Clarke 1968:20) and to decide what the role of cultural anthropology might be in our efforts to

reveal the cultural past, in all of its complexity and unfamiliarity, with the study of archaeological phenomena.

NOTES

1. I exclude from consideration archival and bibliographic issues regarding the by-products of archaeological research, such as field notes and other forms of documentation, which some regard as "archaeological records" of the discipline's primary database (e.g., Fowler and Givens 1992).

2. The Coconino Plateau data represent "average" conditions across an amorphous area north of the San Francisco Peaks, south and east of the Colorado River, and west and south of the Little Colorado River (Jeffrey S. Dean, pers. comm., 2001).

3. In all likelihood, abandonment accelerated as people ran out of occupiable space even

though the surrounding terrain was largely vacant (which explains, in large measure, why indirect predictive models are so inexact).

ACKNOWLEDGMENTS

I thank Dr. John A. Hanson, Kaibab National Forest archaeologist, for his long-term intellectual and administrative support of the Upper Basin Archaeological Research Project (UBARP). UBARP has been supported by grants from the University Research Council (University of Cincinnati), C. P. Taft Research Center (University of Cincinnati), the McMicken College of Arts and Sciences (University of Cincinnati), the Center for Field Research (Earthwatch), the National Park Service (National Center for Preservation Technology and Training), and the USDA Forest Service (Kaibab National Forest). I am grateful to Patrick M. Uphus for producing Figures 2.5 and 2.6. The incisive comments of William A. Parkinson, Sissel Schroeder, and Michael B. Schiffer dramatically improved the logic and content of this chapter.

REFERENCES CITED

Aberle, David F.
1987   What Kind of Science Is Anthropology? *American Anthropologist* 89:551–566.

Andrews, Gill, John C. Barrett, and John S. C. Lewis
2000   Interpretation Not Record: The Practice of Archaeology. *Antiquity* 74:525–530.

Ascher, Robert
1961   Analogy in Archaeological Interpretation. *Southwestern Journal of Anthropology* 17:317–325.
1962   Ethnography for Archeology: A Case from the Seri Indians. *Ethnology* 1:360–369.
1968   Time's Arrow and the Archaeology of a Contemporary Community. In *Settlement Archaeology*, edited by K. C. Chang, pp. 43–52. National Press Books, Palo Alto, California.

Bailey, Geoff
1983   Concepts of Time in Quaternary Prehistory. *Annual Review of Anthropology* 12:165–92.
2007   Time Perspectives, Palimpsests, and the Archaeology of Time. *Journal of Anthropological Archaeology* 26:198–223.

Barrett, John C.
2002   Agency, the Duality of Structure, and the Problem of the Archaeological Record. In *Archaeological Theory Today*, edited by Ian Hodder, pp. 141–164. Polity Press, Cambridge.

Becher, Matthew E.
1992   Archaeological Investigations at a Pueblo II Kayenta Anasazi Ruin Located in the Tusayan Ranger District, Kaibab National Forest, Arizona. Unpublished senior thesis, Department of Anthropology, University of Cincinnati.

Binford, Lewis R.
1964   A Consideration of Archaeological Research Design. *American Antiquity* 29:425–441.
1968   Archeological Perspectives. In *New Perspectives in Archeology*, edited by Sally R. Binford and Lewis R. Binford, pp. 5–32. Aldine, Chicago.
1977   General Introduction. In *For Theory Building in Archaeology: Essays on Faunal Remains, Aquatic Resources, Spatial Analysis, and Systemic Modeling*, edited by Lewis R. Binford, pp. 1–10. Academic Press, New York.
1981   Behavioral Archaeology and the "Pompeii Premise." *Journal of Anthropological Research* 37:195–208.
1983   *In Pursuit of the Past: Decoding the Archaeological Record.* Thames and Hudson, New York.
1987   Data, Relativism, and Archaeological Science. *Man* 22:391–404.
2001a   Where Do Research Problems Come From? *American Antiquity* 66:669–678.
2001b   *Constructing Frames of Reference: An Analytical Method for Archaeological Theory Building Using Hunter-Gatherer and Environmental Data Sets.* University of California Press, Berkeley.
2006   Bands as Characteristic of "Mobile Hunter-Gatherers" May Exist Only in the History of Anthropology. In *Archaeology and Ethnoarchaeology of Mobility*, edited by Frederic Sellet, Russell Greaves, and Pei-Lin Yu, pp. 1–22. University Press of Florida, Gainesville.

Blegen, Carl W.
1941   Preclassical Greece. In *Studies in the Arts and Architecture, University of Pennsylvania Bicentennial Conference*, pp. 1–14. University of Pennsylvania Press, Philadelphia.

Bradfield, Richard M.
1995   *An Interpretation of Hopi Culture.* Derby, United Kingdom.

Chang, K. C.
1958   Study of the Neolithic Social Grouping: Examples from the New World. *American Anthropologist* 60:298–334.

Clarke, David L.
1968 *Analytical Archaeology*. Methuen, London.
1973 Archaeology: The Loss of Innocence. *Antiquity* XLVII:6–18.
Coder, Christopher M.
2000 *An Introduction to Grand Canyon Prehistory*. Grand Canyon Association, Grand Canyon, Arizona.
Cooney, Gabriel
1999 Social Landscapes in Irish Prehistory. In *The Archaeology and Anthropology of Landscape*, edited by Peter J. Ucko and Robert Layton, pp. 46–64. Routledge, London.
David, Nicholas, and Carol Kramer
2001 *Ethnoarchaeology in Action*. Cambridge University Press, Cambridge.
Deal, Michael
1985 Household Pottery Disposal in the Maya Highlands: An Ethnoarchaeological Interpretation. *Journal of Anthropological Archaeology* 4:243–291.
Dean, Jeffrey S.
1988 Dendrochronology and Paleoenvironmental Reconstruction on the Colorado Plateaus. In *The Anasazi in a Changing Environment*, edited by George J. Gumerman, pp. 119–167. Cambridge University Press, Cambridge.
1996 Demography, Environment, and Subsistence Stress. In *Evolving Complexity and Environmental Risk in the Prehistoric Southwest*, edited by Joseph A. Tainter and Bonnie B. Tainter, pp. 25–56. Santa Fe Institute Studies in the Sciences of Complexity, Vol. 24. Addison-Wesley, Reading, Massachusetts.
DeBoer, Warren R.
1983 The Archaeological Record as Preserved Death Assemblage. In *Archaeological Hammers and Theories*, edited by James A. Moore and Arthur S. Keene, pp. 19–36. Academic Press, New York.
de la Torre, Ignacio, and Rafael Mora
2004 Unmodified Lithic Material at Olduvai Bed I: Manuports or Ecofacts? *Journal of Archaeological Science* 32:273–285.
Dincauze, Dena F.
2000 *Environmental Archaeology: Principles and Practice*. Cambridge University Press, Cambridge.
Dolnick, Edward
2001 *Down the Great Unknown: John Wesley Powell's 1969 Journey of Discovery and Tragedy through the Grand Canyon*. Harper Collins, New York.
Dunnell, Robert C.
1982 Science, Social Science, and Common Sense: The Agonizing Dilemma of Modern Archaeology. *Journal of Anthropological Research* 38:1–25.
1989 Aspects of the Application of Evolutionary Theory in Archaeology. In *Archaeological Thought in America*, edited by C. C. Lamberg-Karlovsky, pp. 35–49. Cambridge University Press, Cambridge.
1992 The Notion Site. In *Space, Time, and Archaeological Landscapes*, edited by Jacqueline Rossignol and LuAnn Wandsnider, pp. 21–41. Plenum Press, New York.
Ebert, James I.
1992 *Distributional Archaeology*. University of New Mexico Press, Albuquerque.
Effland, Richard W., Jr., Anne T. Jones, and Robert C. Euler
1981 *The Archaeology of Powell Plateau: Regional Interaction at Grand Canyon*. Grand Canyon Natural History Association, Grand Canyon, Arizona.
Ellis, Florence H.
1978 Small Structures Used by Historic Pueblo Peoples and Their Immediate Ancestors. In *Limited Activity and Occupation Sites*, edited by Albert E. Ward, pp. 59–68. Center for Anthropological Studies, Albuquerque.
Euler, Robert C.
1969 The Archaeology of the Canyon Country. In *John Wesley Powell and the Anthropology of the Canyon Country*, by Don D. Fowler, Robert C. Euler, and Catherine S. Fowler, pp. 8–20. Geological Survey Professional Paper 670. Government Printing Office, Washington, D.C.
Euler, Robert C., and Susan M. Chandler
1978 Aspects of Prehistoric Settlement Patterns in Grand Canyon. In *Investigations of the Southwestern Anthropological Research Group*, edited by Robert C. Euler and George J. Gumerman, pp. 73–84. Museum of Northern Arizona, Flagstaff.
Fowler, Don D., and Douglas R. Givens
1992 Preserving the Archaeological Record. In *Preserving the Anthropological Record*, edited by Sydel Silverman and Nancy J. Parezo, pp. 43–52. Wenner-Gren Foundation for Anthropological Research, New York.
Fugate, Thomas I.
2003 Inferring Settlement Formation Patterns: A

GIS-Based Harris Matrix Analysis of a Prehistoric Masonry Ruin in the Upper Basin, Kaibab National Forest, Northern Arizona. MA thesis, Department of Anthropology, University of Cincinnati.

Gaines, Sylvia W., and Warren M. Gaines
2000   Impact of Small-Group Decision Making in Reducing Stress Conditions. *Journal of Anthropological Archaeology* 19:103–130.

Goldberg, Paul, and Richard I. Macphail
2006   *Practical and Theoretical Geoarchaeology.* Blackwell Publishing, Malden, Massachusetts.

Gosden, Chris, and Gary Lock
1998   Prehistoric Histories. *World Archaeology* 30:2–12.

Gould, Richard A., and Patty Jo Watson
1982   A Dialogue on the Meaning and Use of Analogy in Ethnoarchaeological Reasoning. *Journal of Anthropological Archaeology* 1:355–381.

Gumerman, George J.
1988   A Historical Perspective on Environment and Culture in Anasazi Country. In *The Anasazi in a Changing Environment*, edited by George J. Gumerman, pp. 1–24. Cambridge University Press, Cambridge.

Haury, Emil W.
1931   *Kivas of the Tusayan Ruin, Grand Canyon, Arizona.* Medallion Papers IX. Gila Pueblo, Globe.

Hill, Jane H.
2003   Archaeology and Anthropology. In *Archaeology Is Anthropology*, edited by Susan D. Gillespie and Deborah L. Nichols, pp. 147–153. Archeological Papers No. 13. American Anthropological Association, Arlington, Virginia.

Hodder, Ian
1999   *The Archaeological Process: An Introduction.* Blackwell, Oxford.
2002   (ed.) *Archaeological Theory Today.* Polity Press, Cambridge.

Holliday, Vance T.
2004   *Soils in Archaeological Research.* Oxford University Press, Oxford.

Ingold, Tim
1992   Foraging for Data, Camping with Theories: Hunter-Gatherers and Nomadic Pastoralists in Archaeology and Anthropology. *Antiquity* 66:790–803.

Jochim, Michael A.
1991   Archaeology as Long-Term Ethnography. *American Anthropologist* 93:308–321.

Johnson, Amber L.
2004   On Niche Breadth, System Stability, and the Importance of a Phrase. In *Processual Archaeology: Exploring Analytical Strategies, Frames of Reference, and Culture Process*, edited by Amber L. Johnson, pp. 261–296. Praeger, Westport, Connecticut.

Jones, Andrew
2002   *Archaeological Theory and Scientific Practice.* Cambridge University Press, Cambridge.

Judd, Neil M.
1926   *Archeological Investigations North of the Rio Colorado.* Bureau of American Ethnology Bulletin 82. Smithsonian Institution, Washington, D.C.

Knapp, A. Bernard, and Wendy Ashmore
2000   Archaeological Landscapes: Constructed, Conceptualized, Ideational. In *Archaeologies of Landscape*, edited by Wendy Ashmore and A. Bernard Knapp, pp. 1–30. Blackwell Publishers, Oxford.

Kohler, Timothy A.
1992   Field Houses, Villages, and the Tragedy of the Commons in the Early Northern Anasazi Southwest. *American Antiquity* 57: 617–635.

Kohler, Timothy A., George J. Gumerman, and Robert G. Reynolds
2005   Simulating Ancient Societies. *Scientific American* 293:77–84.

Kosso, Peter
2001   *Knowing the Past: Philosophical Issues of History and Archaeology.* Humanity Books, Amherst, New York.

LaMotta, Vincent M., and Michael B. Schiffer
2002   Behavioral Archaeology: A New Synthesis. In *Archaeological Theory Today*, edited by Ian Hodder, pp. 14–64. Polity Press, Cambridge.

Lucas, Gavin
2005   *The Archaeology of Time.* Routledge, New York.

Mindeleff, Victor
1891   A Study of Pueblo Architecture: Tusayan and Cibola. In *Eighth Annual Report of the Bureau of American Ethnology*, pp. 12–228. Washington, D.C.

Minnis, Paul E.
1992   Earliest Plant Cultivation in the Desert Borderlands of North America. In *The Origins of Agriculture*, edited by C. Wesley Cowan and Patty Jo Watson, pp. 121–141. Smithsonian Institution Press, Washington, D.C.

Moore, Bruce A.
1978   Are Pueblo Field Houses a Function of Urbanization? In *Limited Activity and Occupation Sites*, edited by Albert E. Ward, pp. 9–16. Center for Anthropological Studies, Albuquerque.

Moore, John H.
1994   Putting Anthropology Back Together Again: The Ethnogenetic Critique of Cladistic Theory. *American Anthropologist* 96: 925–948.

Murray, Tim
1999   A Return to the "Pompeii Premise." In *Time and Archaeology*, edited by Tim Murray, pp. 8–27. Routledge, New York.

Nash, David T.
1993   Distinguishing Stone Artifacts from Naturefacts Created by Rockfall Processes. In *Formation Processes in Archaeological Context*, edited by Paul Goldberg, David T. Nash, and Michael D. Petraglia, pp. 125–138. Prehistory Press, Madison, Wisconsin.

Patrik, Linda E.
1985   Is There an Archaeological Record? In *Advances in Archaeological Method and Theory*, Vol. 8, edited by Michael B. Schiffer, pp. 27–61. Academic Press, New York.

Peregrine, Peter N.
2001   Cross-Cultural Comparative Approaches in Archaeology. *Annual Review of Anthropology* 30:1–18.

Pilles, Peter J., Jr.
1978   The Field House and Sinagua Demography. In *Limited Activity and Occupation Sites*, edited by Albert E. Ward, pp. 119–133. Center for Anthropological Studies, Albuquerque.

Pinsky, Valerie
1992   Archaeology, Politics, and Boundary-Formation: The Boas Censure (1919) and the Development of American Archaeology during the Inter-War Years. In *Rediscovering Our Past: Essays on the History of American Archaeology*, edited by Jonathan E. Reyman, pp. 161–189. Aldershot, Avebury.

Porter, Claire C., and Frank W. Marlowe
2007   How Marginal Are Forager Habitats? *Journal of Archaeological Science* 34:59–68.

Powell, John W.
1875   The Cañons of the Colorado. *Scribner's Monthly* 9:523–537.

Preucel, Robert W., Jr.
1990   *Seasonal Circulation and Dual Residence in the Pueblo Southwest: A Prehistoric Example from the Pajarito Plateau, New Mexico*. Garland, New York.

Renfrew, Colin
1980   The Great Tradition versus the Great Divide: Archaeology as Anthropology? *American Journal of Archaeology* 84:287–298.

Rice, Glen, Rick Effland, and Laurie Blank-Roper
1980   *A Sample Survey of Tusayan Planning Unit 1, Kaibab National Forest, Arizona*. Cultural Resources Report No. 33. USDA Forest Service, Southwestern Region, Albuquerque.

Roos, Christopher I., Alan P. Sullivan, III, and Calla McNamee
In   Anthropogenic Fire for Long-Term Landpress. scape Management: Geoarchaeological Evidence for Systematic Burning in the Upland Southwest. In *The Archaeology of Anthropogenic Environments*, edited by Rebecca Dean. Southern Illinois University Press, Carbondale.

Sabloff, Jeremy A., Lewis R. Binford, and Patricia McAnany
1987   Understanding the Archaeological Record. *Antiquity* 61:203–209.

SARG, Members of
1974   SARG: A Cooperative Approach towards Understanding the Locations of Human Settlements. *World Archaeology* 6:107–116.

Schiffer, Michael B.
1972   Archaeological Context and Systemic Context. *American Antiquity* 37:156–165.
1976   *Behavioral Archeology*. Academic Press, New York.
1985   Is There a "Pompeii Premise" in Archaeology? *Journal of Anthropological Research* 41:18–41.
1987   *Formation Processes of the Archaeological Record*. University of New Mexico Press, Albuquerque.

Schoenwetter, James
1981   Prologue to a Contextual Archaeology. *Journal of Archaeological Science* 8:367–379.

Schoenwetter, James, and Alfred E. Dittert
1968   An Ecological Interpretation of Anasazi Settlement Patterns. In *Anthropological Archaeology in the Americas*, pp. 41–66. The Anthropological Society of Washington, Washington, D.C.

Schwartz, Douglas W., Michael P. Marshall, and Jane Kepp

1979   *Archaeology of the Grand Canyon: The Bright Angel Site*. School of American Research Press, Santa Fe.

Schwartz, Douglas W., Richard C. Chapman, and Jane Kepp

1980   *Archaeology of the Grand Canyon: Unkar Delta*. School of American Research Press, Santa Fe.

Schwartz, Douglas W., Jane Kepp, and Richard C. Chapman

1981   *Archaeology of the Grand Canyon: The Walhalla Plateau*. School of American Research Press, Santa Fe.

Simmons, Alan

1998   Exposed Fragments, Buried Hippos: Assessing Surface Archaeology. In *Surface Archaeology*, edited by Alan P. Sullivan, III, pp. 159–167. University of New Mexico Press, Albuquerque.

Simms, Steven R.

1992   Ethnoarchaeology: Obnoxious Spectator, Trivial Pursuit, or the Keys to a Time Machine? In *Quandaries and Quests: Visions of Archaeology's Future*, edited by LuAnn Wandsnider, pp. 186–198. Southern Illinois University Press, Carbondale.

Skinner, S. Alan

1965   A Survey of Field Houses at Sapawe, North Central New Mexico. *Southwestern Lore* 31:18–21.

Speth, John D.

1990   The Study of Hunter-Gatherers in the American Southwest: New Insights from Ethnology. In *Perspectives on Southwestern Prehistory*, edited by Paul E. Minnis and Charles L. Redman, pp. 15–25. Westview Press, Boulder, Colorado.

Sullivan, Alan P., III

1978   Inference and Evidence in Archaeology: A Discussion of the Conceptual Problems. In *Advances in Archaeological Method and Theory*, Vol. 1, edited by Michael B. Schiffer, pp. 183–222. Academic Press, New York.

1986   Occupational Dynamics of a Small Kayenta Anasazi Settlement. In *Prehistory of the Upper Basin, Coconino County, Arizona*, edited by Alan P. Sullivan, III, pp. 47–190. Arizona State Museum Archaeological Series No. 167. University of Arizona, Tucson.

1992   The Role of Theory in Solving Enduring Archaeological Problems. In *Quandaries and Quests: Visions of Archaeology's Future*, edited by LuAnn Wandsnider, pp. 239–253. Southern Illinois University Press, Carbondale.

1995   Artifact Scatters and Subsistence Organization. *Journal of Field Archaeology* 22:49–64.

1996   Risk, Anthropogenic Environments, and Western Anasazi Subsistence. In *Evolving Complexity and Environmental Risk in the Prehistoric Southwest*, edited by Joseph A. Tainter and Bonnie B. Tainter, pp. 145–167. Santa Fe Institute Studies in the Sciences of Complexity, Vol. 24. Addison-Wesley, Reading, Massachusetts.

2000a   Effects of Small-Scale Prehistoric Runoff Agriculture on Soil Fertility: The Developing Picture from Upland Terraces in the American Southwest. *Geoarchaeology: An International Journal* 15:291–313.

2000b   Theory of Archaeological Survey Design. In *Archaeological Method and Theory: An Encyclopedia*, edited by L. Ellis, pp. 600–605. Routledge, New York.

2007   Archaeological Anthropology and Strategies of Knowledge Formation in American Archaeology. In *Archaeological Anthropology: Methodological and Theoretical Approaches*, edited by James M. Skibo, Michael W. Graves, and Miriam L. Stark, pp. 40–56. University of Arizona Press, Tucson.

Sullivan, Alan P., III, and Anthony H. Ruter

2006   The Effect of Environmental Fluctuations on Ancient Livelihood: Implications of Paleoeconomic Data from the Upper Basin, Northern Arizona. In *Environmental Change and Human Adaptation in the Ancient Southwest*, edited by David E. Doyel and Jeffrey S. Dean, pp. 180–203. University of Utah Press, Salt Lake City.

Sullivan, Alan P., III, Philip B. Mink, and Patrick M. Uphus

2002   From John W. Powell to Robert C. Euler: Testing Models of Grand Canyon's Prehistoric Puebloan Settlement History. In *Culture and Environment in the American Southwest: Essays in Honor of Robert C. Euler*, edited by David A. Phillips, Jr. and John A. Ware, pp. 49–68. Anthropological Research Paper No. 8. SWCA, Phoenix.

Sullivan, Alan P., III, Robert A. Cook, Matthew P. Purtill, and Patrick M. Uphus

2003   Economic and Land-Use Implications of Prehistoric Fire-Cracked-Rock Piles,

Northern Arizona. *Journal of Field Archaeology* 28:367–382.

Sullivan, Alan P., III, Philip B. Mink, and Patrick M. Uphus

2007   Archaeological Survey Design, Units of Observation, and the Characterization of Regional Variability. *American Antiquity* 72:322–333.

Tainter, Joseph A.

1998   Surface Archaeology: Perceptions, Values, and Potential. In *Surface Archaeology*, edited by Alan P. Sullivan, III, pp. 169–179. University of New Mexico Press, Albuquerque.

Tainter, Joseph A., and Bonnie Bagley

2005   Shaping and Suppressing the Archaeological Record. In *Heritage of Value, Archaeology of Renown: Reshaping Archaeological Assessment and Significance*, edited by Clay Mathers, Timothy Darville, and Barbara J. Little, pp. 58–73. University Press of Florida, Gainesville.

Taylor, Walter W.

1958   A Brief Survey through the Grand Canyon of the Colorado River. In *Two Archaeological Studies in Northern Arizona*, by Walter W. Taylor, pp. 18–30. Bulletin 30. Museum of Northern Arizona, Flagstaff.

Thomas, Julian

2002   Archaeologies of Place and Landscape. In *Archaeological Theory Today*, edited by Ian Hodder, pp. 165–186. Polity Press, Cambridge.

Trigger, Bruce G.

1968   The Determinants of Settlement Patterns. In *Settlement Archaeology*, edited by K. C. Chang, pp. 53–78. National Press Books, Palo Alto.

2006   *A History of Archaeological Thought*. 2nd ed. Cambridge University Press, Cambridge.

Uphus, Patrick M.

2003   The Influences of Ecosystem Variability on Prehistoric Settlement: Testing Terrain-Based Locational Models for the Upper Basin, Northern Arizona. MA thesis, Department of Anthropology, University of Cincinnati.

Van West, Carla R.

1996   Agricultural Potential and Carrying Capacity in Southwestern Colorado, A.D. 901 to 1300. In *The Prehistoric Pueblo World, A.D. 1150–1350*, edited by Michael A. Adler, pp. 214–227. University of Arizona Press, Tucson.

Varien, Mark D.

1999   *Sedentism and Mobility in a Social Landscape*. University of Arizona Press, Tucson.

Whitley, David S.

2007   Indigenous Knowledge and 21st Century Archaeological Practice: An Introduction. *The SAA Archaeological Record* 7:6–8.

Whittlesey, Stephanie M. (ed.)

1992   *Archaeological Investigations at Lee Canyon: Kayenta Anasazi Farmsteads in the Upper Basin, Coconino County, Arizona*. Statistical Research, Inc., Tucson.

Wilcox, David R.

2005   Big Issues, New Syntheses. *Plateau: The Land and People of the Colorado Plateau* 2(1):9–19.

Willey, Gordon R., and Philip Phillips

1958   *Method and Theory in American Archaeology*. University of Chicago Press, Chicago.

Wobst, H. Martin

1978   The Archaeo-Ethnology of Hunter-Gatherers or the Tyranny of the Ethnographic Record in Archaeology. *American Antiquity* 43:303–308.

Wylie, Alison

2002   Emergent Tensions in the New Archaeology. In *Thinking from Things: Essays in the Philosophy of Archaeology*, by Alison Wylie, pp. 78–96. University of California Press, Berkeley.

3

Raising the Bar

Making Geological and Archaeological Data More Meaningful for Understanding the Archaeological Record

PAUL GOLDBERG

When I was younger, and generally more idealistic and optimistic than I am today, I wrote an article recounting my experiences and interactions as a geologist working with and for archaeologists (Goldberg 1988). My principal points in that article revolved around archaeologists' (here, I use the term to include both "archaeologists" and "prehistorians" as differentiated in the Old World) excavation methods, their treatment of and apparent bondage to the material finds ("goodies"), and their blissful ignorance of some fundamental aspects of what they were actually digging. I wrote the article with the hope that it would raise the awareness of archaeologists to geoarchaeological issues that, in turn, would result in higher quality archeological data, a heightened appreciation for contextual issues (Stein, this volume), and ultimately a greater degree of communication between archaeologists and geologists. I tried to illustrate these issues by providing true-life examples, such as these:

- Geologists were commonly asked to write up "something about the geology of the site" after only a cursory view of some subsurface exposures. This task, as tacitly understood by both parties, would result in a chapter that would either be included as an appendix in a published volume after the last chapter or, equally likely, never see the light of day. In fact, I participated in one project where the stratigraphy chapter (written by a French geoarchaeologist and myself) indeed ended up in the appendix. I was working under the impression that the stratigraphy formed the ultimate backbone of all the finds in the site.

- Geologists were regularly asked to identify objects from the site, but at the same time they were forbidden to alter the materials in any way (e.g., by scratching, chipping, or breaking) in order to analyze them, even if 2,000 beads of the same type had been recovered.

- Archaeologists had an undeveloped grasp of stratigraphic issues and geological phenomena. This situation is exemplified by statements such as "this red color must be due to heating" (when, instead, it may be attributable to decayed vegetation, postdepositional water infiltration, or iron oxide precipitation), or "this brown circular feature is a storage pit" (when, instead, it may be attributable to a hollow produced by a fallen tree ("tree throw"), which is a ubiquitous feature along the hurricane-prone eastern coast of the United States and in Europe (e.g., Langohr 1993; Lutz and Griswold 1939; Macphail and Goldberg 1990).

- Archaeologists displayed a certain degree of inflexibility in modifying entrenched "hunches." When their interpretations conflicted with geoarchaeological data, the response was to go find a "better" geoarchae-ologist or a specialist who would supply the correct/desired information.

- On the other hand, on several occasions I observed arrogant geoscientists whose at-titudes can be epitomized by such lines as "step aside and we'll give you the truth about what you want to know or never thought about knowing." Commonly, this type of attitude supplies irrelevant or over-stated geoarchaeological data and inter-pretations.

In that 1988 article, I had a very simple goal in mind. I thought that by pointing out these issues, even anecdotally, archaeologists and geoarchaeologists would be more mutually cognizant of each others' problems so that in the future such predicaments would be rare or virtually disappear. Nearly two decades later, I have come to realize that these issues have not gone away. Furthermore, I believe that these concerns are not only intrinsically disturbing, but prevent archaeology and geoarchaeology from advancing in absolute terms: new data are collected, but the bar (the overall quality of the data: how they are collected, presented, and ultimately interpreted) is never raised. I will try to recount some new experiences and, as I did previously, attempt to make some sug-gestions about how these problems might be ameliorated or eradicated.

CASE 1: THE ARCHAEOLOGICAL FIELD SCHOOL

I recently participated in an archaeological field school in the Mediterranean area where the focus was on excavating rooms within a complex structure whose finds date from about 1700 BC to AD 1000. As is common for these time periods, the emphasis is on expos-ing architecture and recovering pottery. The site was in its second season of excavation when I arrived as the geoarchaeologist for the latter part of a six-week season. Most of the architectural remains—generally large multi-room structures, several meters wide, built of cut stone—were situated along a moder-ate slope. A large ritual monument was con-spicuous at the top of a hill that slopes down-

ward and radially away to the south. After a brief walk around the site I was struck by the absence of *terra rosa* soils in the area of the excavated structures, although these types of soils occur in fields adjacent to the site. More-over, excavation had revealed that large stone blocks at the base of the building had been placed directly on bedrock; that is, there was no soil sandwiched between bedrock and the first course of construction material.

Back at the excavation, students were busily excavating deposits in buildings that ranged in age from pre-Roman to Islamic periods. The pre-Roman deposits were about 15–25 cm thick and quite silty. The Islamic layers, on the other hand, were concentrated in a certain area of the site, were more local-ized, and were consistently more clayey and darker than the older deposits. In short, the contrast between the 20 cm thick fill in the buildings and the essentially naked slopes outside them was striking, at least to me. Evi-dently, none of the students had thought about what they were excavating, what the material was, where it had come from, or how it got there. It reminded me of one of those closed-door murder mysteries: deposits were found only within the building but not outside it. Al-though it was plain to all that the Islamic de-posits were darker and more clayey than the pre-Roman sediments, the question "why?" was only barely investigated.

The point here is that without having some-one mention these sediment and stratigraphy issues, students were content to keep excavat-ing without ever thinking about what they were digging. Although I do not have all the answers to explain the processes responsible for the above observations (we have some rea-sonably good explanations), I at least was able to open their eyes to the importance of consid-ering the nature and variation of the archaeo-logical fills at the site. Here, as elsewhere, these fills pertain to questions of site formation, ar-chaeological context, and what the former occupants were actually doing besides using (and possibly making) pottery and producing architectural constructions. I suspect that sim-ilar circumstances can be found at other field schools, as well as at more research-oriented excavations, where no earth scientist is present.[1]

CASE 2: RUSH TO JUDGMENT

As I began to get more involved in micromorphology, in addition to geomorphologically oriented fieldwork, I had the chance to work in the western part of North America on a site that contained many semi-subterranean housepits. For me, this place and time frame were new and exciting, and the housepits reminded me of the anthropogenically formed tell sites (Rosen 1986) that dot the Middle East, where I had been working for several years (Goldberg 1979). We were trying to understand the formation processes associated with these housepits, particularly the types of anthropogenic deposits that were present, and the types of activities that might have been responsible for their formation. We were asking difficult questions, such as "Does this layer represent a floor or collapsed roof?" and "Is this feature a hearth or a collapsed, burned beam?"

Particularly interesting to me was the enthusiastic nature of the archaeological interpretations based on limited field data, and certainly little micromorphological data (I was still in the early stages of refining the technique [Goldberg 1983]). There was a tendency to go directly from field observations to inferences of social issues and social structure, an inclination I had previously noted among anthropological archaeologists in the Old World. In any case, geoarchaeological data or observations did not really figure into these jumps from selective site observations to theory. Moreover, the fact that many of the housepits were dug only from rim-center to rim-center, rather than through the rims across the entire structure into the next one, limited our ability to determine temporal sequencing among the different house pits.

CASE 3: WHAT'S IN A FLOOR?

Human burials were commonly placed beneath floors (both unprepared and plastered) of occupied houses and, it is thought, thereby documented relationships among past, present, and future generations (e.g., McAnany 1995). Interestingly, questions regarding the nature of these types of floors—their composition, the technology, the techniques involved in their production, who made them ("plaster specialists" vs. family members)—have been pursued only to a limited extent (Littmann 1967). This not uncommon situation exemplifies the lack of appreciation by archaeologists of the types of information about human activities that can be revealed from the detailed study of construction materials (e.g., plasters) and related cultural deposits. Matthews's work on Middle Eastern tell deposits and floors (Matthews et al. 1996, 1997; see also Goldberg and Arpin 2003; Shahack-Gross et al. 2005; Sherwood 2001; Sherwood and Goldberg 2001) demonstrates that we must begin to view archaeological deposits and materials as being integral parts of the archaeological record and as constituting rich sources of information about human behavior. This approach contrasts with the more commonplace consideration of constructions and fills as being merely "features."

CASE 4: MODELS AND GREAT EXPECTATIONS

I once was invited to participate as the external advisor to an anthropology doctoral student who was studying the petrography of second millennium pottery from the Old World. The student was using petrographic analysis to infer trade routes that were inaccurately or incompletely depicted by historical documents. Coming from a totally nongeological background, the student did a remarkable job of defining major petrographic groups that clearly reflected different sources of the pottery and routes of trade.

The first chapter of the dissertation succinctly set out the problem, and was followed by a "theoretical" chapter in which the student presented a number of models involving trade that had been developed by various social scientists worldwide. The chapter on data was followed by a discussion of the results in which the candidate attempted to find the best fit between the data and one of the models.

To an American anthropological archaeologist, nothing would seem aberrant with the above description. In fact, after having reviewed a number of manuscripts, grant proposals, and PhD proposals during my career, I realized that this scenario would appear to represent the way that archaeology students are taught to write and formulate their research. Research and publication in the natural sciences, on the other hand, normally take a quite different tack: an introductory statement of the problem and why the study was done in the first place is followed by the data, a discussion, and an interpretation of the results. What is absent in this latter approach, but which is so ubiquitous in the archaeological literature, is the presentation of models, theories, or expectations of the results at the beginning of the dissertation. One gets the impression that the data just need to be gathered and then plugged into one of the previously presented theoretical models. Perhaps this approach is a leftover of the "New Archaeology" of the 1970s whereby the researcher was obligated to incorporate "expectations" in a research design to make the research look scientific, even though previous data and the state of the knowledge base might be insufficient to allow one to predict reasonably what to expect. I have been concerned, therefore, that advocates of this pseudoscientific approach rarely considered the following question— "Where is your null hypothesis?"

Similarly, I was a member of the doctoral committee of a student who applied for a National Science Foundation doctoral dissertation improvement grant to conduct research in a Mediterranean country where the archaeological and paleoenvironmental records were, and still are, poorly known. Her proposal requested funds to perform a botanical survey of the area surrounding a Bronze Age site (a project that heretofore had never been undertaken), and then compare these data with those collected from the site. The proposal was not funded because, apparently, an unsympathetic reviewer fatally criticized the proposal on the grounds that "there was no model." I was perplexed by this critique, as

was the student, as to how one can construct a model when there are no data.

GEOSCIENCE INTERACTIONS WITH ARCHAEOLOGY

The purpose of the suggestions that follow is to provide some concrete ways to improve the way research is conducted in archaeology and geoarchaeology, and to elevate the standards —raise the bar—for incorporating geoscience approaches in archaeological research, regardless of geographic location or time period.

Geoscientific Perspectives on Archaeological Fieldwork

Judging by the lack of field preparedness of many students, I think that, rather than drill them with detailed archaeological data, more time should be spent teaching them fundamental skills that are independent of area of specialization, time period, or type of archaeology. Students need to be taught the importance of scrutinizing phenomena in the field, of thinking about where artifacts or deposits could have come from, and of establishing the depositional and post-depositional context of a site within its landscape. Such skills represent the basis of sound archaeological research, because a reasonably accurate archaeological account cannot be developed with incomplete data or deficient field observations.

Furthermore, as has been emphasized only recently, archaeological sediments (as expressed by their composition, texture, form of organization, and other attributes) and their associated field contexts should be considered direct avenues for understanding human activities—by no means an original idea on the part of geoscientists, although the methods for demonstrating it are (Cammas et al. 1996; Courty 2001; Goldberg and Arpin 2003). Such information can often be provided at a finer temporal scale than that furnished by material remains, such as architecture, pottery, and lithics. In other words, archaeological sediments can be thought of as registering individual events (e.g., building, using, and cleaning of hearths, or sweeping and dumping of material) whereas artifacts and other remains commonly pertain to long-term synoptic views of hunting, gathering, economy, and political or social status. Essentially, the analysis of archaeological sediments can supply information about specific short-term events that occurred on the order of days or less (e.g., individual burning episodes [Goldberg and Macphail 2006]).

North American archaeologists are, for the most part, not particularly prone to interpret archaeological sediments in anthropogenic terms (e.g., Stein and Farrand 2002), except for obvious cases, such as large mound sites (e.g., Cahokia, Moundville), where the results of past human activities are striking. The reasons for this inattentiveness are likely complex, but in part may be attributable to the youthfulness of North America's present-day residents, who generally do not have extended temporal links to the landscapes that they inhabit (Goldberg 1999). The same can be said about geoarchaeologists who tend to focus on problems at the landscape and site scales, which is underscored by the fact that geoarchaeology books tend to be written by geoscientists and not by archaeologists (David Sanger, 2004, pers. comm.; cf. Goldberg and Macphail 2006).

On the other hand, there appears to be a greater awareness on the part of Old World archaeologists and geologists of the influence of past human activities, particularly at the site and microstratigraphic level (e.g., occupation deposits). The detailed micromorphological work of Matthews has been significant in elucidating the nature of site constructions and activities, and their social implications from Neolithic and Bronze Age tell sites in the Eastern Mediterranean region (Matthews 1995; Matthews et al. 1994; Matthews et al. 1996, 1997). Similar approaches have been taken for Neolithic, Roman, and Medieval sites in Europe and the United Kingdom by Macphail (e.g., Macphail 1990, 1992, 2003; Macphail and Goldberg 1990, 1995; Macphail et al. 1990; Macphail et al. 1994; Macphail et al. 1998; Macphail et al. 2003).

These developments, as well as the introduction of microstratigraphy and the expansion of stratigraphic concerns in general, raise the following question: What do sediments —the material that encloses the contents of the archaeological record—actually represent and how do we relate them to artifacts? One approach is to separate geological stratigraphy from that of archaeology. This strategy is exemplified by the excavations at Hohle Fels Cave, Germany, where two types of stratigraphic units are recognized, Geological Horizons and Archaeological Horizons (Conard et al. 2000; Goldberg et al. 2003; Hahn 1988), and which do not necessarily coincide. The strength in this approach is that both units are independently recognized and interpreted: the geological horizons are defined along standardized lithostratigraphic criteria (texture, color, boundaries, and so on), whereas the archaeological ones are characterized by the artifact assemblages that they contain. Another approach, one more strictly geological, is taken by Macphail and Cruise (2001) and Courty (2001), who stress the need to examine the microstratigraphic fabric of a site as expressed by its microfacies: the vertical and lithostratigraphic changes within a feature, structure, or site. These changes must be tied to differences in the human and geological processes that produced them, and they therefore have a role in revealing the range of human activities at a site.

Until such microstratigraphic approaches become routine and greater attention is paid to the deposits that enclose material finds, we will be stuck looking at the archaeological record only as traditionally defined (bones, stones, pottery, and architecture), ignoring or screening away fundamental items of archaeological information that are needed to paint a complete picture of human history. For instance, consider the case of the Paleolithic cave of Hayonim, situated in Lower Galilee, in Israel, which was the focus of excavation during the 1990s (Meignen 1999; Stiner 2005; Stiner et al. 2001; Weiner et al. 1995; Weiner et al. 2002). Much of the sediment, as at Kebara Cave nearby, is anthropogenic and consists of combustion features (Figure 3.1) and clayey detritus that has been washed and tracked into the cave and locally trampled (Goldberg and Bar-Yosef 1998). In the field, I

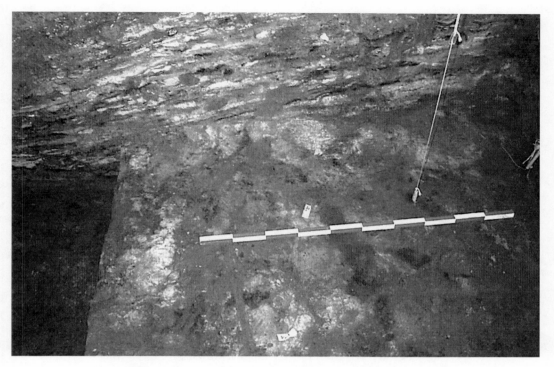

FIGURE 3.1. Field photo from section and floor in the northern part of Hayonim Cave, Israel. Numerous thin features associated with combustion are shown in the vertical profile behind the string and plumb bob. On the floor, upon which the meter stick rests, are remains of more massive ash accumulations and combustion structures from what appear to be larger, more structured burning events. The block from Figure 3.2 comes from the latter type of burning feature.

noted the presence of reddish balls and aggregates of bright red clay (identified in thin section as grains of *terra rosa*, the common soil that covers much of the hillslopes in this area) that appeared to be floating within the mass of many of the cave's ashy sediments. Although they appeared to have been fire heated, the origin of these ubiquitous bright red balls of clay remained a mystery. On balance, ashes should result from the total combustion of charcoal or other combustible material, leaving just a residue of calcium carbonate (Wattez 1988; Wattez and Courty 1987) and not clay. In the case of Hayonim, these ashy sediments consist of calcite or, where they have been diagenetically altered, they are represented by a variety of phosphate minerals (Weiner et al. 2002). Microscopic observation of thin sections and loose sediments also revealed the presence of phytoliths derived from wood/bark, leaves, and grasses (Albert et al. 2003).

These clay balls remained a perplexing problem for several seasons until the mid-1990s, when phytolith specialist Dr. Rosa-Maria Albert came to the cave to excavate and collect phytolith samples of modern vegetation. Among the first items sampled in front of the cave were some of the varied types of grasses that by this time of summer were dry but still standing. Rather than cut them, they were pulled out by the stalks, roots and all, which provided a key piece of information: attached to the roots were numerous balls of soil material, of the same size and shape as those found in the ashes (Figure 3.2). Moreover, after the grasses were burned, the soil aggregates turned a red color similar to that found in the ashes. In sum, the implication was that these balls were likely attached to grasses that might have been used to start these ca. 150,000-year-old fires, which would have been sustained by burning wood and bark from trees. Phytoliths

FIGURE 3.2. Scanned image of Sample 93-32 from Hayonim Cave, Israel. This image was prepared by impregnating a block of undisturbed sediment with polyester resin and then cutting and polishing the block. The block was then scanned on a standard flatbed scanner at 600 dpi. Illustrated here is part of an isolated, relatively massive combustion feature (cf. Figure 3.1) that exhibits a typical structure of a fireplace: an organic rich layer at the base overlain by ash material representing completely combusted products (wood and grass). What is curious here is the presence of the circular dots (TR; normally red but not visible in this black-and-white photograph) that are scattered throughout the ash, notably in the center and upper parts of the photograph. From a geological perspective of sediment source, they should not co-occur with a mass of ashes. In fact, these grains turned out to be balls and aggregates of *terra rossa* soil material that were adhering to roots of grass and that were burned in the fire, possibly to start it. The scale bar is 10 mm.

of wood and bark are the most abundant in the sediments (Albert et al. 2003). Thus, a geo-archaeological curiosity—clay balls are sedimentologically incompatible in a mass of calcitic ashes—provided information about the materials and procedures used in the making of fires, the residues of which constitute a major portion of the cave fill.

GEOSCIENTIFIC PERSPECTIVES ON ARCHAEOLOGICAL TRAINING

One fundamental pedagogical implication of the clay-ball problem relates to the issue of field observation. How can students acquire basic observational skills in the field or tech-nological ones in both the field and lab when they are not components of the curricula of most undergraduate and graduate anthropology programs in the United States? Raising the bar in these areas means providing students with the essential skills needed to design and address problems in an efficient manner, particularly through the use of readily available technology (Killick, this volume). Because archaeology is first and foremost a field-based discipline, researchers should have the basic skills to be able to examine regional landscape data that are pertinent to their sites. Such data can be obtained from satellite images, aerial photos, and topographic, geological, and soil survey maps. These sources provide vital information about potential geological structures, water sources, raw materials, drainage systems, potential migration routes, and the age of the landscape. Courses in remote sensing are commonly available, but those that enable students to interpret a soil survey or read a geological map are not. Information gleaned from the latter can be instrumental in archaeological reconnaissance (for example, locating a source of chert or ceramic temper) and excavation (knowing how shallow the ground water table is likely to be), which can save significant amounts of time and money. Geoarchaeologists involved in cultural resource management (CRM) projects have often complained about the inability of recent graduates in archaeology to read an aerial photograph, use a topographic map, or interpret stratigraphic relationships. This concern is particularly underscored by the fact that most archaeology graduates end up being employed, at least initially, by the CRM sector and not academic institutions.

The ability to observe, document, and interpret microstratigraphic sequences in the field, as discussed above, is necessary in order to fully understand the geological and archaeological history of a site and to infer which activities were conducted by its past occupants. These problems represent difficult assignments for anyone, including geoarchaeologists. Nevertheless, some familiarity with sedimentology, pedology, and microstratigraphy is essential to appreciate what is being excavated and how it got there, especially if a geoscientist is unavailable (Courty 2001).

The most widespread, striking, and readily observable characteristic of sediments is color. It commonly represents the basis for describing stratigraphy in the field and, consequently, for arranging the relative sequence of events that took place during the occupation of a settlement. Yet color can often be misleading and, not uncommonly, can be the result of postdepositional processes (e.g., oxidation or reduction, cementation by secondary minerals, leaching, or bioturbation) that are unrelated to the original depositional event or environment that produced the sediment. Being cognizant of these processes is important in order to avoid making incorrect stratigraphic subdivisions and correlations by grouping or associating sediments solely on the basis of color. Other parameters that should be systematically and correctly recorded are texture, composition, internal organization of clasts, sedimentary and pedogenic structures, the nature of upper and lower contacts, and vertical and lateral changes (Courty 2001). In sum, a basic survey course in geoarchaeology should be a minimal requirement in archaeological studies to ensure that stratigraphic data are observed and recorded correctly (Goldberg and Macphail 2006; Rapp and Hill 2006).

Expertise in operating modern surveying equipment, such as a total station, should also be a standard skill acquired by all archaeology students. This piece of equipment should no longer be thought of as a luxury (or a toy) because of its cost. Prices have declined considerably in the past few years, placing this necessary instrument within the range of most archaeological budgets. Moreover, software has been simplified, making it much easier to use. The total station is indispensable not only in making rapid, accurate, and detailed maps of site topography and features, but also in recording the exact context and provenience of artifacts and ecofacts (McPherron and Dibble 2002; McPherron et al. 2005). This information has significant ramifications for accurately understanding site formation processes (see below). Such analyses can provide powerful guides to excavation and interpretation of both archaeological and geological data by permitting real-time querying of material finds while in the field (e.g., Dibble and McPherron's Newplot program [www.oldstoneage.com]).

The production and plotting of exactly provenienced data with a total station played a key role in understanding the dynamics of site formation at the Mousterian site of Pech de l'Azé IV in the Dordogne region of France. Backplotting of artifacts provenienced with the total station (Figure 3.3), for example, immediately demonstrated that many of the geoarchaeological units are inclined slightly from the interior towards the entrance of the cave.

FIGURE 3.3. Archaeological finds as measured with a total station backplotted along the west profile of Pech de l'Azé IV, France (shown in Figure 3.4). The entrance to the cave is toward the left (south). Note that most of the layers dip slightly toward the left, indicating a source from the right, which turns out to be the interior of the cave (north). Opposite dips are noted for layers in the center of the illustration. These dips, however, are produced by the banking up of sediment over large blocks of roof collapse (generally represented by blacker areas or where the concentrations of dots is lower); these blocks had fallen previously or penecontemporaneously with the finer-grained sediment. The V-like nature of the sediments at the top is quite visible in the field as an erosional surface, which reflects the influx of cryoturbated sediment emanating from within the cave itself, to the right.

This observation, prompted by a geoarchaeological query about artifact dip, was made in the field during the first few days of excavation and thus ruled out the possibility that sediments had been washed into the cave (an expectation based on previous work with cave sediments at Dust Cave, Alabama [Goldberg and Sherwood 1994; Sherwood 2001; Sherwood et al. 2004]). Hence, we were dealing with the void of a true phreatic cave system (not visible in either Figure 3.3 or 3.4) in which sediment found within the cave had accumulated as the result of reworking and redeposition of older phreatic sedimentary relicts derived from the interior of the cave system and not the other way round (Figure 3.3). In short,

access to provenience data obtained by a total station and generated during excavation can be instrumental in furnishing a dynamic understanding of site history and formation processes, and in testing hypotheses in the field.

Representations of Geological and Archaeological Data

From the standpoint of conveying geoarchaeological information, it is often difficult to visualize how tables of bone or lithic artifact counts actually correspond to the stratigraphic framework of a site, even if their recovery contexts are explicitly provided (e.g., Unit H15, Stratum 3). An alternative approach for showing how the frequency of cortical flakes changes with depth, for example, would be to superimpose a set of bar graphs on a photograph of a representative section of the site. With this strategy, one provides the data, where they come from, and what they measure. As a journal editor, I received manuscripts aimed at discussing site formation processes where neither a photograph nor drawing of a representative section is included. In these cases, it is rather difficult for a reader to judge an author's assertions without some independent guide, such as a profile.

Figure 3.4 shows the western profile of the Mousterian site of Pech de l'Azé IV/France at the beginning of the 2003 season. The figure illustrates changes of artifact orientations with depth for the main stratigraphic units in the cave. In this case, the artifact-orientation changes point to differences in sedimentary processes, which in turn reflect upon differences in integrity of the objects' locations (Dibble, this volume).

This kind of direct documentation is even more critical in presenting radiometric dates. The current standard is to provide the dates in a table with some provenience data, perhaps layer number, or square. It is rare, however, to see the exact locations of the samples depicted either on photographs (e.g., Figure 3.4) or on detailed profile drawings. Datable materials (organic materials for radiocarbon dating, sand grains and flints for thermoluminescence dating) can easily be displaced from their original positions, as has been documented for several sites (e.g., Conard et al. 2006; Goldberg and Bar-Yosef 1998; Leigh 2001; Zilhão 2006). Thus, it behooves author(s) to allow readers to see for themselves where dated material originated. An attempt to provide such documentation is shown in Figure 3 of Bar-Yosef et al. 1996, which depicts a complicated profile that exhibits significant evidence of runoff deposition and animal burrowing. It is easy to imagine how difficult it would have been for the reader to understand the recovery contexts of the radiocarbon dates if only a table of "sample locations" had been presented.

Similarly, Courty et al. (1989; see also Kemp 1999) point out that micromorphological analysis involves large-scale observations of profiles in the field and macroscopic views of thin sections at low magnifications (e.g., 1× to 10×; Arpin et al. 2002) or high magnifications (up to 400×). Figure 3.5 illustrates how this process works with a mosaic of photographs from Hohle Fels Cave, Germany (Goldberg et al. 2001). These photos provide evidence that sediments that originated under cold, damp conditions from the interior of the cave (not shown in Figure 3.5) have moved downslope. In this case, interestingly, although the geology indicates sediment movement, the scale of artifact-refits and the "fresh" appearance of the lithics (Dibble, this volume) suggest little or no displacement of the archaeological material (Nicholas Conard, 2006, pers. comm.).

FINAL COMMENTS

This chapter was inspired by problems that have come to light over more than 35 years of my working as a geoarchaeologist with archaeologists, their sites, and their issues. The examples and topics are intended to kindle interest in making archaeology and geoarchaeology more integrated with respect to data collection, presentation, and interpretation. I believe that hands-on experience and observation coupled with the transfer of basic analytical skills should be among the principal goals of teaching archaeology, along with an appreciation of the fundamental role that the geosciences play in studying the cultural past archaeologically. Lord Colin Renfrew (1976) highlighted this point more than 30 years ago:

> This new discipline of geoarchaeology is primarily concerned with the context in which archaeological remains are found. And since archaeology, or at least prehistoric archaeology, recovers almost all its basic data by excavation, every archaeological problem starts as a problem in geoarchaeology.

Because current archaeological practice, particularly in the New World, is often so heavily anthropologically motivated, basic geoscientific issues related to interpreting the variability of the archaeological record are commonly

FIGURE 3.4. Photograph of the western profile of Pech de l'Azé IV, France, at the beginning of the 2003 season, showing orientations of larger (≥ 5 cm) lithic and bone artifacts. The circular plots were produced from measurements made by shooting in the elevations of the uppermost and lowermost edges of the object with the total station. Each dot represents the projection of a line normal to the orientation of the lithic or bone. Thus in layer 6B for example, the concentration of dots on the left side of the diagram indicates a slight inclination of the artifacts in a westerly direction, perhaps reflecting a sediment source from the east, or possible deformation by large blocks of overlying roof fall. Layer 5A, in contrast, shows a more centered concentration reflecting the more flat-lying nature of the artifacts and the deposits as well. The advantage of this type of presentation is that it reveals the orientations of objects that are tied to the sediments as they actually appear in the field, along with their context. As such, it provides the reader with a contextualized data set that can be visualized, critiqued, and interpreted more readily by the researcher in the field during the excavation or independently by the reader at a later time.

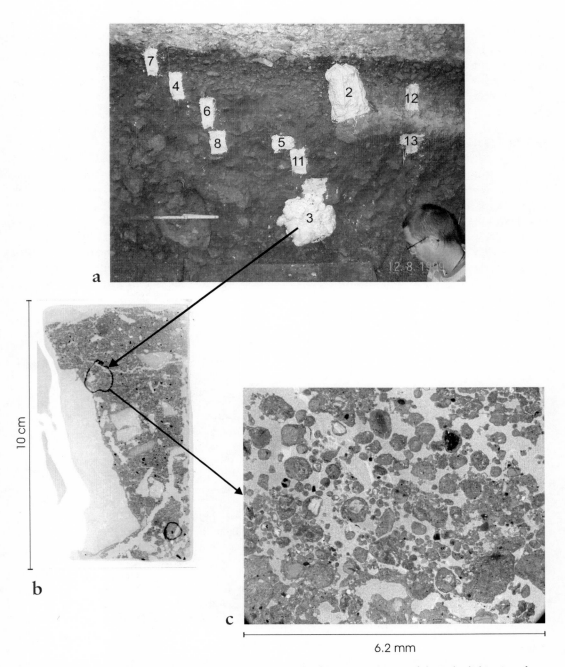

FIGURE 3.5. Series of photographs shown at various scales from excavations of the Paleolithic site of Hohle Fels Cave, Schwabian Jura, Germany. The photos portrayed here range from (*a*) the field scale of the profile; (*b*) through a macro view of an entire thin section (Sample 3A—Gravettian) made with a flatbed scanner; (*c*) down to the scale of the photomicrograph. The photomicrograph (*c*) was taken in plane-polarized light (PPL) and shows aggregates of clay that contain fragments of bone, charcoal, and mineral grains or rock fragments. Significant here is the rounding of the particles produced by cryo-turbation during cold, damp climate conditions. These microscopic details were not visible in the field, where the sediments exposed in the profile consist of large blocks of roof fall embedded and mixed within a silty and clayey matrix, as shown in 3.5a.

overlooked (e.g., the composition of plastered floors and the significance of specific stratigraphic units, such as burned layers). Anthropological theory and the history of archaeological thought are clearly topics that should be taught in order to provide a context for many problems. But perhaps at the undergraduate level we should be concerned more with imparting skills that are needed both in the discipline and in life (e.g., strategies for the acquisition, generation, and organization of data) because theory makes little sense to those who have had little field experience. Furthermore, we cannot ignore the fact that most archaeology students, when first employed as archaeologists, usually begin their careers in CRM, where the realities of day-to-day decisions are based more on field skills than on theoretical ones.

Finally, it might be constructive if archaeologists deemphasized navel gazing or "perpetual introspection" (Tainter and Bagley 2005:58). Geoscientists abandoned such indulgences in the 1960s, with the acceptance of the theory of Plate Tectonics, and essentially have never looked back. Archaeology should learn to live with—and not be afraid of—the fact that it is a discipline that depends on and owes its livelihood to empirically generated data: one really does not know what is under a wall or in a certain layer or feature until after they have been properly excavated. Exploring the origins and behavioral significance of these unknowns, for example, is what makes both geology and archaeology such exciting and, ultimately, enjoyable fields for investigating the past.

NOTE

1. I have sometimes seen a similar lack of questioning in cultural resource management (CRM) projects I have been involved with during the past ten years. This lack, however, is mitigated by the fact that, in most CRM work, there is little time for profound inquiries to be made. Similarly, in many research projects (e.g., those funded by major granting agencies) the principal investigator is often so swamped with logistics, administration, psychological, and practical concerns, that he or she never has time to think about certain key geoarchaeological issues such as "Why is this layer different from the other layers?"

ACKNOWLEDGMENTS

The ideas in this chapter came about as a result of years of interactions and collaborations with archaeologists who are too numerous to name. However, I am very grateful to them. I also benefited from specific comments from friends and colleagues, including T. Arpin, O. Bar-Yosef, N. Conard, H. Dibble, P. Karkanas, D. Killick, C. Marean, S. McPherron, L. Sullivan, and S. C. Sherwood.

REFERENCES CITED

Albert, Rosa M., Ofer Bar-Yosef, Liliane Meignen, and Stephen Weiner
2003   Quantitative Phytolith Study of Hearths from the Natufian and Middle Palaeolithic Levels of Hayonim Cave (Galilee, Israel). *Journal of Archaeological Science* 30: 461–480.

Arpin, Trina L., Carolina Mallol, and Paul Goldberg
2002   A New Method of Analyzing and Documenting Micromorphological Thin Sections Using Flatbed Scanners: Applications in Geoarchaeological Studies. *Geoarchaeology: An International Journal* 17:305–313.

Bar-Yosef, Ofer, Maurice Arnold, Norbert Mercier, Anna Belfer-Cohen, Paul Goldberg, Rupert Housley, Henri Laville, Louis Meignen, John C. Vogel, and Bernard Vandermeersch
1996   The Dating of the Upper Paleolithic Layers in Kebara Cave, Mt. Carmel. *Journal of Archaeological Science* 23:297–306.

Cammas, Cécilia, Julia Wattez, and Marie-Agnès Courty
1996   L'enregistrement Sédimentaire des Modes d'occupation de l'espace. *Paleoecology. XIII International Congress of Prehistoric and Protohistoric Sciences Colloquium VI: Micromorphology of Deposits of Anthropogenic Origin* 3:81–87.

Conard, Nicholas J., M. Bolus, Paul Goldberg, and S. C. Munzel
2006   The Last Neanderthals and First Modern Humans in the Swabian Jura. In *When Neanderthals and Modern Humans Met*, ed-

ited by Nicholas J. Conard, pp. 305–341. Kerns Verlag, Tubingen.

Conard, Nicholas J., Kurt Langguth, and Hans P. Uerpmann

2000 Die Ausgrabungen 1999 in den Gravettien-Schichten des Hohle Fels bei Schelklingen, Alb-Donau-Kreis. *Archäologische Ausgrabungen in Baden-Württemberg* 1999:21–25.

Courty, Marie-Agnès

2001 Microfacies Analysis Assisting Archaeological Stratigraphy. In *Earth Sciences and Archaeology*, edited by Paul Goldberg, Vance T. Holliday, and C. Reid Ferring, pp. 205–239. Kluwer Academic/Plenum, New York.

Courty, Marie-Agnès, Paul Goldberg, and Richard I. Macphail

1989 *Soils and Micromorphology in Archaeology*. Cambridge University Press, Cambridge.

Goldberg, Paul

1979 Geology of Late Bronze Age Mudbrick from Tel Lachish. *Tel Aviv, Journal of the Tel Aviv Institute of Archaeology* 6:60–71.

1983 Applications of Micromorphology in Archaeology. In *Soil Micromorphology*, Vol. 2, edited by Peter Bullock and C. P. Murphy, pp. 139–150. A B Academic, Berkhamsted.

1988 The Archaeologist as Viewed by the Geologist. *Biblical Archaeologist* 51:197–202.

1999 Geoarchaeology in North America. Paper presented at the 64th Annual Meeting of the Society for American Archaeology, Chicago.

Goldberg, Paul, and Trina Arpin

2003 Micromorphology, Sediments, and Artifacts. Paper presented at the 68th Annual Meeting of the Society for American Archaeology, Milwaukee.

Goldberg, Paul, and Ofer Bar-Yosef

1998 Site Formation Processes in Kebara and Hayonim Caves and Their Significance in Levantine Prehistoric Caves. In *Neandertals and Modern Humans in Western Asia*, edited by Takeru Akazawa, Kenichi Aoki, and Ofer Bar-Yosef, pp. 107–125. Plenum, New York.

Goldberg, Paul, and Richard I. Macphail

2006 *Practical and Theoretical Geoarchaeology*. Blackwell Scientific, Oxford.

Goldberg, Paul, Solveig Schiegl, Karen Meligne, C. Dayton, and Nicholas J. Conard

2003 Micromorphology and Site Formation at Hohle Fels Cave, Swabian Jura, Germany. *Eiszeitalter und Gegenwart* 53:1–25.

Goldberg, Paul, and Sarah C. Sherwood

1994 Micromorphology of Dust Cave Sediments: Some Preliminary Results. *Journal of Alabama Archaeology* 40:57–65.

Goldberg, Paul, Stephen Weiner, Ofer Bar-Yosef, Qingi Xu, and Jinyi Liu

2001 Site Formation Processes at Zhoukoudian, China. *Journal of Human Evolution* 41: 483–530.

Hahn, Joachim

1988 *Die Geißenklösterle-Höhle im Achtal bei Blaubeuren I. Fundhorizontbildung und Besiedlung im Mittelpaläolithikum und im Aurignacien*. Forschungen und Berichte zur Vor- und Frühgeschichte in Baden-Württemberg Band 26. Kommissionsverlag, Korad Theiss Verlag, Stuttgart.

Kemp, Robert A.

1999 Soil Micromorphology as a Technique for Reconstructing Paleoenvironmental Change. In *Paleoenvironmental Reconstruction in Arid Lands*, edited by A. K. Singhvi and Edward Derbyshire, pp. 41–71. Oxford and IBH Publishing Co. PVT. LTD., New Delhi.

Langohr, Roger

1993 Types of Tree Windthrow, Their Impact on the Environment and Their Importance for the Understanding of Archaeological Excavation Data. *Helinium* 33:36–49.

Leigh, David S.

2001 Buried Artifacts in Sandy Soils: Techniques for Evaluating Pedoturbation versus Sedimentation. In *Earth Sciences and Archaeology*, edited by Paul Goldberg, Vance T. Holliday, and C. Reid Ferring, pp. 269–293. Kluwer-Plenum, New York.

Littmann, Edwin R.

1967 Patterns in Maya Floor Construction. *American Antiquity* 32:523–533.

Lutz, H. J., and F. S. Griswold

1939 The Influence of Tree Roots on Soil Morphology. *American Journal of Science* 237: 389–400.

Macphail, Richard I.

1990 Soil Micromorphological Evidence of the Impact of Ancient Agriculture. Paper presented at the 14th International Congress of Soil Science, Kyoto, Japan.

1992 Soil Micromorphological Evidence of Ancient Soil Erosion. In *Past and Present Soil Erosion*, edited by Martin Bell and John

Boardman, pp. 197–215. Oxbow Books, Oxford.

2003 Soil Microstratigraphy: A Micromorphological and Chemical Approach. In *Urban Development in North-West Roman Southwark; Excavations 1974–90*, edited by Carrie Cowan, pp. 89–105. MoLAS Monograph 16. Museum of London Archaeological Service, London.

Macphail, Richard I., Marie-Agnès Courty, and Anne Gebhardt

1990 Soil Micromorphological Evidence of Early Agriculture in North-West Europe. *World Archaeology* 22:53–69.

Macphail, Richard I., and Gill M. Cruise

2001 The Soil Micromorphologist as Team Player: A Multianalytical Approach to the Study of European Microstratigraphy. In *Earth Science and Archaeology*, edited by Paul Goldberg, Vance Holliday, and R. Ferring, pp. 241–267. Plenum, New York.

Macphail, Richard I., Gill M. Cruise, S. J. Mellalieu, and Rosalind Niblett

1998 Micromorphological Interpretation of a "Turf-filled" Funerary Shaft at St. Albans, United Kingdom. *Geoarchaeology: An International Journal* 13:617–644.

Macphail, Richard I., Henri Galinié, and Frans Verhaeghe

2003 A Future for Dark Earth? *Antiquity* 77: 349–358.

Macphail, Richard I., and Paul Goldberg

1990 The Micromorphology of Tree Subsoil Hollows: Their Significance to Soil Science and Archaeology. In *Soil-Micromorphology: A Basic and Applied Science*, edited by Lowell A. Douglas, pp. 425–429. Elsevier, Amsterdam.

1995 Recent Advances in Micromorphological Interpretations of Soils and Sediments from Archaeological Sites. In *Archaeological Sediments and Soils: Analysis, Interpretation and Management*, edited by Anthony J. Barham and Richard I. Macphail, pp. 1–24. Institute of Archaeology, University College London.

Macphail, Richard I., John Hather, Scott Hillson, and Roberto Maggi

1994 The Upper Pleistocene Deposits at Arene Candide: Soil Micromorphology of Some Samples from the Cardini 1940–42 Excavation. *Quaternaria Nova* IV:79–100.

Matthews, Wendy

1995 Micromorphological Characterisation and Interpretation of Occupation Deposits and Microstratigraphic Sequences at Abu Salabikh, Iraq. In *Archaeological Sediments and Soils: Analysis, Interpretation and Management*, edited by Anthony J. Barham, M. Bates, and Richard I. Macphail, pp. 41–74. Archetype Books, London.

Matthews, Wendy, Charles A. I. French, Timothy Lawrence, David F. Cutler, and M. K. Jones

1996 Multiple Surfaces: The Micromorphology. In *On the Surface: Catalhoyuk 1993–1995*, edited by Ian Hodder, pp. 301–342. McDonald Institute for Research and British Institute of Archaeology at Ankara, Cambridge.

1997 Microstratigraphic Traces of Site Formation Processes and Human Activities. *World Archaeology* 29:281–308.

Matthews, Wendy, J. Nicholas Postgate, S. Payne, M. P. Charles, and K. Dobney

1994 The Imprint of Living in an Early Mesopotamian City: Questions and Answers. In *Whither Environmental Archaeology?* Vol. 38, edited by Rosemary-Margaret Luff and P. Rowley-Conwy, pp. 171–212. Oxbow Books, Oxford.

McAnany, Patricia A.

1995 *Living with the Ancestors: Kinship and Kingship in Ancient Maya Society.* University of Texas Press, Austin.

McPherron, Shannon P., and Harold L. Dibble

2002 *Using Computers in Archaeology.* McGraw-Hill, Boston.

McPherron, Shannon P., Harold L. Dibble, and Paul Goldberg

2005 Z. *Geoarchaeology: An International Journal* 20:243–262

Meignen, Liliane

1999 Hayonim Cave Lithic Assemblages in the Context of the Near Eastern Middle Paleolithic. In *Neandertals and Modern Humans in Western Asia*, edited by Takeru Akazawa, Kenichi Aoki, and Ofer Bar-Yosef, pp. 165–180. Plenum, New York.

Rapp, George R., Jr., and Christopher L. Hill

2006 *Geoarchaeology: The Earth-Science Approach to Archaeological Interpretation.* 2nd ed. Yale University Press, New Haven.

Renfrew, Colin

1976 Archaeology and the Earth Sciences. In *Geoarchaeology: Earth Science and the Past*, edited by Donald A. Davidson and Myra L. Shackley, pp. 1–5. Duckworth, London.

Rosen, A. M.

1986 *Cities of Clay: The Geoarcheology of Tells.* University of Chicago Press, Chicago

Shahack-Gross, R., R. M. Albert, A. Gilboa, O. Nagar-Hilman, I. Sharon, and S. Weiner
2005   Geoarchaeology in an Urban Context: The Uses of Space in a Phoenician Monumental Building at Tel Dor (Israel). *Journal of Archaeological Science* 32:1417–1431.

Sherwood, Sarah C.
2001   The Geoarchaeology of Dust Cave: A Late Paleoindian Through Middle Archaic Site in the Middle Tennessee River Valley. PhD dissertation, Department of Anthropology, University of Tennessee, Knoxville.

Sherwood, Sarah C., Boyce N. Driskell, Asa R. Randall, and Scott C. Meeks
2004   Chronology and Stratigraphy at Dust Cave, Alabama. *American Antiquity* 69:533–554.

Sherwood, Sarah C., and Paul Goldberg
2001   A Geoarchaeological Framework for the Study of Karstic Cave Sites in the Eastern Woodlands. *Midcontinental Journal of Archaeology* 26:145–167.

Stein, Julie K., and William R. Farrand (editors)
2002   *Sediments in Archaeological Context*. University of Utah Press, Salt Lake City.

Stiner, Mary C. (editor)
2005   *The Faunas of Hayonim Cave, Israel: A 200,000-year Record of Paleolithic Diet, Demography, and Society*. Papers of the Peabody Museum of Archaeology and Ethnology No. 48. Harvard University, Cambridge.

Stiner, Mary C., Steven L. Kuhn, Todd A. Surovell, Paul Goldberg, Liliane Meignen, Stephen Weiner, and Ofer Bar-Yosef
2001   Bone Preservation in Hayonim Cave (Israel): A Macroscopic and Mineralogical Study. *Journal of Archaeological Science* 28:643–659.

Tainter, Joseph A., and Bonnie Bagley
2005   Shaping and Suppressing the Archaeological Record. In *Heritage of Value, Archaeology of Renown: Reshaping Archaeological Assessment and Significance*, pp. 58–73. University Press of Florida, Gainesville.

Wattez, Julia
1988   Contribution à la Connaissance des Foyers Préhistoriques par l'Étude des Cendres. *Bulletin de la Societé Préhistorique Française* 85:352–366.

Wattez, Julia, and Marie-Agnès Courty
1987   Morphology of Ash of Some Plant Materials. In *Micromorphologie des Sols—Soil Micromorphology*, edited by Nicolas Fedoroff, Louis-Marie Bresson, and Marie-Agnès Courty, pp. 677–683. Association Française pour l'Étude du Sol, Plaisir, France.

Weiner, Stephen, Paul Goldberg, and Ofer Bar-Yosef
2002   Three-Dimensional Distribution of Minerals in the Sediments of Hayonim Cave, Israel: Diagenetic Processes and Archaeological Implications. *Journal of Archaeological Science* 29:1289–1308.

Weiner, Stephen, S. Schiegl, Paul Goldberg, and Ofer Bar-Yosef
1995   Mineral Assemblages in Kebara and Hayonim Caves, Israel: Excavation Strategies, Bone Preservation, and Wood Ash Remnants. *Israel Journal of Chemistry* 35:143–154.

Zilhão, J.
2006   Chronostratigraphy of the Middle-to-Upper Paleolithic Transition in the Iberian Peninsula. *Journal of Western Mediterranean Prehistory and Antiquity* 37:7–84.

4

Archaeological Science in America and Britain

DAVID KILLICK

The aboveground floors of the Institute of Archaeology in London look much like those in a typical American anthropology department. Class syllabi, political manifestos, cartoons, and flyers for upcoming talks are taped to doors that open onto cramped offices, whose inhabitants hastily sweep piles of books and papers to the floor to clear a chair for the visitor. Take the elevator down to the basement, however, and one enters a space that has no counterpart in any American anthropology department. The centerpiece of the newly refurbished Wolfson Archaeological Science Laboratories is a vast, clinically clean room that houses four scanning electron microscopes and an electron microprobe, all maintained by a full-time technician and available to graduate students without charge. The basement also contains an X-ray fluorescence unit, a room full of optical microscopes, rooms for extraction of pollen and phytoliths, for chemical and micromorphological analysis of archaeological soils, and for the preparation for microscopy of metals, ceramics, and glasses. On one wall is a discrete plaque thanking several private donors for their support of the laboratory; the name that leaps out at an American is that of Harrison Ford, who was reported by my host to have donated for auction the bullwhip used in his Indiana Jones films.

The Wolfson Laboratories are but one example of the growing role of archaeological science in British archaeology.[1] Archaeological science is certainly nothing new in Britain; the Research Laboratory for Archaeology and the History of Art (RLAHA) at the University of Oxford, the world's first specialist research institute in this area, was established in 1955. The systematic integration of archaeological science into archaeology departments is, however, a more recent development, beginning in the mid-1980s. A pioneer in this movement was the University of Bradford, whose Department of Archaeological Sciences (http://www.bradford.ac.uk/acad/archsci/) offers degrees that blend archaeology with archaeological sciences, and possesses a broader array of in-house scientific expertise and equipment than even the Institute of Archaeology. Other British archaeology departments that have substantial commitments to archaeological science are at the universities of Cambridge, Glasgow, Durham, Nottingham, Sheffield, Southampton, and Cardiff. Outside academia, archaeologists working in heritage management—the British equivalent of our cultural resource management (CRM)—can call upon the services of scientific specialists within English Heritage, the agency charged with conserving Britain's historic and prehistoric legacy. English Heritage (http://www.english-heritage.org.uk/) provides a full range of expert assistance, from geophysical prospecting through dating and materials analysis to conservation of objects and structures, and also commissions fundamental research on new techniques in many of these areas.

These developments, and others to be reviewed below, show that over the last fifteen years the natural sciences have been securely embedded in British archaeological practice. Is this also true of archaeology in the Americas? In this chapter, I attempt a comparison of the state of archaeological science in Britain and in the United States. I readily confess to having divided loyalties; I am a British citizen with a PhD in anthropology from an American university, and teach African archaeology, archaeological science, and the history of technology in a four-field anthropology department. I have been monitoring the growth of archaeological science in Britain and North America for about 15 years (e.g., Killick 1999; Killick and Young 1997). During this time I believe that a serious gap has appeared between British and American archaeology in terms of (1) innovation of scientific methods, (2) their integration into archaeological practice, and (3) the provision of infrastructure (equipment, expertise, funding) to allow significant numbers of archaeologists to use these methods in their field research.

I am not the only archaeological scientist in the United States who thinks that we are lagging seriously behind Britain in these respects. This was one of the topics discussed at the forum "Bridging the Gap: Integrating Archaeological Science and Archaeology" at the 2005 Society for American Archaeology meeting in Salt Lake City. This assertion may, however, be anathema to many American archaeologists, particularly those whose theoretical roots remain grounded in the New Archaeology of the 1970s. British archaeology is often depicted by American archaeologists as divided between minute specializations on the one hand and the outer reaches of postmodern social theory on the other. But then, as Michael Shott has observed (channeling George Bernard Shaw), British and American archaeologists are divided by a common language: few on either side of the Atlantic really know much about the practice of archaeology on the other (Shott 2005). While both of these

tendencies are certainly present in British archaeology, most British archaeologists seem to me to be neither minutely specialized nor wild-eyed postmodernists. My own impression is that the cutting edge in British archaeology today is no more than a commitment to expanding the range and depth of archaeological inquiry, and that archaeological science plays a key role in implementing this aim. Even some postmodern theorists within British archaeology are beginning to understand that archaeological science may serve their interests well (see, for example, Jones 2004 and invited responses in *Archaeometry* [2005] 47: 175–207).[2]

Since 1991, I have taught an annual survey course for seniors and graduate students across the whole range of archaeological sciences, and in revising the syllabus each year I try to at least skim the relevant world literature in English. For this article I have reexamined titles, abstracts, and author affiliations for the last five years (1999–2004) for articles in the international specialist journals, such as *Archaeometry, Journal of Archaeological Science, Geoarchaeology, Radiocarbon, Archaeological Prospection, Quaternary Research,* and *American Journal of Physical Anthropology;* in the general archaeology journals, including *Antiquity, American Antiquity, Latin American Antiquity, Journal of Field Archaeology* and *World Archaeology;* as well as articles on archaeology and quaternary studies in *Nature, Science,* and *Proceedings of the National Academy of Sciences.* I have not attempted a quantitative analysis, which would require awarding fractional shares of authorship for international collaborations as well as tabulation of all the scientific techniques used in each study. Note also that much archaeological science is published in regional archaeology journals, which I have not attempted to scan. To supplement this literature review I searched all the available lists of major research awards for archaeology and archaeological science in both Britain and the United States for the period 2003–2005, and all awards by the National Science Foundation (NSF) Archaeometry competition since its inception in 1973.

CURRENT RESEARCH IN ARCHAEOLOGICAL SCIENCE IN BRITAIN AND THE UNITED STATES

Some subfields of archaeological science seem to be advancing at much the same pace on both sides of the Atlantic. As far as radiocarbon dating is concerned, American and British specialists appear to be in close contact and to be concerned with much the same issues. These include the continuing transition from decay-counting techniques to accelerator mass spectrometry (AMS), issues of inter-laboratory quality control, extension of the radiocarbon calibration curve beyond the last glacial maximum, and advances in compound-specific radiocarbon dating (isolation and dating of pure amino acids, lipids, etc.). The same holds true for the other mainstays of chronometry, which include argon-argon, uranium-series, and luminescence. (All of these are of course widely used outside archaeology, and almost all of the cost of their continuing development is borne by funding agencies for other disciplines, both in Britain and the United States).

New techniques for inorganic chemical analysis, especially inductively coupled plasma mass spectrometry (ICP-MS), seem to be displacing older workhorses such as neutron activation analysis (NAA) and X-ray fluorescence (XRF) in both British and American archaeology. Archaeological geomorphology, human paleobiology, and qualitative and quantitative analysis of macrobotanical and mammalian archaeological assemblages also seem to be running along parallel paths in both nations. So does the use of light stable isotopes (carbon, nitrogen, oxygen) as evidence of past temperatures, the diets of humans and animals, and the former vegetation cover on paleosols. The documentation of past human migrations by strontium isotopes is an equally hot topic on both sides of the Atlantic.

Several techniques are, however, far more frequently applied in European archaeology and paleoenvironmental studies than in the Americas.[3] Some of these disparities can be explained by the different empirical contents of the archaeological and paleoenvironmental records in Eurasia and the Americas (at least until European colonization of the latter).

Thus, British and European archaeologists and archaeological scientists publish many more papers on the technological studies of ancient metals, glasses, and glazes than do American researchers, more on metric criteria for studying domestication of animals, and they make more frequent use of lead isotope ratio analysis in provenance studies. British researchers have made ingenious use of zoological research on the environmental tolerances of extant insect species to reconstruct climatic and environmental changes at archaeological and paleoecological sites (Robinson 2001), but I have not found an example of this approach in American archaeology. Conversely, American papers on phytolith studies in archaeology seem to outnumber British papers on this topic.

I suspect that both observations can be explained by the same fact, which is that Britain is composed of a flotilla of small damp islands with a restricted range of flora and fauna, and abundant "sinks" for pollen and other organic remains. The range of flora and fauna in North America is vast in comparison to Britain, and thus the environmental tolerances of most individual species are as yet less well known. In many areas of the New World conditions are also less favorable for the accumulation and preservation of pollen than they are in Britain. Conversely, phytoliths have proven most useful in the study of grasslands, which occupy a large proportion of the North American continent but are much less abundant in Europe (Vance Holliday, 2005, pers. comm.). The strength of phytolith studies in the United States is also partly explained by consistent support of research on this topic by the NSF Archaeometry competition over the past 15 years.

But other disparities cannot be explained by invoking differences in the empirical content of the past. For example, optical petrography—a technique perfected a century ago—is very widely used in British and European archaeology (either as a stand-alone method or in conjunction with trace-element analysis) for provenance studies of pottery and lithic artifacts (Alpine greenstone axes, jet, Roman millstones, Stonehenge bluestones, and much more). Petrographic analysis has become a widely accepted area of specialization within British archaeology, due in large part to the example set by David Peacock and his students at the University of Southampton.

Although the value of optical petrography is almost universally acknowledged by American specialists in ceramic provenance, it is far less often applied in American than in European archaeology because of an acute shortage of skilled practitioners. While many American graduate students are willing to spend several years training to become archaeological zoologists, botanists, or geomorphologists, very few have been willing to devote an equivalent period of time to achieving proficiency in optical petrography. This is particularly odd when one recalls the pioneering studies published by Anna Shepard from the 1930s through the 1960s. Contributors to a volume assessing her legacy (Bishop and Lange 1991) note that she never held a university position, and thus trained no students. Nor did she establish close working relationships with leading archaeologists who might have championed her approach. Whatever the reasons, her shining example failed to establish optical petrography as a standard method in American archaeology.

A less obvious disparity between British and American archaeology is in the use of micromorphology, which is the study of thin-sections of undisturbed profiles of archaeological soils, sediments, and occupation surfaces (Goldberg, this volume). Micromorphology is revolutionizing the study of site formation processes, and appears from a simple count of published papers to be nearly as often applied by American as by British researchers. In this case, appearances are deceptive, for nearly two-thirds of the published case studies that I have noted by American micromorphologists are the product of a single scholar (Paul Goldberg of Boston University), and most of his studies are of Old World archaeological sites. Applications of micromorphology are still relatively uncommon in New World archaeology.[4]

British researchers also seem to publish many more papers on methodological as-pects of geophysical prospecting in archaeology than do their American counterparts (Kvamme, this volume). Bayesian calibration of radiocarbon dates and the Bayesian statistical approach in general (Buck 2001) are spreading rapidly in British archaeology and paleoecological studies, but are as yet little used in the Americas. The two available software packages for Bayesian radiocarbon calibration (OxCal and BCal) were both developed in Britain. British specialists in paleoclimatic reconstruction for archaeology also seem to employ a wider range of techniques than is usual in American archaeology.

The abundance of paleoenvironmental "sinks" in Britain has also motivated recent advances in tephrochronology as a means of dating them. The dates of major volcanic eruptions, and the chemistry of the tephra produced in individual eruptions, are often well established at source by vulcanologists (usually by radiocarbon dating of organic matter buried under ashfalls). Tiny shards of volcanic glass from the eruptions may be carried hundreds of miles before deposition. If layers of microtephra can be detected in sediments, and linked though their chemical composition (usually determined by electron microprobe) to particular eruptions dated at source, then they provide dates for those levels. This technique is very widely used in European quaternary studies and is the focus of a major research program at the University of Oxford's RLAHA. Much work on tephrochronology has been done in the Americas by geologists, but surprisingly few American archaeologists seem to be aware of the potential of microtephra for dating archaeological and paleoenvironmental sites in Central America and in the western half of North and South America.

The widest gap between British and American archaeological science is in applications of organic chemistry. This is a field that the British practically own, except perhaps for ancient DNA, where Britain would have to wrestle Germany for the world heavyweight title. The major centers for the study of organic residues other than DNA in Britain are at Bristol and Bradford, but inspection of recent British grant awards (see below) shows that expertise in this field is in fact quite widely dispersed. There is relatively little action in the United States in archaeological organic residues other than DNA, with barely half a dozen active scholars. Methodological innovation in the analysis of organic residues has been particularly rapid in the last decade, but techniques like compound-specific stable isotope analysis of organic residues (Copley et al. 2003) have seen little archaeological application by researchers based at American institutions.

THE AVAILABILITY OF
INSTRUMENTS AND EXPERTISE

In this section I ask whether there is adequate capacity to satisfy demand from archaeologists for scientific techniques. The critical issue here is not usually the availability of analytical instruments, but whether there are enough archaeological scientists. Any scientist can undertake an analysis of archaeological materials, but it takes an experienced archaeological scientist to ensure that techniques are appropriate to the archaeological questions posed, that the data produced are of good quality, and that the interpretations made of them are both scientifically and archaeologically sound. I studied the distribution of expertise issue by noting the institutional affiliations of archaeological scientists listed in published articles, and supplemented this information with web searches.

There is clearly plenty of capacity in radiocarbon laboratories in both Europe and North America. Nor have I found any suggestion that there are too few zooarchaeologists, archaeobotanists, palynologists, or specialists in geographic information systems (GIS) in either Europe or North America (though all of these are in critically short supply in other parts of the world, especially in Africa and Southeast Asia). But some techniques that were initially developed in the United States are now much more widely available in Britain, and in Europe at large, than they are here.

There are now only two laboratories for archaeological dendrochronology in the United States, one of which (Arizona) specializes in North America, while the other (Cornell) is

devoted to dendrochronology of the Aegean and Near East. Each has one tenured faculty member. There are least six such laboratories in Britain. Casting the search wider, there are 55 dendrochronology laboratories in Western and Eastern Europe, Scandinavia, and the Baltic countries at time of writing (11/12/05), three-quarters of which list dating as a major research area (http://www.dendro.bf.uni-lj.si /laboratoriji.html). These numbers highlight the extreme fragility of archaeological dendrochronology in the United States. Malcolm Hughes, former head of the University of Arizona's Laboratory of Tree-Ring Research, once joked to me that he probably should not have allowed Jeff Dean and his technicians to go out to lunch together, lest North American archaeological dendrochronology be wiped out at a stroke by a misguided truck. Then there is the fragility of the data. More than 75 years of research in archaeological dendrochronology at the University of Arizona exists only as single paper copies; none of several proposals to build an electronic database were ever funded.

There is a particularly stark contrast between Europe and the United States in the current status of archaeomagnetic dating. American researchers played a major role in developing this technique, but it is now almost extinct in the United States. Laboratories at Colorado State University and the University of Arizona have shut down, leaving only Franklin and Marshall College (which does not have a graduate program) in the academic sector, and the laboratory at the Museum of New Mexico. My brief web search found six archaeomagnetic laboratories in Britain: four in universities, one at English Heritage, and one in the private sector. Two of these are participants in AARCH, a network of 12 European archaeomagnetic laboratories with a current grant of 1.48 million euros (at time of writing, 1€ = $1.33) from the European Commission to train a new generation of specialists (http://www.bradford.ac.uk/arch sci/aarch/). Why are Europeans putting serious money into archaeomagnetic dating when Americans have largely given up on the technique? The answer lies in the relative states of development of archaeomagnetic master curves in the two continents. Europeans have invested the time and funding to refine these curves to the point where they are archaeologically useful, whereas large portions of even the best developed North American curve—that for the American Southwest—still have large sections that are poorly defined nearly 40 years after Robert Dubois began work on the master curve for this region (Lengyel and Eighmy 2002).

Several other subfields of archaeological science have only three or fewer dedicated laboratories in American universities or museums. Among these are luminescence dating, organic residue analysis, uranium-series dating, argon-argon dating, electron spin resonance dating, ceramic and glass technology, and archaeometallurgy. How many experts do we actually need in each field? No definite answer can be given, as no attempt has been made to estimate actual or potential demand for these services. Lacking this information, we have to resort to cruder indicators. One symptom of demand exceeding supply is when American archaeologists find it necessary to go overseas for technical expertise or training. This is certainly the case in archaeometallurgy, my own field of specialization. I know six American graduate students in this field who have recently obtained, or are working on, degrees in British universities, or who are enrolled in American universities but have done dissertation research with British archaeometallurgists. Similarly, recently published work on identifying maize in organic residues is a collaboration between an American archaeologist and a British archaeological scientist (Reber and Evershed 2004). It required expertise in a branch of analytical organic chemistry that no American archaeological scientist could provide.

These observations are merely suggestive of a lack of capacity in the United States, and in any case only a small fraction of the more than seven thousand members of the Society for American Archaeology will yet want to make use any of the methods listed in the previous paragraph. Ceramic and lithic provenance studies are, however, of vital interest to most of the membership, and thus make a better test case.

The first archaeological uses of neutron activation analysis (NAA) in the United States were in made in the late 1950s and in the context of classical archaeology (Matson 2003). The 1960s saw the application of NAA in anthropological archaeology for provenance studies of inorganic materials, and by the 1970s NAA had become the technique of choice for provenance studies in the Americas. The choice of this technique over alternatives largely reflects the fact that NAA was then almost free to American archaeologists. The research nuclear reactors in which samples were irradiated were heavily subsidized by the federal government as part of a program (initially titled Atoms for Peace) that was intended to show a nervous American public that nuclear technology had civilian as well as military uses. In practice, the major constraint for American archaeologists eager to employ NAA has not been access to equipment—at least a dozen American reactors have run archaeological samples at some point—but access to persons skilled at seeking archaeologically meaningful structure in the blizzards of trace-element data generated by NAA. Four programs (those at Brookhaven National Laboratories [BNL], the University of Missouri Research Reactor [MURR], Lawrence Berkeley National Laboratory (LBNL), and the Smithsonian Institution) developed particular expertise in archaeological applications of NAA. Each has been further subsidized through laboratory grants from the NSF Archaeometry program (MURR) or through federal block grants to the parent institution (Smithsonian, LBNL, and BNL).

European governments did not subsidize civilian research access to nuclear reactors nearly as generously. I suspect that differences in the apparent cost of NAA led to the emergence of different "technological styles" of provenance analysis in the United States and Europe. While provenance analysis became practically synonymous with NAA in America, Europeans tended to employ optical petrography in the first instance for ceramics and lithics (except obsidian), supplemented by a more varied mix of techniques for trace element analysis than in the United States. NAA is employed in Europe, but there is much more extensive use of optical emission spectroscopy (OES), X-ray fluorescence (XRF), particle-induced X-ray emission analysis (PIXE), and atomic absorption spectroscopy (AAS) than in the United States. European expertise in archaeological provenance work is therefore dispersed among many laboratories rather than being concentrated in a few, as in the United States and Canada.

But even in America the demand for NAA from archaeologists far exceeded the supply of archaeological scientists who are expert in its application. In the immortal words of Crown (1991), most American archaeologists felt obligated by the mid-1980s to "nuke them sherds," but in practice, archaeologists in federal agencies and in the CRM sector have rarely been able to obtain access to NAA. Even within the academic sector there was much more demand than the few experts in archaeological NAA could accommodate. The few experts in this technique were free to choose their collaborators from the pool of applicants. In provenance analysis of obsidian, for example, NAA laboratories gave priority to academic archaeologists working in Mesoamerica and the Near East. The unmet demand for obsidian analysis in the western United States provided the incentive for Steven Shackley to develop the XRF facility at the University of California, Berkeley, which now provides most of the obsidian analyses for this region to academic, government, and CRM clients.

There were, however, far more archaeologists seeking expert help with ceramic provenance studies, and a desperate search for alternatives to NAA ensued. Some archaeologists turned to the relatively new technique of inductively coupled plasma optical emission spectroscopy (ICP-OES). In the late 1980s and early 1990s, a consortium of academic archaeologists studying northern Rio Grande White wares had large numbers of sherds analyzed at the ICP-OES laboratory at Royal Holloway College, University of London.

Ronald L. Bishop (2005, pers. comm.) recalls that he recommended that the consortium approach the Royal Holloway laboratory because the Smithsonian NAA program could not take on any new partners at that time. Another participant notes that while this solved one problem—the British laboratory proved fast, cheap, and accurate—it raised another difficult issue, which was that the collaborating archaeologists had to assume total responsibility for statistical interrogation of the data (Patricia L. Crown, 2005, pers. comm.). For this reason the partnership did not endure.

In 1987 the National Science Foundation awarded the Laboratory of Archaeological Chemistry at the University of Wisconsin, Madison, funds to install an ICP-OES dedicated to archaeological samples. Unfortunately, the Wisconsin laboratory developed an idiosyncratic method (weak-acid extraction) of preparing ceramic samples for analysis (Burton and Simon 1993). This method was shown by a controlled comparison (Triadan et al. 1997) to produce data structures that are not comparable to data obtained by NAA, probably because weak-acid extractions reflect post-depositional chemical alteration to a much greater extent than do whole-sherd NAA or ICP analyses (Killick 1999). Weak-acid extraction is no longer used for ceramic provenance analysis (James Burton, 2005, pers. comm.), and the several thousand ceramic analyses made by this technique are, at this point, of historical interest only.

A more recent response to demand was the establishment in the 1990s of a private-sector ceramic petrography laboratory (at Desert Archaeology, Inc.) specializing in the archaeology of southern Arizona (http://www.desert.com/petroweb/petrology.php). This facility serves academic, government, and private-sector clients. Ceramic provenance studies have also been attempted in this region by a combination of petrography and electron microprobe analysis of ceramic pastes (Abbott 2000). The latter method is incapable of detecting trace elements, and thus can be compared to XRF and NAA data only to a very limited extent. (And then only if one accepts that electron microprobe analyses of porous earthenware pastes can be accurate, which I strongly doubt.)

Conventional ICP-MS (in which the sample is completely dissolved) compares very favorably to NAA in sensitivity across a broad range of elements, and the data produced should in theory be compatible with those produced by NAA and XRF. ICP-MS is now widely available in the United States, is fast and relatively cheap, and thus should make trace-element analysis readily available to most archaeologists; my scan of affiliations listed by authors suggests that this is indeed happening. Increasingly, it appears, American archaeologists are collaborating with their local geology or chemistry departments. While such collaboration will lessen the pressure upon the five established centers for trace-element provenance (MURR, Smithsonian/NIST, LBNL, the Berkeley XRF laboratory, and the new ICP-MS center at California State University, Long Beach) there are some potential dangers in decentralization. One is that the archaeologists involved will usually have to assume full responsibility for data analysis and interpretation. As noted above in the case of the Rio Grande ceramics project, this can be a daunting task. A less obvious problem is that of ensuring the accuracy of the data. The five laboratories cited have taken great care with inter-laboratory calibration, through regular exchange of samples and standards, so that all of their data on (for example) obsidian sources can be merged with confidence into a single database. Will archaeologists working with their local ICP-MS laboratory be as careful? As one who is from time to time asked to review archaeological research proposals involving inorganic chemical analysis, I am alarmed by the frequent lack of discussion of calibration issues in proposals submitted by archaeologists not affiliated with one of the five established centers. Archaeological science should, like any other branch of science, be a cumulative and progressive enterprise, but far too many American archaeologists seem to regard each provenance study as an island unto itself.

In summary, the demand for ceramic and lithic provenance analyses in the United States has consistently outpaced growth in the supply of experienced analysts. Access to these analysts has been strongly skewed by place of employment (academic archaeology has been favored over CRM) and by region (Mesoamerican archaeologists have had precedence for NAA). Ad hoc solutions have sprung up at various points in time to meet the unsatisfied demand. Some of these solutions have been successful, some have failed, and the jury is still out on others. Demand for provenance analysis still greatly exceeds supply of experienced practitioners of the art.

There is only one center of archaeological NAA in Europe that is comparable to the American centers listed above. This is at the National Center for Scientific Research in Greece (http://www.ims.demokritos.gr/arch aeoceramics/index.html), which provides analytical services for Aegean archaeologists from many nations. But elsewhere in Europe archaeological provenance analysis by trace elements and isotopes tends to be both initiated and carried out by geochemists with at least a part-time specialization in archaeological science. Geochemists who produce inaccurate data do not last long in their profession. Whereas American archaeologists tend to discard data produced by older methods when a newer one becomes available, Europeans try to retain older, less precise data if it can be shown by newer methods to be sufficiently accurate for archaeological goals. An outstanding example of how to consolidate previous research in ceramic provenance studies is the GEOPRO program, funded by the European Union from 1998 through 2001 (total funding: €1.3 million). This has allowed leading experts in Greece, Britain, Spain, and Germany to cross-calibrate data sets developed by different analytical techniques (NAA, XRF, AA, ICP-MS; see Hein et al. 2002) and to develop "mixed-mode" statistical approaches to allow both chemical and petrographic data to be used in assignments of provenance.

The major conclusion to be drawn from this extended example is that provenance analysis in the United States is still constructed around separate communities of practice, both with respect to analytical techniques and geographical regions. While the same was true of Europe at an earlier time, European provenance studies—and European archaeological science in general—have entered a new phase that is marked by consolidation of previous research, critical evaluation of methods and data, and systematic coordination of training, research, conferences, and publication across Europe as a whole. More generally, European archaeological science today displays many of the characteristics of a mature field of science. American archaeological science has achieved this state only in some forms of chronometry (radiocarbon, dendrochronology, argon-argon dating) and arguably in light stable isotope studies of diet and paleoclimates.

PLANNING FOR ARCHAEOLOGICAL SCIENCE AT THE NATIONAL LEVEL

Perhaps the most striking difference between archaeological science in the United States and Britain is in planning. Neither the Society for American Archaeology nor the National Science Foundation has any mechanism to monitor demand for archaeological science, to make periodic evaluations of the state of the art, or to make recommendations for future investments. In Britain, all of these functions were undertaken from 1994 to 2004 by the Science-Based Archaeology Strategy Group (SBASG), which was created by the British Parliament to monitor the capacity of both physical infrastructure and human capital (including postgraduate training) for archaeological science in Britain and to advise the Natural Environment Research Council (NERC) on priorities for funding.

SBASG was the latest manifestation of a committee that has advised British science funding agencies on archaeological science since the mid-1970s. One of its most important roles was to identify important emerging research questions that were worthy of targeted funding. NERC funded several of these Key Initiatives (listed at http://www.nerc.ac.uk/funding/sbarchaeology/strategy.shtml). The last one was "Environmental Factors in the Chronology of Human Evolution and Dispersals" (http://www.nerc.ac.uk/funding/thematics/efched/index.shtml), which awarded £2 million in grants in 2002, to be spent over four years (at time of writing, £1 = $1.75). The prominence of British researchers in the fields of organic residue analysis and studies of ancient DNA is attributable in large part to the success of an earlier NERC Key Initiative on biomolecular archaeology.

The abolition of SBASG in 2004 marked the coming of age of archaeological science in Britain. At this point, NERC decided that it was sufficiently mature that it could compete on a level playing ground with the other sciences that fall under NERC's mandate. Hence, the "ring-fenced" allocation of funds for archaeological science was also abandoned, and proposals for research in this field now compete for funding with those in other areas that NERC supports.

It is tempting to explain these differences in oversight at the national level by appealing to pop psychology, contrasting the European preference for planning to the American preference for free-market competition. There is undoubtedly some truth to this explanation, but it is far from the whole story. Most public and private funding for archaeology and archaeological science in the United States is awarded on the basis of peer-reviewed proposals, which are arguably a type of free-market competition, but then so is much of the available funding for archaeology and archaeological science in Britain. In the United States, the National Science Foundation is constantly trying to steer scholars into emerging areas of research by funding interdisciplinary programs around themes such as distributed supercomputing or nanotechnology, or around geographical areas, as in the Department of Polar Programs, which has funded some archaeology at high latitudes. The NSF Archaeology Program has tried to stimulate submission of proposals in two very broad areas (archaeometry and human origins) through annual competitions. This is the passive approach to funding: one sets out the bait and waits to see what sorts of proposals it attracts. The British use this approach, as well, but they also combine it with an active strategy that involves making educated guesses about which areas of archaeological science will be particularly valuable to archaeology in the near future. I believe that SBASG deserves much of the credit for Britain's excellent record of innovation in archaeological sciences over the last decade.

The United States has no permanent and transparent mechanism for periodic review of the state of archaeological sciences. Even in so fundamental a technique as radiocarbon dating, it was left to the British to devise, fund, and conduct statistical studies of inter-laboratory variation. Since the 1950s, the United States has consistently had more radiocarbon laboratories, and has produced more dates, than any other nation. Archaeologists have long suspected that quality control in radiocarbon dating was not all that it should have been, and some American archaeologists have been able to show statistically significant offsets in sets of dates from different laboratories for archaeological components of short duration (e.g., Shott 1992). Yet no systematic attempt to assess inter-laboratory variation was made until 1978, when sets of samples of known radiocarbon content (wood, peat, grain, sediment, etc.) were prepared in Glasgow and sent to 20 laboratories around the world for multiple blind measurements, with the results submitted to British statisticians for analysis. The first and second studies, funded entirely by NERC, were completed in 1982 and 1990, and revealed a truly shocking lack of consistency among participating laboratories (International Study Group 1982; Scott et al. 1990). These studies prompted many laboratories to pay more attention to sources of internal error. By the fourth inter-laboratory study, completed in 2003, 85 radiocarbon laboratories participated—about 75 percent of all laboratories worldwide—and the statistical analyses of the results show generally improved accuracy and precision (Scott 2003). But some laboratories are still producing inaccurate dates, understating their real errors, or both.

Periodic assessments of quality control and periodic reviews of priorities are hallmarks of mature sciences, but as yet neither the Society for American Archaeology nor NSF Archaeology seems to be much concerned with these issues. If archaeological science is to become a mature science in the United States, as in Britain, there needs to be some guidance and oversight at the national level by one or more panels of appointed experts, whose findings and recommendations should be posted as public documents.

FUNDING

The focus in this section is on funding for research and development (including research infrastructure) in archaeological science. Research and development spending is the motor of innovation, and is therefore a better indicator of the state of archaeological science than is the amount spent on consumption of scientific services in archaeological projects.

In the United States, the principal source of funding for basic research on techniques, other than radiometric dating, is the annual archaeometry competition of the NSF Archaeology and Archaeometry Program.[5] The archaeometry competition was introduced in 1973, but the funding allocated to it has fluctuated within the same window since its inception. Annual awards have oscillated between $0.7 million and $1.4 million, averaging around $1.1 million per year.[6]

The archaeometry competition makes two types of awards: one for research, and the other for laboratory support. Research awards are primarily for technique development; proposals to make use of established techniques within specific archaeological field projects are directed instead to the Archaeology Program. Laboratory-support awards provide funds for personnel salaries, equipment, and sometimes to subsidize the cost of analyses for collaborating archaeologists. Four laboratories have been consistently supported under this program: the University of Missouri Research Reactor (MURR), the University of Arizona's Laboratory of Tree-Ring Research, the Cornell University Dendrochronology Laboratory, and the Laboratory of Archaeological Chemistry at the University of Wisconsin, Madison. Each of these has received at least four multiyear awards and at least $1 million in archaeometry competition funding since 1985. Other laboratories that have received sporadic support include the Berkeley Geochronology Unit/Institute for Human Origins (argon-argon dating), several radiocarbon laboratories, and several laboratories providing luminescence or electron spin resonance dating.

Archaeological science in Britain is mostly funded by the Natural Environment Research Council (NERC), whereas other aspects of archaeological research are funded by agencies such as the Arts and Humanities Research Council (AHRC), the British Academy, and English Heritage (though, as noted below, both the AHRC and English Heritage may also fund archaeological science). As noted above, within NERC there is no longer any predetermined pot of funds for archaeological science; proposals in this field must compete against those in other fields funded by NERC. Thus, proposals in archaeological science must, above all, be demonstrably good science to be funded. In the United States, most archaeological science proposals are submitted for the archaeometry competition and reviewed by a panel composed solely of archaeologists and archaeological scientists. Over the last 15 years, by far the most common complaint that I have heard about the reviewing of proposals submitted to the NSF Archaeometry competition is that the review panels focus too much upon the anthropological rationale for the research and not enough on the science.

British archaeological scientists complain about the scarcity of funding, but in comparison to the United States, spending has been generous. The NERC grants web site (http://gotw.nerc.ac.uk) lists 38 awards for science-based archaeology with starting dates in 2003, 2004, and 2005. In sum, the amount awarded was £4.983 million (accessed 11/12/05, at which time £1.00 = $ 1.74). Over the same period the NSF Archaeometry competition made 16 awards (13 current, 3 expired) with a total value of $1.798 million (retrieved 11/12/05 through http://www.nsf.gov/awardsearch). If one converts the pound at the exchange rate listed above, NERC's spending on archaeological science from 2003 to 2005 was 4.8

times that of the NSF Archaeometry competition. The comparison becomes even more unfavorable when adjusted for relative population size. In 2004, the United States had 293 million inhabitants and Britain 60.2 million (http://www.census.gov/ipc/www/idbsum .html). Thus core funding (i.e., funding specifically labeled as archaeometry or science-based archaeology) per capita for the period 2003–2005 was 23.5 times as large in Britain as in the United States.

This is not the whole story, for there are other sources of funds for archaeological science in both the United States and Britain that are not labeled as such. Some proposals funded by NSF Archaeology seem to me to be better characterized as research and development (R&D) than as applied archaeological science. I read all online abstracts for NSF awards (both current and expired) in archaeology with starting dates in 2003, 2004, and 2005, and consider the following to be R&D awards: freshwater bivalve morphometrics and hydrological conditions (2003: $28,464); stable isotopes as a tool for studying California hunter-gatherer strategies (2003: $120,667); airborne radar for site mapping in Mesoamerica (2004: $78,421); isotopic studies of past human migration in Mesoamerica (2004: $256,369); multidisciplinary study of horse domestication (2004: $173,089); interdisciplinary paleoecology at Makapansgat (2004: $50,464); techniques for provenance of flint in France (2005: $58,454); and domestication of the donkey (2005: $79,882). I excluded, however, funding for genomic studies of living human populations, even when the rationale for these focuses upon human origins. NSF Archaeology has partially funded one large grant in this field (2004: $1.14 million) but almost all other research on this topic has been funded, both in the United States and Europe, by funding agencies for human biology and health sciences, or by private foundations. In any case, research in this area has been far more heavily funded in Europe than in the United States over the last decade (see for example Renfrew and Boyle 2000).

In marked contrast to British practice, there has been little direct support for archaeology from divisions responsible for funding natural science or engineering research at NSF. Archaeologists have however indirectly benefited from core support from other NSF programs for the NSF/University of Arizona AMS radiocarbon dating facility, though only about 15 percent of the dates run there are on archaeological samples (T. M. Jull, 2005, pers. comm.). Block grants to the Smithsonian Institution, the National Institute for Standards and Technology, and the Lawrence Berkeley National Laboratories also benefit archaeology, but the dollar amount of such subsidy is not accessible. Other branches of government do not contribute much. While applied archaeological science is funded by many federal and state agencies (especially state departments of transportation) and by the private sector (largely in the context of CRM projects), there are almost no sources of funding for technique development and laboratory support outside NSF. NASA has occasionally funded demonstrations of its new technologies, such as airborne and space-shuttle radar, on archaeological projects, but these seem to be publicity-generating activities for NASA rather than evidence of any genuine interest in archaeology. A few archaeological applications of DNA and immunoassay studies have been slipped into research supported by the National Institutes of Health. The National Center for Preservation Technology and Training, a unit of the National Park Service, has occasionally funded technique development, and there is episodic "spin-off" funding from the Department of Energy, such as research on glass hydration and desert varnish, both of which are relevant to long-term disposal of nuclear wastes. But these examples are few and far between.

Private and corporate support for archaeological research is increasingly common, but is comparatively rare for laboratory-based archaeological science. I am aware of only six instances of private endowments for this purpose in the United States, one of which is the Landon T. Clay Chair of Scientific Archaeology at Harvard University, created in 1987.[7]

The Arts and Humanities Research Council is the main source of funding for academic archaeology in Britain. It appears to be increasingly willing to make major grants for archaeological science. In my search of the 392 AHRC awards from 1999 to 2005 (http://www.ahrc.ac.uk/awards/), I found 21 awards that I would consider to be research and development in archaeological science, 13 of which were made from 2003 to 2005. Among these are awards for organic residue analysis from Niah Cave, Sarawak (2003: £52,645), predictive modeling by GIS of the locations of submerged postglacial sites (2003: £51,558), paleopathological studies of early horse husbandry (2003: £315,660), stable isotope studies of mobility, migration, and diet of Beaker people (2004: £531,079), and DNA studies of tools and soils from Neanderthal sites (2004: £116,097).

Archaeological scientists in Britain can also apply to NERC for support for MSc and PhD students to undertake specific research projects or to be trained in particular skills. At time of writing, 24 current studentships in archaeological science were listed on the NERC web site (http://sotw.nerc.ac.uk). An increasingly important source of funding for training young researchers in archaeological science is the European Commission, through the various categories of training and cooperation grants available through its "Marie Curie" programs (http://mc-opportunities.cordis.lu/). All five Marie Curie awards made to date for archaeological training and coordination are, or were, coordinated by British universities. I have already noted the GEOPRO program for ceramic provenance studies, which ended in 2001, and the AARCH program for training in archaeomagnetism, which ended in 2006. Other current Marie Curie grants are for archeological biogeochemistry, which currently funds four PhD students at the University of Bradford, and a grant of €1 million to the Institute of Archaeology in London for training European students to both MSc and PhD levels in archaeological and conservation science. Marine archaeology is also a component of a large Marie Curie grant to the University of Southampton for seafloor acoustic imaging.

The only comparable source of funds for

training in the United States is the NSF/ University of Arizona IGERT Program in Archaeological Science, which fully funds 14 graduate students each year. This was a competitive award from NSF's Integrative Graduate Education and Research Training program, and funding for it expires in 2008. Archaeological science is not a recognized category for NSF Graduate Research Fellowships, and in any case there were only eight awards for archaeology among the 1,100 GRF awarded in 2005. NSF Archaeology has made an average of 21 Doctoral Dissertation Improvement Grants (capped at $12,000) each year from 2003 to 2005, but based on the online abstracts (http://www.nsf.gov/awardsearch), it appears that almost none of these involved research and development in archaeological science.

Last but not least in the British context is English Heritage, which was founded by an Act of Parliament in 1983. In 2003–2004, it had a combined income (from government grants and admission charges) of £145 million. English Heritage is charged with preservation and interpretation of British historic and prehistoric monuments and buildings, and manages more than 400 cultural properties. It therefore performs many of the same functions as the Cultural Resources division of the U.S. National Park Service. Both the archaeology and archaeological science teams of English Heritage are housed at Fort Cumberland, near Portsmouth. The archaeological science laboratories there offer a wide range of techniques and services, including remote sensing; scanning electron microscopy; chemical, botanical, zoological, metallurgical, and ceramic analysis; analysis of human remains; and conservation of finds. They also purchase from the academic sector analyses that they cannot provide in-house (e.g., strontium isotopes, radiocarbon dating) and commission fundamental research—on conservation treatments, for example—from universities and industry. The archaeological science team supports English Heritage's own team of about 60 archaeologists, and also undertakes projects referred to them by nine regional archaeological science officers. The cost of this support is unfortunately not given as a line item in the annual reports. English Heritage also manages the Aggregates Levy Sustainability Fund (http://www.english-heritage.org.uk/server/show/nav.1315), which puts about £7 million per year into archaeology, some of which goes into basic scientific research (A. M. Pollard, 2005, pers. comm.).

This listing is far from exhaustive. Both NSF and NERC also have competitions for major research equipment (mass spectrometers, electron microprobes, scanning electron microscopes, etc.) but these instruments are not usually for the exclusive use of archaeologists or archaeological scientists. Private and public universities in the United States also put some funding into archaeological science through start-up funding for newly hired faculty, and through internal research funding, but the amounts of these investments cannot be retrieved. There are no private research universities in Britain.

There is certainly plenty of room for argument about what else should be included in this comparison. But it seems highly improbable that missing records would alter the major conclusion to be drawn from the data presented above: in terms of funding designated for research and development of archaeological science, the United States is being massively outspent by Britain.

INSTITUTIONAL SETTINGS FOR ARCHAEOLOGICAL SCIENCE

The disparity in research funding is certainly an important reason why Britain has in recent years been more innovative than the United States in many aspects of archaeological science. But there are other factors that need critical examination. Who accepts responsibility for nurturing archaeological scientists? Who pays their salaries and provides them with laboratory space? And who takes responsibility for training more of them?

The modern era in archaeological science began with a series of ad hoc liaisons between individual archaeologists and individual scientists. In the United States, we can point to the pivotal collaboration in the early 1930s between Emil Haury and the astronomer A. E.

Douglass on dendrochronology (Nash 1999) and to collaboration between the chemist Willard Libby and the archaeologist Froehlich Rainey in the development of radiocarbon dating during the early 1950s (Libby 1955). From the late 1950s through the 1960s, nuclear chemists (Edward Sayre, Garman Harbottle, Adnan Gordus, Frank Asaro) worked with both classical archaeologists (Frederick Matson, Homer Thomson, Hetty Goldman) and anthropological archaeologists (James Griffin, Robert Rands, Kent Flannery) to establish the chemical approach to provenance of non-metallic materials (Matson 2003). In the mid-1960s, there were fertile interactions at Yale University between the archaeologists K. C. Chang and Michael Coe, the geochemist Karl Turekian, and the radiocarbon guru Minze Stuiver. These pioneers trained the first generation of archaeological scientists—those with graduate training in both science and archaeology—in the United States, including Nikolaas van der Merwe and Ronald L. Bishop.

Archaeological science in Britain also began with a series of ad hoc collaborations. In late 1953, the young Oxford physicist E. T. Hall, working with anatomist Joseph Weiner and archaeologist Kenneth Oakley, proved that Piltdown Man was a fake. This revelation created an international sensation, as a result of which Hall, Weiner, and archaeologist Christopher Hawkes persuaded the University of Oxford to establish the Research Laboratory for Archaeology and the History of Art. This facility was established in 1955 with Hall as founding director. Cambridge University was also at the forefront in the 1950s, largely through Grahame Clark's pathbreaking use of zoological and botanical evidence to reconstruct the seasons of occupation at the Mesolithic site of Star Carr. In the 1960s, ecological archaeology became the main focus at Cambridge through the research of Eric Higgs and his students, while Arnold Aspinall and colleagues developed geophysical remote sensing for archaeology at the University of Bradford, and David Peacock pioneered geological approaches to provenance at the University of Southampton. Colin Renfrew, then at the University of Sheffield, was a key figure in ar-

chaeological science in the 1960s because of his pioneering geochemical studies of obsidian exchange, and his advocacy for radiocarbon dating at a time when many European archaeologists were openly skeptical of it. He has been a strong promoter of innovations in archaeological science ever since (e.g., Renfrew and Boyle 2000). Other major figures in the development of archaeological science in Britain were Don Brothwell and Michael Tite, each of whom produced a key text that that helped define the field of archaeological science (Brothwell and Higgs 1963; Tite 1972).

A second setting for collaboration, in both Britain and North America, was in the conservation laboratories of major museums. These labs were equipped to conduct chemical and physical research on object conservation (and, in the aftermath of Piltdown, to spot fakes). The British Museum Research Laboratories became a powerhouse in archaeological science in the 1970s, providing expertise ranging from thermoluminescence and radiocarbon dating to ancient pyrotechnology (metals, ceramics, glasses). The laboratory of the Boston Museum of Fine Arts began collaborating with Classical archaeologists in the late 1950s, as did (much later) the laboratories of the Getty Museum, the Metropolitan Museum of Art, and the Los Angeles County Museum.

In the 1960s, the Museum of Anthropology and Archaeology at the University of Pennsylvania, building upon Froehlich Rainey's collaboration with Libby, founded the Museum Applied Science Center for Anthropology (MASCA). In the 1960s and 1970s, MASCA's Elizabeth Ralph developed one of the first radiocarbon calibration tables and helped to develop the cesium magnetometer. Subsequently, MASCA has made major contributions to archaeometallurgy (Vince Pigott and Stuart Fleming), archaeobotany (Naomi Miller), organic residue analysis (Patrick McGovern), and the development of chemical analysis by PIXE (Fleming, with Charles P. Swann [now Professor Emeritus, Bartol Research Institute, University of Delaware]). Its publication series (MASCA Papers in Science and Archaeology), edited by Kathleen Ryan, was notable for its exemplary integration of scientific analysis with anthropological theory.

In the 1970s, the Conservation Analytical Laboratory (CAL) of the Smithsonian Institution became a major contributor to anthropological archaeology through its neutron activation program (Ronald Bishop, James Blackman, Edward Sayre) and studies of ceramic technology (Pamela Vandiver) and metallurgy (Martha Goodway). CAL and its successors were also an important training ground for archaeological scientists; many leading figures in the field today have held predoctoral or postdoctoral fellowships there.

In 1977, a consortium of eight universities around Boston established the Center for Materials Research in Archaeology and Ethnography (CMRAE), the laboratories for which were located at the Massachusetts Institute of Technology under the directorship of Heather Lechtman. During the academic year, the Center provides courses taught by faculty from the participating universities, all of whom allow their students to take these courses for credit. CMRAE also provides summer courses of several weeks duration, and more than 200 students from universities throughout the United States have learned the basics of zooarchaeology, archaeobotany, archaeometallurgy, ceramic petrography, geoarchaeology, and statistics from resident or visiting instructors. CMRAE is a unique institution that has gone largely unappreciated within MIT. In the mid 1990s, it fought off a determined attempt by the provost to close the program, and subsequently it was forced to sever its connection with the Department of Anthropology; it now resides in the Department of Materials Science. In retrospect, it would probably have been better placed at an institution more sympathetic to its educational mission, such as Boston University.

From the mid-1980s, however, American and British strategies in archaeological science began to diverge (Killick and Young 1997). While American anthropological and Classical archaeologists continued to work primarily with scientists in other academic departments and in museums, some archaeology departments in Britain began to offer positions to experts with degrees in other fields. Among the first wave were metallurgist Ronald Tylecote at the Institute of Archaeology in London and chemist Mark Pollard, who was hired as founding head of the Department of Archaeological Sciences at the University of Bradford. The success of these early experiments led to a second wave of appointments from the end of the 1990s to the present.

In the context of British archaeology, these were not radical moves. British archaeology departments house prehistorians, Classical archaeologists, Egyptologists, and Near Eastern archaeologists together, whereas in the United States these are segregated in separate departments of anthropology, classics, and Near Eastern studies, each of which has a distinct habitus. British archaeology departments are collections of specialists in particular areas, and there is no expectation that all members should share the same theoretical orientation, or have had the same intellectual preparation. In Britain, archaeological scientists are evaluated for their expertise and for their prior achievements in the field, without having to pass the litmus test (can he/she teach survey courses in archaeology and physical anthropology?) to which any candidate for an assistant professorship in archaeology would be subjected in most American anthropology departments.

While many British archaeologists acknowledge the relevance of anthropological theory for archaeology, social anthropologists have no influence on hiring in any facet of British archaeology. They are located in separate university departments, and are in any case vastly outnumbered by archaeologists—32 universities in Britain offer at least one degree in archaeology, while only seven offer a degree in social anthropology (A. M. Pollard, 2005, pers. comm.).

American anthropology departments have been much more reluctant to offer faculty appointments to scholars who do not have degrees in anthropology. In the great majority of these departments, archaeologists are numerically subordinate to cultural and social anthropologists, many of whom display a degree of antipathy towards science that ranges from mild to violent.[8] Fundamental disagreements about the role of science divide archaeologists and biological anthropologists in many American anthropology departments from their colleagues in cultural anthropology, and in some cases have contributed to fission into separate departments (Stanford University, Boston University), to de facto division (Harvard University), or to disaffected archaeologists and biological anthropologists moving their appointments into other units (University of California, Berkeley, MIT).

In spite of the veiled or overt hostility towards archaeology on the part of cultural anthropologists, many American anthropological archaeologists of a certain age continue to insist that American archaeology is superior to European archaeology because "We have anthropology and they do not."[9] I agree that long cohabitation with cultural anthropologists has given American archaeology its distinctive character (Sullivan, this volume), but I am equally convinced that it is a major reason why the United States lags behind Europe in archaeological science.

Even in American anthropological archaeology, archaeological science is still regarded in most departments as an area of specialization that is added to the usual list of requirements that includes mastery of the history of anthropology, archaeological method and theory, and the archaeological literature of at least one region of the world. These expectations make it very difficult to train archaeological scientists, as graduate students must spend at least two extra years acquiring the scientific training that they need in other departments. At the faculty level, it is exceedingly unusual for anthropology departments to hire archaeological scientists with graduate degrees in other disciplines.[10] Then, there is the problem of equipping laboratories. American anthropology departments are commonly located in colleges of social science, which can rarely afford to offer new appointees laboratories outfitted with the tools needed for cutting-edge research in genetics, organic residue analysis, materials analysis, or chronometry. This situation explains why most of the archaeological scientists in faculty positions in American

anthropology departments today specialize in zooarchaeology or archaeobotany, which do not generally require expensive equipment, or in statistical or spatial technologies that are still relatively inexpensive when compared to the bench sciences.

There are a few exceptions to these generalizations. Harvard University has spent lavishly on laboratories for archaeological science. It can well afford to do so, but so can at least another two dozen well-endowed universities that have not chosen to invest in this area.[11] What made the difference at Harvard was pressure from a private citizen, Landon Clay, who endowed a Chair in Scientific Archaeology in 1987. While the first incumbent (Nikolaas van der Merwe) had his PhD in anthropology, the second (Noreen Tuross) has her PhD in biochemistry.

The University of Arizona is a state university, and relatively poor when compared to leading private universities, yet it has the largest number of archaeological scientists on any American or Canadian campus. How did this happen? The short answer is that Emil Haury made it happen, for he was a fervent believer in interdisciplinary research before that phrase even entered the lexicon. In addition to cofounding the Laboratory of Tree-Ring Research in 1937, he had a long-standing collaboration with the geologist Ernst Antevs, and was the main force behind the establishment of a radiocarbon laboratory at the university in 1957 (Vance Haynes, 2005, pers. comm.). Though he retired in 1964, the example that he set has remained the template for doing archaeology at the University of Arizona ever since. In 1973, the geology and anthropology departments established a joint geoarchaeology program headed by Vance Haynes, who held faculty appointments in both departments until his retirement in 2001. David Kingery held joint appointments in anthropology and in materials science and engineering from 1988 until 2000, and Vance Holliday is currently a joint appointment between anthropology and geosciences. None of these scholars has a PhD degree in anthropology, yet each has made profound contributions to archaeology. This interdisciplinary philosophy also extends to training. About half of the students funded by the current IGERT Program in Archaeological Sciences at the University of Arizona (http://datamonster.sbs.arizona.edu/IGERT/) are registered for graduate degrees in anthropology. The other half are graduate students in chemistry, geosciences, geography, and materials science. All are required to take at least three courses in archaeological method and theory, and to have advisory committees that include at least one archaeologist.

Although few of the larger archaeology programs around the United States have ventured beyond zooarchaeology, archaeobotany, and (less commonly) geoarchaeology when hiring faculty, a few small departments evidently see opportunities in archaeological applications of inorganic chemistry and light stable isotopes. The University of South Florida, California State University at Long Beach, Purdue University, and the Rochester Institute of Technology have all made recent hires in one or both of these areas. At both South Florida and Long Beach, the anthropology departments have formed innovative alliances with departments of natural sciences to equip joint laboratories, and Long Beach has recently introduced an MSc program in archaeological sciences.

These are encouraging developments, but they are not nearly sufficient. Demand from American archaeologists for archaeological science continues to increase, but few archaeological scientists are being trained, and most anthropology departments seem unwilling to hire them (Goldberg, this volume). Unfortunately, the museum laboratories that were such an important component of archaeological science from the 1960s through the 1990s have all been casualties of the fiscal crisis that has afflicted many museums since 2001. The British Museum's Department of Scientific Research, the University of Pennsylvania's MASCA, and the Smithsonian Institution's Science Center for Materials Research and Education (SCMRE, formerly CAL) have all shrunk drastically in the last five years and have largely abandoned archaeology for a narrower focus on conservation science. The loss of the British Museum laboratories has

been more than countered by the commitment of British archaeology departments to natural sciences. In the United States, however, there has been little growth to compensate for the collapse of MASCA and SCMRE. The loss of SCMRE is particularly damaging, as the internships that it provided at both the predoctoral and postdoctoral levels were an extremely important part of the training of many American archaeological scientists. Fortunately the neutron activation program lives on in the Smithsonian's Museum of Natural History.

Cultural resource management companies in the United States have been increasingly willing to hire specialists in some areas of archaeological science. Specialists in basic faunal and botanical identification, GIS, and geoarchaeology can be found in most large CRM firms. In southern Arizona, home to the largest cluster of CRM companies in the United States, two firms now house a ceramic petrology unit (Desert Archaeology, Inc.) and an archaeomagnetic laboratory (Statistical Research, Inc.).[12] From my conversations with archaeological scientists in these labs, it seems that the main problem with specialized techniques in CRM settings lies in generating enough billable hours. In CRM, revenues must cover salaries, rental of space, depreciation of equipment, and utilities, whereas in academic and museum laboratories these costs are partly or wholly subsidized by the institution. In CRM, where the lowest bidder usually wins the contract, many companies balk at paying the real costs of scientific analyses.

One way to lower costs in the private sector is to increase productivity by specializing in a few services and focusing on rapid throughput. Most of the archaeological radiocarbon dates run in the United States are processed by two private companies, Beta Analytic and Geochron. They offer much better turnaround time than university-based laboratories, but they do not undertake much research on development of the techniques, as university laboratories do. And even these private companies cannot afford the capital outlay for AMS radiocarbon dating—both firms prepare targets, but subcontract the measure-

ARCHAEOLOGICAL SCIENCE IN AMERICA AND BRITAIN

ments to AMS facilities at universities or national laboratories. More generally, the high cost of analytical instruments makes it very difficult to see the private sector as a reliable source of innovation in many fields of archaeological science.

Although solid research commonly transpires in the context of CRM, this sector can also offer cover for obsolete and dubious methods. Because most CRM reports are not peer-reviewed, some techniques are still widely used in CRM that would not usually survive scrutiny in front-line academic journals. For example, it has been shown conclusively that optical measurement of obsidian hydration is unreliable (Anowitz et al. 1999; Riciputi et al. 2002), yet (at time of writing) four of the five American obsidian hydration laboratories advertising on the web page of the International Association of Obsidian Studies are still offering "dates" by this method. All four are located in the western United States and serve mostly clients in CRM. The fifth laboratory has acknowledged the force of the critique and has switched to a different method of measuring hydration that is calibrated against secondary ion mass spectrometry (SIMS), the technique used by Anowitz and his colleagues to measure the actual depth of penetration of hydrogen ions within obsidian.

Then there is the case of oxidizable carbon ratio (OCR) "dating." Although this method appears to contravene basic principles of physical chemistry (Killick et al. 1999), and has never been submitted to peer review at a journal of geochronology or archaeological science, its sole provider has nevertheless supplied more than 6,000 "dates" to dozens of paying clients (http://members.aol.com/dsfrink/ocr/ocrpage_2.htm). Although the list of clients includes some academics, most are in CRM or in government agencies working in the southeastern United States. The inventor of OCR has worked the cracks in the system with great skill. His main marketing devices are an impressive web site and the annual meetings of the Society for American Archaeology, at which he is a regular author or coauthor. (The SAA does not require peer review of submitted papers.)[13]

These examples (and there are others) suggest that some archaeologists in CRM either do not keep up with the technical literature or cannot evaluate what is published. (Nor, it appears, can some of the state and federal officials who are responsible for quality control in CRM.) In Britain, non-academic archaeologists can turn for advice to one of nine regional science officers appointed by English Heritage, but there is no such resource in the United States.

There is certainly some deplorable science in American academic archaeology, and for the same reasons, but many of the worst errors are screened out by peer review by granting agencies, by leading journals (though regional archaeological journals are often lax in reviewing scientific content), and by scholarly presses considering manuscript submissions. Furthermore, almost all project managers in American CRM were trained in American anthropology departments; if some of them cannot evaluate archaeological science, then the fault lies in part with the academic programs from which they graduated. What are these graduate programs doing to educate the next generation of archaeologists—most of whom will work in CRM—about scientific methods?

Almost all anthropology graduate programs in the United States offer training in particular aspects of archaeological science, most commonly in GIS and zooarchaeology. But very few offer an overview of archaeological science for archaeologists, and none currently require that all graduate students in archeology take such a course. This point has been made before (De Atley and Bishop 1991; Killick and Young 1997; Sabloff 1991) but seems to fall on deaf ears each time. Even at the University of Arizona, with its long focus on interdisciplinary archaeology, only about 12 percent of graduate students in the archaeology program over the last 14 years have taken the survey course in archaeometry.

DISCUSSION AND RECOMMENDATIONS
The practice of archaeology in America and in Europe has changed irrevocably in the last decade. Archaeological sites are a nonrenewable

57

resource, and the days of excavation on a large scale with minimal post-excavation analysis are gone in all rich countries. (This development may explain why so many leading American processual archaeologists are now eager to work in China.) Except for CRM excavations in advance of large construction projects, most future excavations in Europe and the United States will be on a relatively small scale, but will involve much more intensive analysis during and after excavation. Archaeological science will play an ever-expanding role in survey, excavation, and studies of materials recovered by excavation. I have argued in this chapter that the United States is lagging behind Britain in many aspects of archaeological science. In conclusion, I suggest that if American archaeologists wish to remain at the forefront of archaeological practice, some fundamental changes need to be made.

Funding

The gap between Britain and the United States in archaeological science is partly attributable to disparities in national support for research in this area. Funding for the NSF Archaeometry competition has been essentially flat in dollar amounts for 30 years and is at about 22 percent of its level in 1973 when corrected for inflation. Since the private sector is unlikely to contribute much to research and development in archaeological science, a substantial increase in federal funding will be needed if we are to catch up to Britain.

Here, of course, we run into the brick wall of the U.S. Congress, which over the last decade has shown little enthusiasm for supporting science unless it has obvious applications in warfare, medicine, or the exploration of space. American leadership in many areas of basic and applied science is being undermined by the insatiable appetite for tax cuts.[14] To give but one example, I work closely with several geochemists, who tell me that the flow of European post-doctoral fellows in geochemistry and cosmochemistry to the United States is drying up because recent PhDs in these areas can now find better equipped and better funded laboratories in Europe.

Obviously we should join other concerned scientists in working for political change and lobbying for more funding for science. But even if the NSF were to receive substantially increased funding, there is no guarantee that any of it would flow to the Archaeology and Archaeometry Program. We urgently need to work to expand public support of archaeology, and the relevant professional societies—the Society for American Archaeology, the Archaeological Institute of America, and the Society for Archaeological Sciences—ought to join forces to make a case to NSF and to congressional representatives for increased funding for both archaeology and archaeological science. The SAA has shown little inclination to support archaeological science (and certainly much less than the AIA). It needs to lobby vigorously for more funding for research and development in this area. The SAA, AIA, and SAS should also form a joint committee to study the current state of training in archaeological science in the United States and to make recommendations for its inclusion in undergraduate and graduate curricula. NSF should establish and fund an advisory body for archaeological science, modeled upon the British SBASG, to review the state of the field and recommend specific priorities for future funding. We also need federal funding for a program, similar to that run by English Heritage, to which any field archaeologist can go for informed advice about archaeological science.

Must Anthropological Archaeology Always Set the Agenda?

The lone archaeologist is now an endangered species. As archaeology has grown, the knowledge required to do cutting-edge archaeological research has expanded far beyond the capabilities of any single individual. Archaeological field research is increasingly carried out by teams of specialists, and the best archaeologists today are those who have the management skills to integrate other specialists productively, and the humility to share information at all stages of the project. The days when boxes of finds were sent to specialists who mailed their reports back to the archaeologist are largely gone too (except in radiocarbon dating). Most leading specialists in archaeological science will no longer accept samples unless they understand the contexts from which they came and had a role in their selection.

Publication, too, is increasingly a team effort, which can create problems when archaeologists are evaluated for tenure in university departments dominated by cultural anthropologists, for whom single authorship remains the norm. With archaeological science now welcome in more mainstream journals of natural science and engineering, the price of collaboration for archaeologists will increasingly be dual publication. Archaeologists will be the senior authors on articles submitted to standard archaeological journals, but junior authors on articles submitted to journals of natural science or engineering.

These changing realities call into question the mantra of processual archaeology: that archaeology is anthropology or it is nothing. However dear this phrase may be to the currently dominant generation of American archaeologists (those who received their PhDs between 1965 and 1985) it is no longer convincing (Sullivan, this volume). Yes, archaeology can be anthropology, but it can also be environmental history, Quaternary paleoecology, evolutionary ecology, history of technology, world history, Classical archaeology, or Near Eastern archaeology. Archaeological scientists work in all of these areas. In retrospect, the insistence upon archaeology as anthropology looks like a power play, a stratagem to ensure that only card-carrying anthropologists should get to decide what the relevant questions are. Anthropological archaeologists did get to set much of the archaeological agenda in the United States from the early 1970s to the present (though Classical and Near Eastern archaeologists contributed too) but the monolithic façade of anthropology is now riven by cracks.

Far fewer cultural or social anthropologists have any interest in archaeology today than was the case 20 years ago, and many of their main theoretical concerns revolve around identity, globalization, transnational migration, and consumption. Because these issues

are theorized almost exclusively within the context of global capitalism, there is little here that can be transplanted to the archaeology of precapitalist societies. Most British archaeologists, and an increasing number of their American counterparts, go directly to European sociology and political science for theory, rather than waiting a decade or more for these same theories to be digested in social or cultural anthropology. At the same time, some archaeologists look to evolutionary ecology or to neo-Darwinian cultural transmission theories for models rather than to social or cultural anthropology (Kuhn 2004).

World archaeology today is therefore theoretically and methodologically more diverse than it was in the 1980s. Some older American processual archaeologists appear to want to fight diversity to the death, but they will not succeed in reasserting their earlier dominance. More open-minded archaeologists need to be paying serious attention to the question of how to accommodate these changes. One of the most pressing issues is determining how to integrate archaeological science into American archaeology.

Before the 1990s, most collaborating scientists were content to stick to their areas of special expertise and to let archaeologists set the agenda. Archaeological scientists today are more knowledgeable about archaeology and want some say in setting the questions and drawing the conclusions. The best interdisciplinary archaeological projects, like those headed by Ofer Bar-Yosef (Harvard University) and Izumi Shimada (Southern Illinois University), are committed to sharing information, publications, and credit among participants. They also ensure that archaeological scientists get into the field so that they understand the context of the materials on which they will undertake laboratory analyses. In some recent excavations, notably those headed by Bar-Yosef at Kebara and Hayonim Caves, some laboratory work has actually been carried out on site, providing near-instant feedback to the excavators (e.g., Weiner et al. 1995; Goldberg, this volume).

An important corollary to this point is that most archaeological scientists today are not waiting for archaeologists to bring them problems to study; instead, they actively look for archaeological problems that their expertise can address. For one example, consider the brilliant work of Richard Evershed and colleagues in distinguishing milk residues from other animal and plant fats in organic residues from British Neolithic pottery (Copley et al. 2003). This study shows how to solve a question of long standing in European prehistory (when did the "secondary products" revolution begin?), but the project was initiated by an archaeological scientist, and six of the eight authors were at that time in a chemistry department.[15]

Where Can Archaeological Scientists Find Homes in the United States?

British archaeology departments have responded to the growing role of science in archaeology by hiring archaeological scientists and equipping them with laboratories. As noted above, it is almost impossible to do this in American anthropology departments that are dominated by cultural anthropologists. It is equally unlikely that American departments of classics or Near Eastern studies are going to start offering positions to persons whose primary area of expertise lies, for example, in organic chemistry or geomorphology.

One potential solution to this impasse is to create British-style departments of archaeology that bring together anthropological archaeologists, classical archaeologists, Near Eastern archaeologists, and archaeological scientists. Thus far, only Boston University has gone this route in the United States, but we can expect to see more universities following its example as some leading anthropology departments grind inexorably towards internal divorces. But a few anthropology departments, like my own, have reached a *modus vivendi* that works well for archaeology, so some three- or four-field anthropology departments will certainly endure. How should these adjust to the increasingly important role of science in archaeology?

The old model in the United States—of ad hoc collaboration between archaeologists and scientists in other departments—is increasingly untenable. Most museum laboratories have withdrawn their support of archaeological science, and informal interdisciplinary programs within universities tend to work to the detriment of the participating scientists. Most departments of natural sciences or engineering do not like it when their faculty members switch significant amounts of research time into pursuits other than those for which they were hired. It is usually professional suicide for untenured scientists or engineers to put much time into archaeology, and even tenured science and engineering faculty in many universities suffer for sustained collaboration by being denied promotions or salary increases.

The only viable solution to these problems seems to be to press for formal interdepartmental collaborations, leading to the creation of joint faculty appointments between anthropology departments and departments of natural science or engineering (Killick and Young 1997; Sabloff 1991). Joint appointments will bypass the usual requirement that all hires in anthropology departments have PhDs in anthropology. They would also offer protection to the scientists involved because (1) there would be explicit approval from time of appointment for undertaking research in archaeological science, (2) there would a formal agreement of criteria for promotion and tenure, and (3) faculties of science are better able to fund start-up costs and technical support for laboratories than are faculties of social science.

Joint hires will also provide better contexts for training archaeological scientists. The rate of expansion of knowledge in some areas of science (such as molecular biology, biochemistry, geochemistry, or materials science) is such that students with a BA in anthropology cannot realistically expect to make up their deficits in science after entering a PhD program. The best preparation for many graduate students in archaeological science will be a PhD in a department of natural science or engineering, with a PhD minor in anthropology. Another viable option is to admit students with both BSc and MSc degrees in science and engineering to PhD programs in anthropology. It is undoubtedly much easier to pick up the essentials of archaeological method and theory at the graduate level than it is for anyone with a BA or MA degree in anthropology to make up the background in science at the graduate level.

CONCLUSIONS

In 1993, Robert C. Dunnell ignited a minor firestorm with a short review article entitled "Why Archaeologists Don't Care about Archaeometry." This article infuriated most archaeological scientists of my acquaintance, but Dunnell did have a valid point, which was that much archaeological science did not seem to be addressing any issues in which archaeologists were interested.

Times have changed. Most archaeological scientists are now much more knowledgeable about the aims of archaeology, and are consequently much better at selecting research problems of real archaeological interest. Even the journal *Archaeometry* now publishes occasional debates on the integration of archaeological theory with archaeological science. The well-publicized successes of integrated teams of archaeologists and archaeological scientists, like those led by Bar-Yosef and Shimada, have also sharply raised the bar for professional standards in field archaeology. For archaeological deposits that are in very limited supply, such as deeply stratified caves, it should by now be unacceptable—perhaps even unethical—to undertake excavations unless the lead archaeologist takes an interdisciplinary team into the field. Both Paul Goldberg (this volume) and Vance Holliday (2005, pers. comm.) condemn what the latter calls "cigar-box archaeology." This is the deplorably common practice in which an archaeologist without any training in geoarchaeology or soil science decides which sediment samples should be selected for later analysis in the laboratory. Decisions like these should always be made jointly, in the field, by the archaeologist and the specialists, working together in a partnership of equals.

Many (though not all) archaeological scientists on both sides of the Atlantic have made the effort to learn more about archaeological method and theory. But have archaeologists made comparable efforts to learn more about archaeological science? The evidence suggests that many British archaeologists have learned more about it, and that they care sufficiently to make space for archaeological scientists within archaeology departments. Physical proximity is the best stimulus for interdisciplinary research and training, and builds mutual understanding between generalists and specialists (Killick and Young 1997). In my opinion, this development is partly responsible for Britain's remarkable record of innovation in archaeological and paleoenvironmental research over the last decade.

I can, however, find little evidence that most American archaeologists care much more about archaeological science than they did in 1993; the principal areas of application are still radiocarbon dating, dendrochronology, geomorphology, provenance of inorganic materials, light stable isotope studies of diet, and zoological and botanical studies at the scale of whole organisms. While these analyses are as important as ever, a much wider range of natural science techniques are in routine use in European archaeology today (Brothwell and Pollard 2001).

There has certainly been little change at the level of American graduate education. A few archaeology graduate students—a small minority—do acquire advanced training in the natural sciences, but they have to add this to all the usual required courses in anthropology, and thus take much longer ·to complete their degrees. The great majority of American archaeologists still get their PhDs without having taken even a survey course in archaeological science or a course in chronometry. Radiocarbon dating is certainly as important a tool for modern archaeology as ceramic typology, plane-table surveying, or database management software. Professional archaeologists are expected to be proficient in these techniques. Why then are graduating PhDs in archaeology not expected to understand why radiocarbon ages need to be corrected for variation in $^{13}C/^{12}C$ ratios before they are calibrated, or what the standard error on a radiocarbon age actually entails?

American archaeology does not, of course, have to embrace archaeological science just because the Europeans are doing so. We should follow their lead because the natural sciences provide us with powerful tools that we can use to explore the predictions of archaeological theories in the empirical archaeological record. American anthropological archaeology has compiled an impressive track record of innovation in both theory and methods, but in the last two decades we have been lagging behind the Europeans in the advancement of methods, if not in theory. Catching up in the area of archaeological science will certainly require a large infusion of research funding, but this alone will not be sufficient. We will need to think carefully about what changes we need to make in training archaeologists, and especially about our reflexive commitment to archaeology as anthropology. The time has come to consider a wider range of affiliations, and to make a serious commitment to the training and employment of archaeological scientists.

NOTES

1. The terms *archaeometry* and *archaeological science* are used interchangeably in the United States, but in Britain the former is considered a subset of the latter. In British usage, archaeometry includes archaeological applications of physics, inorganic chemistry, mathematics, statistics, and engineering, but excludes biology and biochemistry. Some archaeologists consider archaeology itself to be a science, but this view ignores the fact that many archaeologists work within the disciplinary frameworks of the humanities, such as Classics, Near Eastern, or East Asian studies.

2. This change of mind was probably prompted by the intensive use of archaeological sciences in the Çatalhöyük excavations, directed since 1993 by Ian Hodder (http://www.catalhoyuk .com/). I recognize that the label *postmodern* is by now stale and without specific referent, but lack the space here for more extensive definitions.

3. For more documentation of this claim than can be provided here, examine Brothwell and Pollard 2001.

4. Vance Holliday (pers. comm.) suggests that the neglect of micromorphology in American archaeology reflects the fact that the technique is rarely used by American soil scientists, who have tended to concentrate upon soil classification and mapping rather than soil genesis.

5. Research and development of most radiometric dating techniques (radiocarbon and other cosmogenic isotopes, electron spin resonance, argon-argon, and uranium series dating) is supported in both the United States and in Britain mostly by research budgets for physics and for geosciences.

6. This value was calculated from data supplied by Dr. John Yellen, program director for NSF Archaeology, for awards from 1973 to 1997, and from data on the NSF web site from 1998 to 2005. When adjusted for inflation, the current purchasing power of a dollar is only 22 percent of its worth in 1973.

7. A second endowed chair—the Emil Haury Chair of Archaeological Dendrochronology —was created at the University of Arizona in 2007.

8. Although "science studies" are currently trendy in American cultural anthropology, these do not signal a change of attitude, for these simply treat science as a form of discourse. Social anthropologist Ana María Alonso (pers. comm.) suggests that in these studies scientists substitute for natives in the role of Exotic Other.

9. Adapted from Hilaire Belloc's flippant explanation, a century ago, for British imperial domination of its colonies: "The difference is / that we have got / the Gatling gun / and they have not."

10. Nor do Classics or Near Eastern studies departments, whose archaeologists are often equally keen on archaeological science. In these departments the barrier to admission is the insistence upon mastery of modern and ancient languages before embarking upon other training.

11. In spite of its name, the Department of Anthropological Sciences at Stanford University has no archaeological scientist among its faculty.

12. The archaeomagnetic laboratory at Statistical Research closed in 2007.

13. Peer review is clearly not infallible. Even though no paper on the methodological aspects of OCR has ever been accepted in a journal of geochronology or archaeological science, OCR "dates" have been listed in papers

published in *Science, Radiocarbon,* and the *Journal of Archaeological Science.*

14. Trends in federal funding of research are discussed in the January 2006 report of the National Academy of Sciences (http://www.aaas.org/spp/rd/upd1205.htm).

15. This was one of the projects funded under NERC's Key Initiative on Ancient Biomolecules.

ACKNOWLEDGMENTS

I am most grateful to John Yellen for supplying lists of awards by NSF Archaeometry, and to the several dozen archaeologists and archaeological scientists on both sides of the Atlantic who took the time to respond to my e-mailed requests for information. The idea of writing this chapter arose out of many conversations and e-mail exchanges with Mark Pollard over the past decade; he also showed me where to find information on awards in Britain. I am also much indebted to Jeff Dean, Jeff Homburg, Vance Holliday, Beth Miksa, Vince Pigott, Steve Shackley, Michael Shott, Julie Stein, Rob Tykot, Nikolaas van der Merwe, Pamela Vandiver, and Patrick Wrinn for their comments on previous drafts of this chapter.

REFERENCES CITED

Abbott, David R.

2000 *Ceramics and Community Organization among the Hohokam.* University of Arizona Press, Tucson.

Anowitz, Lawrence M., J. Michael Elam, Lee R. Riciputi, and David R. Cole

1999 The Failure of Obsidian Hydration Dating: Sources, Implications, and New Directions. *Journal of Archaeological Science* 26:735–754.

Archaeometry

2005 Comments on A. Jones, Archaeometry and Materiality: Materials-Based Analysis in Theory and Practice, *Archaeometry* 46(3) (2004):327–338 and Reply, *Archaeometry* 47:175–207.

Bishop, Ronald L., and Frederick W. Lange (editors)

1991 *The Ceramic Legacy of Anna O. Shepard.* University Press of Colorado, Niwot.

Brothwell, Donald R., and Eric Higgs (editors)

1963 *Science in Archaeology.* Thames and Hudson, London.

Brothwell, Donald R., and A. Mark Pollard (editors)

2001 *Handbook of Archaeological Sciences.* John Wiley and Sons, Chichester.

Buck, Caitlin E.

2001 Applications of the Bayesian Statistical Paradigm. In *Handbook of Archaeological Sciences*, edited by Don R. Brothwell and A. Mark Pollard, pp. 695–702. John Wiley and Sons, Chichester.

Burton, James H., and Arleyn W. Simon

1993 Acid Extraction as a Simple and Inexpensive Method for Compositional Characterization of Archaeological Ceramics. *American Antiquity* 58:45–59.

Copley, M. S., R. Berstan, S. N. Dudd, G. Docherty, A. J. Mukherjee, V. Straker, S. Payne, and R. P. Evershed

2003 Direct Chemical Evidence for Widespread Dairying in Prehistoric Britain. *Proceedings of the National Academy of Sciences* 100:1524–1529.

Crown, Patricia L.

1991 Appraising the Legacy: A Thematic Synthesis. In *The Ceramic Legacy of Anna O. Shepard*, edited by Ronald L. Bishop and Frederick W. Lange, pp. 383–393. University Press of Colorado, Niwot.

De Atley, Suzanne P., and Ronald L Bishop

1991 Toward an Integrated Interface for Archaeology and Archaeometry. In *The Ceramic Legacy of Anna O. Shepard*, edited by Ronald L. Bishop and Frederick W. Lange, pp. 358–380. University Press of Colorado, Niwot.

Dunnell, Robert C.

1993 Why Archaeologists Don't Care about Archaeometry. *Archeomaterials* 7:161–165.

Hein, A., A. Tsolakidou, I. Iliopoulos, H. Mommsen, J. Buxeda i Garrigós, G. Montana, and V. Kilikoglou

2002 Standardisation of Elemental Analytical Techniques Applied to Provenance Studies of Ancient Ceramics. *The Analyst* 127:542–553.

International Study Group

1982 An Inter-Laboratory Comparison of Radiocarbon Measurements in Tree Rings. *Nature* 298:619–623.

Jones, Andrew

2004 Archaeometry and Materiality: Materials-Based Analysis in Theory and Practice. *Archaeometry* 46:327–338.

Killick, David

1999 Archaeometry Is Good Science or It Is Nothing: Some Concerns about Current Practice in the United States. Paper presented at the workshop Archaeology as Anthropology: Material Culture and Technology, Center for Archaeological Investigations, Southern Illinois University, Carbondale.

Killick, David, Tim Jull, and George Burr
1999   Querying OCR Dating. *Society for American Archaeology Newsletter* 17(5):32–37.

Killick, David, and Suzanne M. Young
1997   Archaeology and Archaeometry: From Casual Dating to a Meaningful Relationship? *Antiquity* 71:518–524.

Kuhn, Steven L.
2004   Evolutionary Perspectives on Technology and Technological Change. *World Archaeology* 36:561–570.

Lengyel, Stacey N., and Jeffrey L. Eighmy
2002   A Revision to the U.S. Southwest Archaeomagnetic Master Curve. *Journal of Archaeological Science* 29:1423–1431.

Libby, Willard
1955   *Radiocarbon Dating*. 2nd ed. University of Chicago Press, Chicago.

Matson, Frederick R.
2003   Ed Sayre So Far. In *Patterns and Process: A Festschrift in Honor of Dr. Edward V. Sayre*, edited by Lambertus van Zelst, pp. 19–25. Smithsonian Center for Materials Research and Education, Suitland, Maryland.

Nash, Stephen
1999   *Time, Trees and Prehistory: Tree-Ring Dating and the Development of North American Archaeology, 1914–1950*. University of Utah Press, Salt Lake City.

Reber, E. A., and Richard P. Evershed
2004   How Did Mississippians Prepare Maize? The Application of Compound-Specific Stable Isotope Analysis to Absorbed Organic Residues from Several Mississippian Sites. *Archaeometry* 46:19–33.

Renfrew, Colin, and Katie Boyle
2000   *Archaeogenetics: DNA and the Population History of Europe*. McDonald Institute, Cambridge.

Riciputi, Lee R., J. Michael Elam, Lawrence M. Anovitz, and David R. Cole
2002   Obsidian Diffusion Dating by Secondary Ion Mass Spectrometry: A Test Using Results from Mound 65, Chalco, Mexico. *Journal of Archaeological Science* 29:1055–1075.

Robinson, Mark
2001   Insects as Paleoenvironmental Indicators. In *Handbook of Archaeological Sciences*, edited by Don R. Brothwell and A. Mark Pollard, pp. 121–134. John Wiley and Sons, Chichester.

Sabloff, Jeremy
1991   Brief Observations from a Conference. In *The Ceramic Legacy of Anna O. Shepard*, edited by Ronald L. Bishop and Frederick W. Lange, pp. 394–399. University Press of Colorado, Niwot.

Scott, E. M., T. C. Aitchison, D. D. Harkness, G. T. Cook, and M. S. Baxter
1990   An Overview of All Three Stages of the International Radiocarbon Comparison. *Radiocarbon* 32(3):309–319.

Scott, Marion (editor)
2003   The Third International Radiocarbon Comparison and the Fourth International Radiocarbon Comparison, 1990–2002: Results, Analyses, and Conclusions. *Radiocarbon* 45(2):135–408.

Shott, Michael J.
1992   Radiocarbon Dating as a Probabilistic Technique: The Childers Site and Late Woodland Occupation in the Ohio Valley. *American Antiquity* 57:202–230.
2005   Two Cultures: Thought and Practice in British and North American Archaeology. *World Archaeology* 37:1–10.

Tite, Michael S.
1972   *Methods of Physical Examination in Archaeology*. Seminar Press, London and New York.

Triadan, Daniela, Hector Neff, and Michael Glascock
1997   Evaluation of the Archaeological Relevance of Weak-Acid Extraction ICP: The Case of White Mountain Redware. *Journal of Archaeological Science* 24:997–1002.

Weiner, Stephen, Solveig Schlegel, Paul Goldberg, and Ofer Bar-Yosef
1995   Mineral Assemblages in Kebara and Hayonim Caves, Israel: Excavation Strategies, Bone Preservation, and Wood Ash Remnants. *Israel Journal of Chemistry* 35:143–154.

5

Remote Sensing Approaches to Archaeological Reasoning: Pattern Recognition and Physical Principles

KENNETH L. KVAMME

Remote sensing refers to techniques that acquire information about a subject through indirect means. Remote sensing in archaeology includes many such methods, ranging from ground-based geophysics (e.g., magnetometry, ground-penetrating radar), to aerial surveys (e.g., photography, thermography), to satellite imaging. Its goals include the recording, mapping, and interpretation of detectable physical characteristics that reflect the nature of surface and subsurface archaeological deposits; its *modus operandi* presents a way of doing archaeology that relies primarily on fundamental behavioral and physical principles. Remote sensing is capable of revealing much about archaeological sites, settlements, and regions, and benefits from its ability to evaluate large areas efficiently and non-invasively.

Archaeological remote sensing has rapidly evolved owing to advances in technology and changing needs and goals of the discipline. With global population expansion, massive changes to the landscape are occurring at an unprecedented scale. There is a need for cost-effective methods to locate, map, and acquire information about archaeological sites before they are obliterated. Traditional excavations and pedestrian surveys are becoming increasingly expensive, and only trivial areas are commonly examined owing to labor and cost limitations. Excavations commonly investigate

areas measured only in square meters, but remote sensing can yield information about *entire settlements* covering many hectares or even square kilometers. Moreover, when conditions are favorable, it can detect features unseen on the surface, precisely map them, and offer reliable archaeological interpretations based on characteristic measurements, form, distribution, and context, and do so often without reference to anthropological analogs or models. In short, remote sensing may offer the only effective means to inventory much of the world's archaeological resources, which it accomplishes by relying on basic physical laws and fundamentally different signatures between human and natural features.

BACKGROUND CONCEPTS AND DEFINITIONS

Archaeological remote sensing utilizes a variety of techniques that measure physical properties of surface or near-surface deposits —usually within 1 to 3 m of the ground surface. Some methods record variations only at the surface, but others penetrate the subsurface with depth limitations that vary with soil properties, vegetation cover, and types of archaeological features.

Active technologies record responses to an electrical current or radar beam transmitted into the earth, whereas *passive* technologies measure natural properties detectable at the surface, such as reflected light or the strength of local magnetic fields. While information gained by a single sensor can be insightful, most respond only to a narrow range of physical properties. In general, the use of multiple methods offers greater insights because buried anthropogenic features not revealed by one may be made visible by another, and several sensors can provide complementary information, such as when a hearth and burned-house elements are detected by magnetometry and its compacted floor by ground-penetrating radar (Clay 2001; Donoghue 2001; Kvamme 2006a).

Useful remote sensing results are obtained from *contrasts* between archaeological features and "natural" background conditions. Archaeological features become visible if they possess physical properties sufficiently different from the surrounding matrix. A buried stone foundation might be more magnetic, better reflect radar waves, retain more thermal energy, and stunt overlying plant life, compared with surrounding deposits. Such contrasts are referred to as "anomalies" until their sources can be identified. Anomaly identification is a crucial issue in contemporary remote sensing and the focus of this chapter. Detection of anthropogenic anomalies is the goal of remote sensing because we want to locate, map, and interpret those that reflect buried cultural features: the subsurface archaeology. Anomalies may also be generated by biological (e.g., rodent holes, animal burrows, dens, tree roots, tree throws), geological (e.g., buried paleo-channels, rising bedrock), or pedological (e.g., natural soil changes) phenomena. Moreover, recent cultural practices (e.g., plowing, landscaping, buried pipes) generate many anomalies not of interest. The task, then, is to separate the cultural from the natural, and within the former to filter out unwanted intrusions from periods not of interest —a challenging proposition!

Identifying the loci of cultural features through remote sensing is important to archaeology because large cost savings can be realized by making projects more efficient. Field teams may go directly to potential features, reducing the amount of excavation required to effectively evaluate a site for management purposes (Weymouth 1986; Wynn 1986). It is also a far more efficient methodology for locating archaeological features compared to the primitive prospecting method of "shovel test pits" (popular in North America), where numerous small holes are excavated systematically across an area in an effort to directly locate buried cultural materials and features, despite notoriously low discovery probabilities (Kintigh 1988). Yet, a commonly held view in archaeological remote sensing is that anomaly identification must be accomplished through excavation, often referred to as "ground-truthing" (Hargrave 2006). Unquestionably, this is the most reliable method because one can frequently reveal an anomaly's source by exposing it, but excavating *every* anomaly is impractical and may actually defeat a principal goal of remote sensing: to say something about a place without having to alter or destroy it. Such an approach is also not realistic because most remote sensing surveys cover large areas. Aerial and space-based methods typically image square kilometers, but even ground-based geophysical surveys can examine a hectare (10,000 m²) or more per day, and a single archaeological settlement may disclose thousands of anomalies! Clearly, not every anomaly can be excavated to ascertain what it represents; there are far too many, and exposing each one is generally impossible given cost and time issues. Ethical and preservationist concerns arise, as well. These perspectives suggest that remote sensing may not be very useful if we cannot determine what anomalies represent without excavation. But what are the alternatives? The following sections emphasize multiple approaches to anomaly identification that do not rely on the spade. A goal is to clarify how inferences and conclusions are derived from remotely sensed data.

Remote sensing specialists utilize two fundamental tactics to distinguish between culturally generated and naturally produced anomalies and to infer something about their origins. The first is a realization of their *pattern* in the landscape, which includes characteristics of form, size, distribution, and context. The second approach is based on knowledge of *fundamental physical principles:* laws that dictate how sensors will respond to various archaeological features and deposits. The latter approach has always formed the core method of interpretation, but in recent years the former has achieved great importance owing largely to new forms of computer processing and graphic portrayals that better reveal anomalies, their form, and distribution (Kvamme 2001). This result has engendered entirely new domains of inquiry, goals, and uses of remote sensing.

PATTERN RECOGNITION APPROACHES TO ARCHAEOLOGICAL INTERPRETATION

A fundamental characteristic of archaeological features and the anomalies they produce in remotely sensed data sets is their high spatial frequency or small size. Postholes might vary between 0.1 and 0.7 m in diameter, hearths and storage pits from 1 to 1.5 m, walls might be 0.5 m thick, dwellings can be as small as 3 m wide, trails might measure 0.5 m across, whereas prepared roads might be 2 m in width. For such features to be detected and recognized by remote sensing, the spatial resolution of acquired data must be high, results must be imaged to facilitate visualization of anomalies, and large areas must be surveyed to permit recognition of culturally generated patterns in their distributions.

Early satellites offered spatial resolutions between 10 and 80 m, with 30 m being most common—far too coarse for defining within-site components of archaeological sites. It is only in the last decade that panchromatic photography from space became available in the form of Cold War photographs by the Russian KVR-1000 and U.S. Corona spy satellites, with spatial resolutions in the 2–4 m range. Better still, since 1999 two high-resolution satellites have been launched, IKONOS and Quickbird, that offer panchromatic imagery at 1 m and 0.6 m spatial resolutions, and multispectral data at 4 m and 2.4 m, respectively. With these data, it is finally possible to detect and map individual features and components of archaeological sites from space, as various

studies are beginning to show (Fowler 1996, 2002; Kennedy 1998). Aerial remote sensing, initially based entirely on photography and always of high (sub-meter) spatial resolution (Wilson 2000), has now incorporated other domains including multispectral scanners (Barnes 2003), thermography (Dabas and Tabbagh 2000), and laser altimetry (Barnes 2003) that offer great spatial detail. Finally, ground-based geophysical remote sensing has also seen significant advances: instruments are now faster, allowing large areas to be surveyed at very high sampling densities in the sub-meter range (Clark 2000; Conyers 2004).

In addition to high spatial resolution, the data must be effectively displayed in order for anomalies to be readily visualized. Applications of digital image processing and computer graphics methods represent additional revolutionary improvements to remote sensing. Sensors either yield photographs, which can be digitized, or matrices of digital data that are treatable as imagery. Image processing techniques allow enhancements to be made, enabling significant features to be clarified and subtle ones to be seen. The use of continuous-tone colors or gray scales allows photo-quality imaging, even of non-photographic data like radar or magnetometry. Culturally produced features can sometimes be imaged with sufficient clarity that the specialist and non-specialist alike can instantly interpret and understand results, as when the floor plan of a house or the layout of an entire settlement is unambiguously expressed (Clay 2001; Hesse et al. 1997; Toom and Kvamme 2002; Walker 2000). In other words, the results of remote sensing surveys can now *look like* the buried archaeology thanks to computer graphics.

Although a geophysical survey of a small area might illustrate anomalies of potential cultural origin, it can be difficult or impossible to realize what they represent without excavation. A small segment of a linear anomaly could, for example, represent part of a room, a house wall, the edge of a ditch, pavement, trail, or road. Consequently, one must be able to see the complete form of an anomaly and its relationships with others in order to interpret its meaning or significance. Large survey areas increase the likelihood that complete cultural features with regular, interpretable shapes will be encountered and recognized in remotely sensed imagery (e.g., houses, house clusters, other structures, walls, trails, roads, fortifications [Buteux et al. 2000; Dalan 1993; David 1995:28; Kvamme 2003]). Ironically, the ability to image hundreds or thousands of potential cultural anomalies in large-area surveys means that it is no longer practical to rigorously evaluate or scientifically model more than a few (a common practice decades ago in geophysics when areas of survey were small and anomalies few in number [Clark 2000]). Contemporary work is oriented more toward the visualization of culturally produced patterns in remotely sensed imagery. Nevertheless, the benefits of being able to image, locate, and document likely cultural features within large regions far outweighs this shortcoming.

The following sections examine the kinds of knowledge and interpretations that can be arrived at by making use of "pattern recognition" principles applied to remotely sensed imagery. These principles are taken from standard guidelines that have been developed for nearly a century in the field of air photo interpretation (Avery and Berlin 1992).

Pattern Recognition Based on Shape

A fundamental tenet of air photo interpretation is that regular geometric shapes in the landscape—circles, ellipses, squares, rectangles, or straight lines—are generally of human origin. They occur much less frequently as products of nature, although some natural features, such as alluvial fans, floodplain meanders, and volcanic cones, possess distinctive shapes (Avery and Berlin 1992:52). Moreover, cultural features such as walls, houses, plazas, and roads usually disclose distinct boundaries, unlike natural features that tend toward irregular shapes and "fuzzy" edges. Consequently, if one sees a rectangle in remotely sensed imagery, it most likely represents a human construction, and depending on scale, it could represent the floor plan of a house, a larger administrative building or monument,

a plaza or courtyard, or even the boundaries of an agricultural field. This principle is probably the most fundamental one in the domain of pattern recognition and frequently allows classification of anomalies as particular types of cultural features without the need for excavation.

Examples of the recognition of archaeological features based on shape are easy to find. The Great Pyramids at Giza are instantly identified from space, even at the very coarse spatial resolutions available in the 1970s (Quann and Bevan 1977), but recent 1 m imagery from the IKONOS satellite also shows the many rectangular tombs (*mastaba*) surrounding them (Figure 5.1a). Likewise, large reservoirs at Anghor Wat, Cambodia, are instantly seen as cultural features by their rectangular shapes and distinct edges in a high altitude radar image taken from space (Figure 5.1b). Within a settlement, a house in the fourteenth-century Whistling Elk Village, in South Dakota, is clearly defined by electrical resistance and magnetic gradiometry data because of its square form and southeast-facing linear entryway (Figure 5.2a, b [Toom and Kvamme 2002]). Historic paintings by George Catlin and Karl Bodmer of the Mandan village (ca. 1822–1837; later occupied by the Arikara from 1837 to 1861) at Fort Clark, in North Dakota, depict circular earthlodges (a conical wooden-framed dwelling covered with earth). However, we do not need to rely on ethnographic or historical evidence to infer the presence of dwellings, some of which overlap, that register as circles in an electrical resistance survey transect through this site (Figure 5.2c [Kvamme 2003]). Similarly, the fortification ditches and associated bastions at the site of Double Ditch (late AD 1400s–1785), also in North Dakota, are recognized in a magnetic gradiometry image by their parallel, linear components and the inverted "U" shapes of their bastions (Figure 5.2e). Finally, the locus of the historic Mount Comfort Church (1840s–1863), burned during the American Civil War in Arkansas, is revealed by its rectangular shape within an electrical resistance data set (Figure 5.2f).

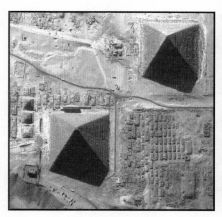 

a   b

FIGURE 5.1. Cultural features exhibit regular geometric shapes: (a) the Great Pyramids at Giza, Egypt, are recognized by their triangular faces in this 1 m resolution IKONOS image, as are nearby rectangular tombs (credit: Space Imaging; collected November 17, 1999); (b) large rectangular reservoirs and linear roadways are identified in this X-band synthetic aperture radar image of Anghor Wat, Cambodia (credit: NASA/JPL).

Pattern Recognition Based on Systematic Repetition

Seen from the air, trees in forests are irregularly distributed, but they occur in systematic rows and columns in orchards. Similarly, in remote sensing, a collection of small anomalies 1–2 m in size can represent badger dens, tree throws, or prehistoric storage pits. When occurring in regularly spaced rows and columns in an electrical resistance data set, one might make a strong argument for graves, as in the mid-nineteenth century Bozeman Cemetery, near Arkadelphia, Arkansas, where few burials are actually marked on the surface (Figure 5.3a). Likewise, when small electrical resistance anomalies define the perimeter of a rectangular space in an early twentieth century village, the presence of building footings is suggested (Figure 5.3b). These anomalies were recorded at Army City, a commercial complex associated with Camp Funston (now Fort Riley), Kansas, during World War I (Hargrave et al. [2002] illustrate a photograph of the original structure). Under the manicured lawns of the historic Sylvester Manor estate on Shelter Island, New York, repetitive lineations that meet at right angles in a shallow electrical resistance survey reveal the layout of a street or building grid of a sixteenth century Dutch-English settlement. Two such grid orientations suggest the possibility of two cycles of building (Figure 5.3c [Kvamme 2003]). At Huff Village, a fifteenth century fortified settlement in North Dakota, an aerial photograph illustrates repetitive shallow depressions, known to represent houses. Row upon row of systematically spaced rectangular houses can be seen within the village's defensive ditch (Figure 5.3d).

Pattern Recognition Based on Relative Size

Size differences are common among many types of archaeological features. Public buildings versus dwellings, dwellings versus smaller outbuildings and privies, and roads versus trails provide examples of how functionality might be inferred from size characteristics. This phenomenon is illustrated in Figure 5.4a–c, which compares the relative sizes of the footprints of a pioneer period cowboy cabin of the 1870s in central Kansas (Kvamme 2001), the previously described Mount Comfort Church (1840s–1863), in Arkansas, and the Fort Clark Trading Post (1832–1861) of the American fur trade in North Dakota (Kvamme 2003). Obviously, the last cannot

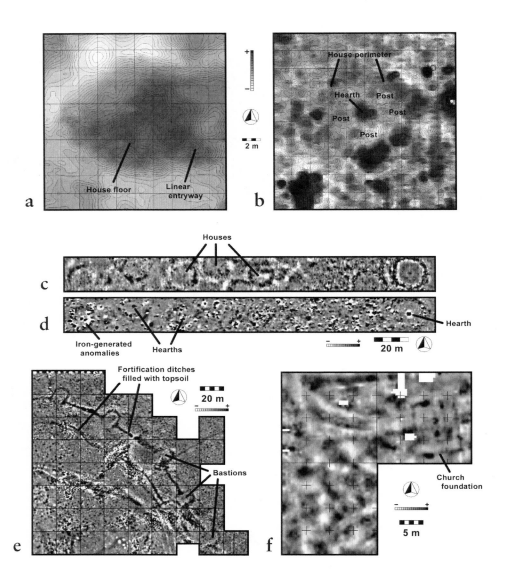

FIGURE 5.2. Recognition of cultural features by shape; (a) a square structure with southeast-facing linear entryway revealed by electrical resistance survey at fourteenth century Whistling Elk Village, South Dakota; (b) a magnetic gradiometry image of the same area in 5.2a, showing its burned perimeter, central hearth, and the loci of roof support posts; (c) earthlodges revealed by their circular form in an electrical resistance image from the mid-nineteenth century Mandan-Arikara village at Fort Clark, North Dakota; (d) a magnetic gradiometry image of the same area in 5.2c, showing central hearths, storage pits, and iron artifacts, including one particularly iron-rich house (left); (e) fortification ditches and bastions, recognized by their respective linear and U-shaped forms in magnetometry data from the fourteenth to eighteenth century Double Ditch Village, North Dakota; (f) the rectangular footprint of the foundation of Mount Comfort Church (1840s–1863) in Arkansas, destroyed during the Civil War, is recognized in an electrical resistance data set.

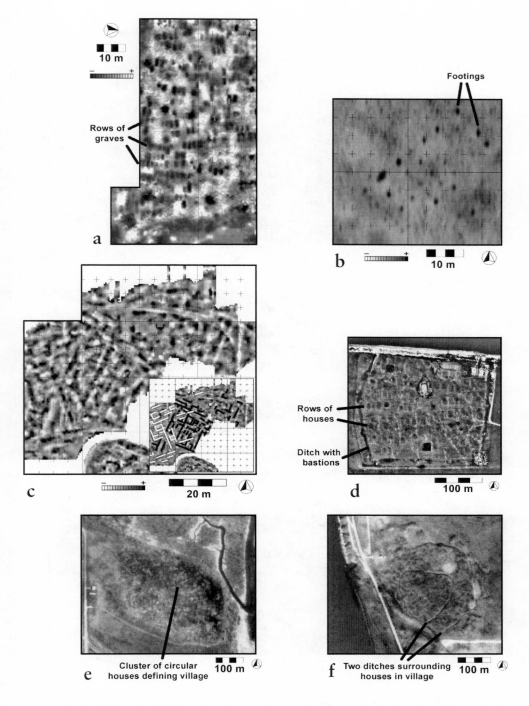

FIGURE 5.3. (*a*) Repetitive occurrences of 1 × 2 m oval-to-rectangular shaped anomalies in an electrical resistance data set point to unmarked graves at the Bozeman Cemetery, Arkansas; (*b*) the regular pattern of electrical resistance anomalies(forming a rectangle) points to building footings at the World War I era commercial center of Army City, Kansas; (*c*) multiple parallel and right-angle lineations suggest two different orientations in the layout of a sixteenth century Dutch-English street or building grid in New York (inset shows an interpretation); (*d*) an aerial photograph of the fifteenth century Huff Village, North Dakota, shows systematically spaced rectangular anomalies known to be houses organized in rows within the village's fortified ditch system; the Missouri River lies to the north (1960s photo courtesy of W. R. Wood, University of Missouri, showing several open excavations); (*e*) aerial photograph of the nineteenth century Mandan-Arikara village at Fort Clark, North Dakota, showing circular earthlodges; the Missouri River lies to the east; (*f*) aerial photograph of fourteenth to eighteenth century earthlodges within two fortification systems at Double Ditch Village, North Dakota; the Missouri River lies to the west.

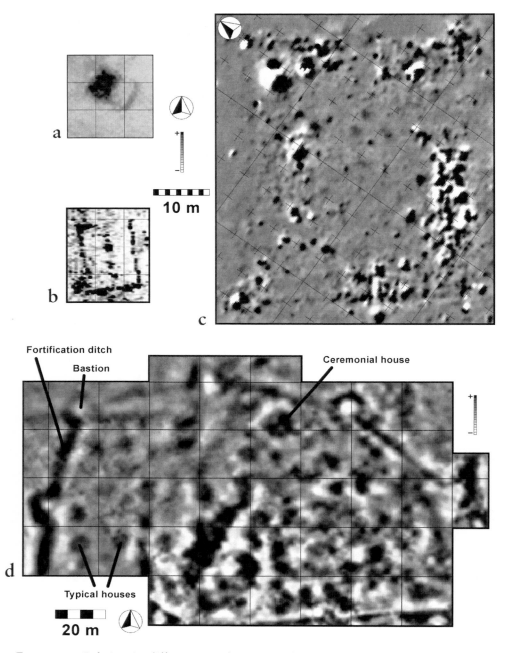

a

b

10 m

c

Fortification ditch

Bastion

Ceremonial house

d

Typical houses

20 m

FIGURE 5.4. Relative size differences can be associated with functionality, as suggested by comparisons between (*a*) an 1870s cowboy cabin in central Kansas revealed by electrical resistance survey, (*b*) the mid-nineteenth century Mount Comfort Church, Arkansas, portrayed by ground-penetrating radar, and (*c*) the Fort Clark Trading Post (1832–1861), North Dakota, magnetically revealed by magnetic foundation stones. About 60 roughly circular anomalies (*d*) are interpreted primarily as houses in an electrical resistance image from the fourteenth century Whistling Elk Village, South Dakota; the larger one is interpreted as a structure of special communal or ceremonial significance.

represent a dwelling, while such a conclusion is entirely possible given the size of the first.

At Whistling Elk Village, described earlier, electrical resistance surveys revealed about 60 anomalies interpreted as dwellings by shape and size, yet a single anomaly stands out by virtue of its abnormally large dimensions, which supports the interpretation that it is the remains of a ceremonial structure or communal lodge (Figure 5.4d; shown in detail in Figure 5.2a [Toom and Kvamme 2002]). At a larger scale, the magnetic gradiometry data from this "Big House" reveal multiple interior anomalies (Figure 5.2b). The large central one (about 1.5 m in diameter) is interpreted as a hearth; four small anomalies (about 25 to 50 cm in size) arranged in a regular quadrilateral are interpreted as likely roof support posts (an inference based on prior archaeological knowledge from similar excavated houses); the bounding square (10 m wide) can only represent the house perimeter. These features were detected because the house had burned and the hearth had been used repeatedly (see below)—inferences later validated by excavation (Toom and Kvamme 2002).

Pattern Recognition Based on Association

Association refers to relationships between anthropogenic anomalies or features. Houses combine to form settlements, fortifications and plazas go with villages, and roads and trails emanate from them, for example. A single house-sized anomaly in a field could represent almost anything, from a large tree throw to a silted-in pond, but combine a series of such anomalies in a relatively tight cluster and the probability of them representing houses within a village increases. For instance, at Huff and Double Ditch villages in North Dakota, the association between the fortification systems and the village's dwellings is clear (Figure 5.3d–f; the ditches visible at Double Ditch are different from those revealed by geophysics in Figure 5.2e). Associations also occur at a larger scale. Hearths go with houses, as do roof support posts and entryways, such as those at the Big House of Whistling Elk (Figure 5.2a, b). The same situation occurs in the many circular earthlodges

at the Mandan-Arikara village at Fort Clark, where central hearths and interior storage pits are prominent in the magnetic gradiometry data (Figure 5.2d) and fit nicely within the bounding house perimeters defined by the resistance survey (Figure 5.2c).

Pattern Recognition Based on Context

Context, as used here, refers to relationships such as correlations between characteristics of terrain and types of archaeological phenomena, which figure prominently in predictive models of archaeological site location (Kvamme 2006b; Wescott and Brandon 2000). Most settlements of the Plains Village Tradition of the Middle Missouri River, for example, tend to be located on high terraces adjacent to the river (Figure 5.3d–f). The within-site use of context may be more problematic, but examples can be contrived. For instance, in the case of riverine settlements certain anomalies might be inferred to represent boat quays owing to their form and their proximity to navigable channels. Similarly, and not surprisingly, historic period flour mills and saw mills typically co-exist with millponds.

Experience as a Basis for Pattern Recognition

When remote sensing projects are first initiated in a region, many anomalies may be unambiguously cultural in origin, as determined by means of the foregoing recognition elements. Yet, a great amount of uncertainty may remain concerning the identity of other anomalies. In these cases, one must turn to archaeological excavations as a means of anomaly identification. Published archaeological reports illustrate plans of dwellings, public buildings, storage facilities, and other features. House plans from 1970s excavations at Whistling Elk indicated square houses with southeast-facing linear entryways, for example, as well as basic size data that matched exactly many anomalies interpreted as houses (Figure 5.2a [Toom and Kvamme 2002:11]).

Beyond consulting the published literature, one may also conduct limited archaeological tests over a sample of anomalies of a given type and form. If consistent identifications are

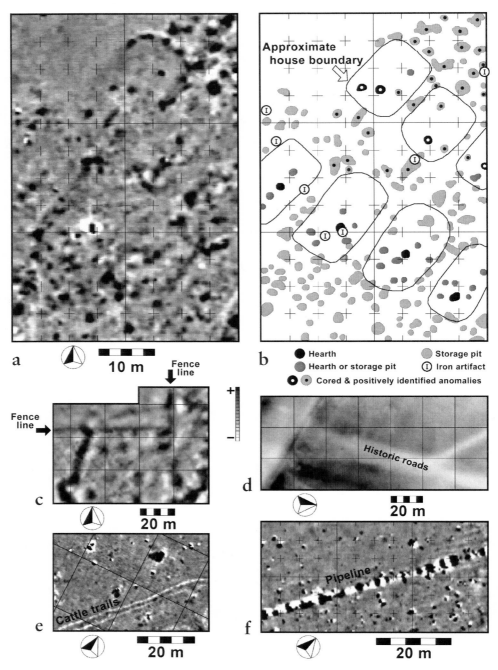

FIGURE 5.5. Interpreting anomalies from past and recent sources: (*a*) small, 1–1.5 m, circular magnetic anomalies at the fifteenth century Huff Village, North Dakota; (*b*) interpretation of significant anomalies in 5.5a based on a limited coring program (conducted at anomalies with dots) that revealed most were storage pits or hearths; (*c*) vegetation along field boundary fences cause high electrical resistance anomalies at Whistling Elk Village, South Dakota; (*d*) a late nineteenth to early twentieth century road network is partially revealed in an electrical resistance data set; (*e*) incisions in the surface along parallel cattle trails produce negative magnetic anomalies; (*f*) a buried steel pipe produces a series of dipolar magnetic anomalies at each joint.

made, then other anomalies of the same type and form likely represent the same cultural feature. For example, at Huff Village hundreds of roughly circular anomalies about 1 to 1.5 m in diameter were detected by magnetic gradiometry (Figure 5.5a). A systematic soil coring program over a representative area, using a 1 in. (2.54 cm) corer, established relatively secure identifications; in this case, about 74 percent were subterranean storage pits, 16 percent were hearths, and the remaining ones were small middens (Kvamme 2003). Moreover, hearths yielded characteristically higher measurements (Bales and Kvamme 2005) and were usually located along house centerlines. Storage pits, on the other hand, were often located under house entryways, off-centerline within houses, and around house perimeters (Ahler and Kvamme 2000). This knowledge allowed remaining anomalies of this size and type to be classified with a high degree of confidence (Figure 5.5b).

By testing samples of anomalies of a particular type, size, and form, and archiving the results, a regional "anomaly library" can be developed as a reference source for future work. For example, anomalies with a characteristic range of measurements, sizes, and shapes might point to a specific kind of archaeological feature, while other anomalies with different ranges of measurements, sizes, or shapes might point to other types. Anomaly form, size, and type will vary, of course, according to remote sensing technique and particular soil and environmental conditions at the time of data acquisition. Examples of on-line archives of remote sensing studies include the *English Heritage Geophysics Database* (http://www.eng-h.gov.uk/SDB) and the *North American Database of Archaeological Geophysics* (http://www.cast.uark.edu/nadag).

Pattern Recognition
Approaches: Summary
The foregoing anomaly recognition domains are not independent of each other or of inference strategies based on knowledge of physical principles, discussed below. As a rule, we might state, for example, that a hearth goes with a house (association), the hearth is smaller

than a house (size), each might be recognized by circular forms (shape), and postholes might be regularly arranged (repetitive patterns). At the same time, the physics of magnetometry suggest that hearths should yield larger magnitude magnetic measurements compared to fired postholes, whereas burned house walls might exhibit moderate values (see below). These patterns, in fact, were all combined to confirm the magnetic interpretations of the Big House at Whistling Elk Village (Figure 5.2b [Toom and Kvamme 2002]).

Pattern recognition is not a foolproof method. Complex archaeological deposits may make anomaly identification difficult. Intensive occupations with dense stratigraphy or superimposed constructions can "jumble" signals that might be remotely detected, making patterns unclear. Even in the most interpretable sites, there are always anomalies that cannot be explained with high certainty. Moreover, every site will also contain anomalies of biological, pedological, geological, or recent cultural origin that can mimic archaeological phenomena. In other words, a small percentage of the anomalies classified as storage pits in Figure 5.5b might actually represent recent badger dens. Modern cultural practices introduce anomalies that are particularly numerous. Something as mundane as mow marks and as silly as tethered, grazing goats can generate linear or circular anomalies, respectively, in remotely sensed imagery. Former field boundaries (Figure 5.5c), recent roads (Figure 5.5d), trails, cattle tracks (Figure 5.5e), and pipelines (Figure 5.5f) can all be linear in form and point to anomalies that might be prone to misinterpretation as features of possible interest. Thorough background research and frequent on-site field visits are essential to reducing potential errors of interpretation.

BEYOND PATTERN RECOGNITION: INTERPRETATIONS BASED ON PHYSICAL PRINCIPLES
Not all culturally generated anomalies exhibit clear and recognizable spatial patterns. We must also react to remote sensing by identifying the *physical properties* of archaeological materials and features in the ground

and deducing how various sensors might respond to them. It is therefore prudent to first examine basic characteristics of the source of anthropogenic anomalies—the archaeological record (Sullivan, this volume).

The Nature of Archaeological Sites

After more than a century of excavation of a wide range of archaeological phenomena (Stein, this volume), a great deal has been learned about the nature of archaeological sites. This knowledge can be applied to determine the kinds of cultural features that might be remotely detected and the nature of sensor responses (see Scollar et al. 1990:4–7). It is a well-known dictum that an archaeological site is a three-dimensional matrix of materials, containing artifacts, ecofacts (floral and faunal remains), human-generated constructions (features), and the deposits in which they lie (Goldberg, this volume). *Artifacts* are material objects modified by people. Portable artifacts include small items that are easily moved, such as tools employed in day-to-day activities (e.g., spear points, pots, knives). Non-portable artifacts include such larger items as posts, building timbers, bricks, or shaped stones used in architectural constructions. *Constructions* include the many types of buildings and other facilities that people make, including places of occupancy (e.g., dwellings, public structures), non-occupancy (e.g., storage pits, wells, burial mounds, fortification ditches), and transportation facilities (e.g., roads, trails).

Sediments and soils from the matrix within which artifacts and constructions lie. Most result from natural processes, but many are anthropogenic or are altered by human activity. *Additive deposits* occur where materials have been accumulated by people, such as refuse dumps (e.g., middens containing food waste, bones, discarded portable artifacts, ash from fires) or where earth materials have been used in constructions (e.g., burial mounds, platforms, prepared house floors, raised berms). *Reductive deposits* form where sediments and soils have been removed, as when ditches, pits, or cellars are excavated or where incisions in the surface have been caused by foot traffic.

Altered deposits are those whose properties have been changed as a consequence of intensive fires in hearths or kilns, for example. Similarly, soil compaction commonly occurs under living floors or along pathways.

Properties of Archaeological Sites: What Can Be Remotely Detected?

Large, non-portable artifacts, such as building foundations or pavement stones, generally can be remotely sensed, but the same may not be said of small portable artifacts (an exception is metallic artifacts that may be located with metal detectors). Large masses of small portable artifacts or ecofacts *might* occasionally be revealed by remote sensing, as when a concentration of ceramic sherds subtly raises the local magnetic field.

Human constructions receive attention in remote sensing because their larger volumes of contrasting physical properties increase detection probabilities relative to common sensor resolutions and sampling densities (their regular geometric shapes also make them more easily recognized by means of pattern recognition principles). Moreover, additive deposits generally vary in their characteristics. Middens filled with refuse might contain more air voids, solids (such as bone and discarded artifacts), soil nutrients, or different levels of moisture, which would alter their subsurface electrical, thermal, or surface vegetation patterns (Scollar et al. 1990; Weymouth 1986). Mound formation often employs topsoil, which generally raises the local magnetic field, whereas areas where topsoil was removed for cellars or ditches tend to deflate it. Heavily fired features, including kilns or burned houses, are particularly detectable because they profoundly increase soil magnetism (Clark 2000). Large constructions near the surface can impact vegetation patterns, as when a buried stone wall retards growth or moist sediments in a former ditch promote it (forming the "crop mark" phenomenon). In either case, the spectral properties of the plants may be altered (Scollar et al. 1990; Wilson 2000). Differences in deposit materials, their compaction, moisture retention, and other factors affect absorption and emissivity rates of solar radiation; consequently, when this energy is re-radiated, thermal variation can occur (Dabas and Tabbagh 2000).

Sensor Mixes and Detection Probabilities

The likelihood of detecting a buried archaeological feature depends on (1) matching the contrasting physical properties of the feature with sensors capable of detecting those properties, (2) the amount of physical contrast between the feature and surrounding deposits with respect to sensor sensitivity, (3) the size of the feature relative to the spatial resolution of the measurements, (4) the depth of the feature below the surface with respect to signal attenuation and the level of confounding noise factors that might overly it, (5) the degree of regular pattern the feature exhibits (pattern recognition property), and (6) use of multiple sensors that allow detection of different physical consequences of buried materials or deposits.

The spatial resolution of measurements determines the size of archaeological features that can be resolved, with a rule of thumb that the interval between measurements should be no greater than *half* the size of the smallest feature one wishes to detect (so that multiple measurements may delineate it [Weymouth 1986:347]). It should be obvious why larger features like houses or ditches are relatively easy to locate (many measurements define them), and why resolving small portable artifacts and features is so difficult. Ground-based and aerial methods offer very high spatial detail, well into the sub-meter range, and recent satellite systems now deliver a similar capability with meter-level spatial resolutions (Figure 5.1 [Fowler 1996; Kennedy 1998]). Detection probabilities are also affected by instrument sensitivity. A magnetometer with a precision of 0.001 nT (*nanotesla*, or 10^{-9} Tesla) can detect smaller, deeper, and more subtle anomalies than one that measures only to the 0.1 nT level (Becker 1995).

Environmental conditions at the time of data acquisition also influence results. Daylight is necessary for many forms of air or space imaging, but may be undesirable for thermal remote sensing. Low sunlight is necessary to achieve terrain shadowing (necessary to detect relief changes) in aerial photography. Seasonal effects must also be considered because vegetation at a particular stage of development is necessary for "crop marking," visible from the air or space, and resistivity-conductivity methods cannot be employed in frozen ground. Too much or too little soil moisture can negatively affect electrical resistance, conductivity, or thermal surveys, while too much moisture may impede transmission of radar energy. Deeply buried archaeological features are more difficult to detect than shallowly buried ones because the soil above acts like a filter that degrades signals from lower levels. Buried pipes, electrical lines, and radio or cell phone transmissions can negatively impact many ground-based instruments. In general, remote sensing of any kind is more successful in open fields with uniform ground cover; heavily vegetated, wooded, or urban landscapes can pose great difficulties or make many methods of remote detection impossible (Bewley 2000; Clark 2000; Dabas and Tabbagh 2000; Scollar et al. 1990).

A REMOTE SENSING CASE STUDY: MAGNETOMETRY

Much about the character of the archaeological record can be deduced by exploring its physical principles alone, but it is impossible to examine all remote sensing techniques here. Instead, I focus on demonstrating the inferential possibilities of magnetometry, which is a passive, ground-based remote sensing method that is arguably one of the most productive prospecting tools available to archaeologists (Kvamme 2006c). To fully understand its basic principles, it is first necessary to review some background theory.

Types of Magnetism

Few materials exhibit magnetism in the absence of a magnetic field. Any that exists is considered "remanent" because it remains after the generating process. Most soils, clays, and rocks contain small magnetic 'domains oriented in random directions with little magnetic effect. At temperatures beyond the Curie point (about 600° C), the domains align themselves parallel to the Earth's magnetic field and remain in this situation upon cooling, creating an appreciable total effect because their magnetic fields add together, making fired features readily detectable by magnetometry (Aitken 1970:683; Clark 2000:64). This form of magnetism is known as *thermoremanent magnetism*, which is permanent and is carried by all igneous rocks.

Because all materials exist within Earth's magnetic field, a second form of magnetism is introduced, known as *induced magnetism*. The ability of a material to become magnetized depends on its *magnetic susceptibility*, which requires the presence of magnetizable minerals (e.g., hematite, magnetite, and maghemite [Clark 2000:100]). Soils generally possess a magnetic susceptibility larger than the rocks from which they originate (except for those that develop from highly magnetic volcanic rocks) owing to a variety of physical and biological processes. Relatively insoluble iron minerals tend to accumulate in topsoil. A natural "fermentation process" also occurs with alternating periods of wetness and dryness that affects oxides and the transmutation of hematites to more magnetic maghemites. Natural or anthropogenic firing reduces hematite to magnetite, which upon cooling is partially reoxidized to maghemite, thereby increasing magnetic susceptibility (Clark 2000). Within topsoil layers magnetotactic and other bacteria concentrate magnetic compounds (Fassbinder et al. 1990), and extended human occupations tend to exacerbate these effects through the introduction of organic and fired materials to the topsoil (see below). Magnetometers measure the *sum* of induced magnetism due to susceptibility and all forms of remanent magnetism.

Earth's Magnetic Field

Earth's magnetic field arises from currents produced by the molten iron core and has a total field strength ranging from about 30,000 nT at the magnetic equator to about 60,000 nT at the magnetic poles (Weymouth 1986:341). This range is noteworthy because magnetic anomalies of potential archaeological interest often lie within ±5 nT of background levels.

Instrumentation is therefore incredibly sensitive, capable of detecting on the order of one part in a half million of Earth's total magnetic field.

In effect, Earth's magnetic field acts as if a giant bar magnet lies at its center. The angle between geographic north and geomagnetic north measured with a compass in the horizontal plane is known as *declination*. The lines of magnetic force also intersect the Earth's surface at various angles in the vertical plane, depending on location. At the magnetic equator this *inclination* angle is horizontal, at the magnetic poles it is vertical, and at mid-latitudes it varies from about 55 to 75 degrees (Mussett and Kahn 2000:139–142). This angle causes a characteristic phenomenon in magnetometry data sets. The magnetic field of an anomaly is added to Earth's, with north and south poles of the induced component generally aligned parallel to the current magnetic axis (although deviations can occur depending on the source's shape and other factors). A separation between the poles occurs as a result of the inclination angle causing a *dipolar* phenomenon, with a positive peak generally lying south of the true locus of the source, and a depression (or negative) in the magnetic field occurring to the north at mid-northern latitudes (see Figure 5.5f).

Instrumentation and Field Methods

Many different types of magnetometers and magnetic gradiometers (a twin-sensor instrument that measures vertical changes in the magnetic field) are commonly used in archaeology (see Clark 2000; Weymouth 1986). Most are capable of 0.1 nT resolution and are equipped with data memory devices that store tens of thousands of measurements for later downloading and computer processing. With high data acquisition rates, surveys of large areas are possible, from 0.5 to 4.0 hectares per day, making them the workhorse of archaeogeophysics. Magnetic surveys are typically performed in gridded blocks that range from 20 to 50 m square. Most practitioners use ropes or tapes with meter marks placed parallel to each other on the ground to form grids. The instruments are then moved along these guides to accurately locate measurements. Spatial resolution is controlled by the separation between transects, the number of samples taken per meter, and the sampling capabilities of the instrument (see Clark 2000:158–164). While early surveys usually acquired only one measurement per m², current high-speed instrumentation typically allows sampling densities of 16–32 measurements per m² for improved anomaly definition.

Cultural Causes of Magnetic Variation in the Archaeological Record

The foregoing discussion suggests that three natural processes are primarily responsible for magnetic variations: (1) *inherent differences in magnetic susceptibilities* occur among various materials, deposits, and soils; (2) *magnetic enrichment of topsoils* stems from physical and chemical processes (e.g., weathering) and biogenic processes (e.g., magnetotactic bacteria); and (3) *firing effects on soil magnetism* produce a thermoremanent effect. Yet, people live within their environment, generally on topsoil, and modify it and other deposits, leading to the formation of magnetic anomalies within archaeological sites that are attributable to seven principal anthropogenic processes (Clark 2000; Scollar et al. 1990; Weymouth 1986).

1. *People create fires.* Cooking fires occur in hearths (Figure 5.2b, d), fireplaces, and ovens within and outside of structures. Certain technologies require intensive firing —for ceramics, glass, or metallurgy—usually in specialized kilns or furnaces. Fires also occur accidentally when a structure burns (Figure 5.2b), or purposefully when a village is razed in warfare. In all cases, the high temperatures introduce thermoremanent anomalies to the archaeological record.

   Implications: Extremely high and concentrated magnetic measurements may be indicative of a burned house or structure. Concentrated burning often produces broad dipolar anomalies, a characteristic signature of hearths.

2. *People make constructions and artifacts composed of fired materials.* Bricks are made of moderately fired clay, which increases their magnetic susceptibilities, and are common construction materials employed in large numbers. Prominent anomalies therefore result owing to their large cumulative mass (Figure 5.6a). Although ceramic vessels are also fired artifacts, the small masses of individual sherds and the relatively low magnetic contrasts they produce generally make them undetectable. On the other hand, whole vessels or dense sherd concentrations might possibly be detected.

   Implications: A rectangular or linear anomaly might suggest a foundation or wall. Marked positive measurements can lead to an inference of brick walls, foundations, or pavements.

3. *Human occupations exacerbate magnetic enrichment of surface soils.* Fired materials within settlements become dispersed through time owing to hearth cleanings or subsequent constructions that redistribute materials from earlier hearths or burned structures. Additionally, occupations introduce organic materials to the topsoil (food, waste products) that promote bacterial growth, including magnetotactic and other bacteria that concentrate magnetic compounds (Fassbinder et al. 1990). The rise in magnetic susceptibility that occurs is generally small in magnitude and must be recorded with a specialized magnetic susceptibility meter, an active instrument that artificially induces a magnetic field in samples to be measured.

   Implications: Areas of intensive occupation or activity should exhibit raised levels of magnetic susceptibility.

4. *Human constructions accumulate topsoil.* Many constructed features are built of topsoil, causing a local increase in the magnetic field. Small burial or effigy mounds may be accumulations of nearby topsoil and exhibit large magnetic contrasts (Figure 5.6b). Excavated ditches often mound removed topsoil nearby, forming a raised berm and an enlarged magnetic contrast (Figure 5.6c). In turn, ditches may eventually become filled with surface soils,

forming concentrated zones of high magnetism owing to the large volume of magnetically enriched material composing their fills (Figure 5.2e). Similarly, small storage pits ultimately become packed with magnetically enriched topsoil after their abandonment, making them readily detectable (Figure 5.5a, b).

Implications: Moderately high magnetic measurement in and about former houses may point to earth or sod constructions. High measurements over mounds and earthworks may indicate topsoil compositions. Storage pits with high readings suggest topsoil fills.

5. *Human constructions remove topsoil.* Many constructed features require the removal of topsoil, resulting in a net lowering of the magnetic field over those features or a "negative" anomaly, because the amount of overlying magnetic material is less than in neighboring areas. Unfilled ditches (Figure 5.6c), recessed house floors, subterranean storage pits, cellars, and even excavations and looter's "pot holes" (Figure 5.6d) effectively remove small to large volumes of magnetically enriched topsoil, causing negative contrasts. Simple incisions in the ground caused by foot traffic along trails (Figure 5.5e) or roads (Figure 5.6d) can produce the same effect, where topsoil has been kicked or pushed aside. Occasionally, sediments and soils removed during the excavation of a grave are not replaced in their original order. If the more magnetic topsoil does not lie at the surface after a grave is filled, negative anomalies can sometimes be expressed (Figure 5.6e).

Implications: Anomalies indicated by negative measurements register something about construction methods, whether topsoil was removed, deeply buried, or whether a void may exist below the surface.

6. *People import stone and other materials for constructions.* Building foundations, pavements, and floors are often constructed of stone. Many rocks tend to be more magnetic (e.g., igneous rocks), but some are less magnetic (e.g., most limestones), than surrounding soils, thereby generating magnetic contrasts. For example, foundation blocks made of somewhat magnetic sandstone yielded positive anomalies that defined the Fort Clark Trading Post, North Dakota (Figure 5.4c). Likewise, specialized sediments are sometimes imported for desirable characteristics, such as clay for prepared floors or pit linings, and sand or gravel for trails, walkways, or base substrates for larger constructions. These materials, too, can produce detectable contrasts depending on their inherent magnetic susceptibilities, volume, and depth.

Implications: A rectangular or linear anomaly might suggest the presence of a foundation, pavement, or wall. Positive or negative magnetic values can lead to inferences concerning material types if common building materials in a region are known.

7. *People make iron artifacts.* Iron artifacts tend to be readily detected by magnetometry depending on their size, shape, orientation, mass, and depth below the surface (Figures 5.2d; 5.5a, b, f; 5.6a). Iron is nearly ubiquitous in historic period sites and markedly alters the Earth's magnetic field, commonly producing large and easily recognized dipolar anomalies. For instance, one of the circular earthlodges at the Mandan-Arikara village at Fort Clark revealed a ring of dipolar anomalies about its perimeter, indicative of iron artifacts (Figure 5.2d, left).

Implications: The magnetic signature of iron artifacts is usually unambiguous owing to its concentrated, large magnitude, and dipolar form, leading immediately to an inference of ferrous metal. In historic sites, iron litter may point to significant artifacts, dumping areas, or the loci of former wooden structures that employed nails in their construction.

CONCLUSIONS

Archaeological inferences in remote sensing studies are based on the twin pillars of pattern recognition and knowledge of fundamental physical principles. For instance, a house might be recognized by its shape, and a centrally placed circular hearth by its size, shape,

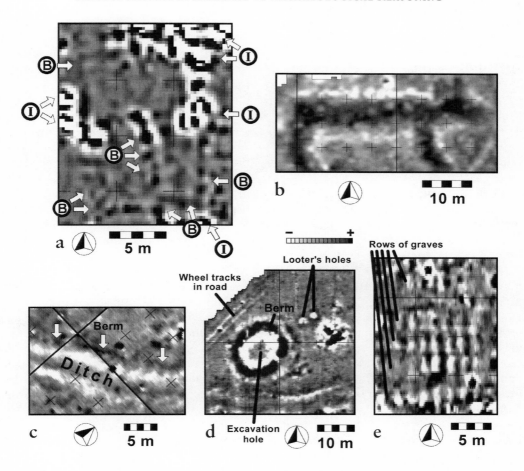

FIGURE 5.6. Anomalies illustrating fundamental magnetic principles: (*a*) the fired-brick foundation of the Mount Comfort Church (1840s–1863), Arkansas, is visible among numerous iron-produced anomalies from stove parts, nails, and other artifacts about 35 cm below the surface, as revealed by excavation (B = brick; I = iron); (*b*) topsoil mounded to a height of about 1 m forming the Great Bear Effigy (Mound 31; ca. AD 650–1300) at Effigy Mounds National Monument, Iowa, causes positive magnetic anomalies; (*c*) topsoil mounded in a raised berm adjacent to the open fortification ditch at the thirteenth century Menoken Village, North Dakota, causes positive magnetic anomalies; negative anomalies occur over the ditch itself; (*d*) incised truck tracks, an unfilled excavation, and looter's pits form negative magnetic anomalies at Menoken Village; (*e*) at the Confederate Cemetery at the University of Mississippi (founded in 1862), graves are indicated as negative magnetic anomalies, most likely because topsoil was not replaced at the surface of each one (data source courtesy of Jay Johnson, University of Mississippi).

relative position, and association, but characteristically high magnetic readings in dipolar form lend certainty to the inference of a hearth.

Practically speaking, remote sensing surveys provide a rapid means of data collection over large areas, with costs far less than excavation, and results that are generally more fruitful than primitive "shovel test pit" methodologies. Remote sensing can guide expensive excavations to features of potential archaeological interest, producing cost savings by making site explorations more efficient. Indications can be given about depth, areal extent, and distribution of cultural features, as well as of soil types and other subsurface conditions. By reliably locating archaeological features, the volume of excavations can be reduced, causing smaller artifact collections to be recovered, thereby lowering curation costs. Moreover, while traditional invasive methods destroy the very resources they investigate, remote sensing methods are nondestructive, an important consideration when exploring culturally sensitive or protected sites.

Remote sensing is not a panacea. It is constrained by the particular characteristics that might be present at the time and place of data acquisition (e.g., soil type, ground moisture, ground cover), potentially leading to poor or no archaeological feature detection, and it is particularly difficult to conduct within urban or forested landscapes (Bewley 2000; Donoghue 2001). Costs may be viewed as a drawback, but they are comparable to digging hundreds of less informative shovel test pits across an area (Johnson and Haley 2006) and must be balanced against such issues as making management and planning decisions based on little knowledge of what lies beneath the ground, the expense of incorrectly placing costly excavations, and the possibility of failing to locate significant archaeological features, human remains, and other culturally sensitive deposits prior to their disturbance (with expensive and complex actions required for their mitigation [Hargrave 2006]).

Under suitable conditions, archaeological remote sensing can yield detailed maps portraying subsurface features over large areas. This capability has potentially large implications because it makes the direct study of settlement form and content possible through remotely sensed imagery alone, as *primary data* (e.g., Gaffney et al. 2000; Kvamme 2003). Such data may be suitable for the study of site structure, content, and organization, for examining spatial patterns and relationships. Although excavations provide rich chronological information, material culture samples, and more secure identifications of subsurface features, they often miss the larger picture— the structure, layout, and size of settlements, the number of houses they might contain, how they are distributed, the presence of lanes, trails, roads, public buildings, plazas, gardens, graves, defenses, and the like. Remote sensing methods, therefore, offer a rich adjunct to regional or landscape archaeologies in addition to their utility as feature discovery tools.

ACKNOWLEDGMENTS

Jeff Grathwohl and the University of Utah Press are thanked for the wonderful venue of the Snowbird Conference that brought the volume's participants together. At that conference many excellent ideas and comments were fielded by the participants, to whom I owe my thanks. Two anonymous reviewers provided useful remarks that improved this presentation. This work benefited from the aerial photograph of Huff Village; Ray Wood of the University of Missouri kindly volunteered a scan. The Confederate cemetery data were provided by Jay Johnson of the University of Mississippi. Many ideas arose in discussions with Lew Somers (Geoscan Research), Bruce Bevan (Geosight), Rinita Dalan (Minnesota State University—Moorhead), and many students of the University of Arkansas who demanded explanations about how we know what lies beneath the earth. Work at Huff, Fort Clark, Menoken, and Double Ditch was made possible by grants from the State Historical Society of North Dakota and the PaleoCultural Research Group of Flagstaff, Arizona, supported by Fern Swenson and the late Stan Ahler, respectively.

Investigations at Whistling Elk were supported by a grant from the National Center for Preservation Technology and Training, National Park Service, and conducted under an ARPA permit. The survey at Sylvester Manor was sponsored by the Andrew Fiske Memorial Center for Archaeological Research and its director, Steven Mrozowski. Research at Fort Riley was funded by the Strategic Environmental Research and Development Program, Department of Defense. Work at other sites was largely the result of University of Arkansas class projects conducted with students, whose efforts are greatly appreciated.

REFERENCES CITED

Ahler, Stanley A., and Kenneth L. Kvamme
2000 *New Geophysical and Archaeological Investigations at Huff Village State Historic Site (32MO11), Morton County, North Dakota.* Report submitted to the State

Historical Society of North Dakota, Bismarck.

Aitken, Melvin J.
1970 Magnetic Location. In *Science in Archaeology*, edited by Don R. Brothwell and Eric S. Higgs, pp. 681–707. Praeger, New York.

Avery, Thomas E., and Graydon L. Berlin
1992 *Fundamentals of Remote Sensing and Air Photo Interpretation.* 5th ed. Macmillan, New York.

Bales, Jennifer R., and Kenneth L. Kvamme
2005 Geophysical Signatures of Earthlodges in the Dakotas. In *Plains Earthlodges: Ethnographic and Archaeological Perspectives*, edited by Donna Roper and Elizabeth Pauls, pp. 157–183. University of Alabama Press, Tuscaloosa.

Barnes, Ian
2003 Aerial Remote-Sensing Techniques Used in the Management of Archaeological Monuments on the British Army's Salisbury Plain Training Area. *Archaeological Prospection* 10:83–90.

Becker, Helmut
1995 From Nanotesla to Picotesla—A New Window for Magnetic Prospecting in Archaeology. *Archaeological Prospection* 2:217–228.

Bewley, Robert H.
2000 Aerial Photography for Archaeology. In *Archaeological Method and Theory: An Encyclopedia*, edited by Linda Ellis, pp. 3–10. Garland, New York.

Buteux, Simon, Vince Gaffney, Roger White, and Martign van Leusen
2000 Wroxeter Hinterland Project and Geophysical Survey at Wroxeter. *Archaeological Prospection* 7:69–80.

Clark, Anthony
2000 *Seeing Beneath the Soil: Prospection Methods in Archaeology.* Reprinted. Routledge, London. Originally published 1990, B. T. Batsford Ltd., London.

Clay, R. Berle
2001 Complementary Geophysical Survey Techniques: Why Two Ways are Always Better than One. *Southeastern Archaeology* 20: 31–43.

Conyers, Lawrence B.
2004 *Ground-Penetrating Radar for Archaeology.* AltaMira Press, Walnut Creek, California.

Dabas, Michel, and Alain Tabbagh
2000 Thermal Prospecting. In *Archaeological Method and Theory: An Encyclopedia*, edited by Linda Ellis, pp. 626–630. Garland, New York.

Dalan, Rinita A.
1993 Issues of Scale in Archaeological Research. In *Effects of Scale on Archaeological and Geoscientific Perspectives*, edited by Julie K. Stein and Angela R. Linse, pp. 67–78. Geological Society of America Special Paper 283. Boulder.

David, Andrew
1995 *Geophysical Survey in Archaeological Field Evaluation.* English Heritage Society, London.

Donoghue, D. N. M.
2001 Remote Sensing. In *Handbook of Archaeological Sciences*, edited by Don R. Brothwell and A. M. Pollard, pp. 555–563. John Wiley, New York.

Fassbinder, Jorg W. E., Helge Stanjek, and Hojatollah Vali
1990 Occurrence of Magnetic Bacteria in Soil. *Nature* 343:161–163.

Fowler, Martin J. F.
1996 High-Resolution Satellite Imagery in Archaeological Application: A Russian Satellite Photograph of the Stonehenge Region. *Antiquity* 70:667–671.

2002 Satellite Remote Sensing and Archaeology: A Comparative Study of Satellite Imagery of the Environs of Figsbury Ring, Wiltshire. *Archaeological Prospection* 9:55–69.

Gaffney, C. F., J. A. Gater, P. Linford, V. L. Gaffney, and R. White
2000 Large-Scale Systematic Fluxgate Gradiometry at the Roman City of Wroxeter. *Archaeological Prospection* 7:81–99.

Hargrave, Michael L.
2006 Ground Truthing the Results of Geophysical Surveys. In *Remote Sensing in Archaeology: An Explicitly North American Perspective*, edited by Jay K. Johnson, pp. 269–304. University of Alabama Press, Tuscaloosa.

Hargrave, Michael L., Lewis E. Somers, Thomas K. Larson, Richard Shields, and John Dendy
2002 The Role of Resistivity Survey in Historic Site Assessment and Management: An Example from Fort Riley, Kansas. *Historical Archaeology* 36:89–110.

Hesse, Albert, Luis Barba, Karl Link, and Agustin Ortiz
1997 A Magnetic and Electrical Study of Archaeological Structures at Loma Alta, Michoacan, Mexico. *Archaeological Prospection* 4:53–67.

Johnson, Jay K., and Bryan S. Haley
2006   A Cost Benefit Evaluation of Remote Sensing Applications. In *Remote Sensing in Archaeology: An Explicitly North American Perspective*, edited by Jay K. Johnson, pp. 33–45. University of Alabama Press, Tuscaloosa.

Kennedy, David
1998   Declassified Satellite Photographs and Archaeology in the Middle East: Case Studies from Turkey. *Antiquity* 72:553–561.

Kintigh, Keith W.
1988   The Effectiveness of Subsurface Testing: A Simulation Approach. *American Antiquity* 53:686–707.

Kvamme, Kenneth L.
2001   Current Practices in Archaeogeophysics: Magnetics, Resistivity, Conductivity, and Ground-Penetrating Radar. In *Earth Sciences and Archaeology*, edited by Paul Goldberg, Vance Holliday, and C. Reid Ferring, pp. 353–384. Kluwer Academic/Plenum, New York.
2003   Geophysical Surveys as Landscape Archaeology. *American Antiquity* 68:435–457.
2006a   Integrating Multidimensional Geophysical Data. *Archaeological Prospection* 13:57–72.
2006b   There and Back Again: Revisiting Archaeological Location Modeling. In *GIS and Archaeological Predictive Modeling*, edited by M. W. Mehrer and Konstance Wescott, pp. 5–47. CRC Press, New York.
2006c   Magnetometry: Nature's Gift to Archaeology. In *Remote Sensing in Archaeology: An Explicitly North American Perspective*, edited by Jay K. Johnson, pp. 205–234. University of Alabama Press, Tuscaloosa.

Mussett, Alan E., and M. Aftab Khan
2000   *Looking into the Earth: An Introduction to Geological Geophysics.* Cambridge University Press, Cambridge.

Quann, J., and B. Bevan
1977   The Pyramids from 900 Kilometers. *MASCA Newsletter* 13:12–14.

Scollar, I., A. Tabbagh, A. Hesse, and I. Herzog
1990   *Archaeological Prospecting and Remote Sensing.* Cambridge University Press, Cambridge.

Toom, Dennis L., and Kenneth L. Kvamme
2002   The "Big House" at Whistling Elk Village (39HU242): Geophysical Findings and Archaeological Truths. *Plains Anthropologist* 47:5–16.

Walker, A. R.
2000   Multiplexed Resistivity Survey at the Roman Town of Wroxeter. *Archaeological Prospection* 7:119–132.

Wescott, Konnie L., and R. Joe Brandon (eds.)
2000   *Practical Applications of GIS for Archaeologists: A Predictive Modeling Toolkit.* Taylor & Francis, London.

Weymouth, John W.
1986   Geophysical Methods of Archaeological Site Surveying. In *Advances in Archaeological Method and Theory*, Vol. 9, edited by Michael B. Schiffer, pp. 311–395. Academic Press, New York.

Wilson, D. R.
2000   *Air Photo Interpretation for Archaeologists.* Arcadia Publishing, Charleston, South Carolina.

Wynn, J.C.
1986   A Review of Geophysical Methods Used in Archaeology. *Geoarchaeology: An International Journal* 1:245–257.

6

Non-Anthropological Approaches to Understanding Lithic Artifact and Assemblage Variability

Most, if not all, American archaeologists who study lithic assemblages do so in the context of analyzing prehistoric industries. Thus, their research falls into the general area of "anthropological archaeology" in contrast to other, more humanistically oriented archaeological disciplines such as classical archaeology, history, and art history. This state of affairs is not due to a lack of lithic materials in later historic periods, but rather it appears to be a result of archaeologists having stressed the analysis of other artifact classes, such as ceramics.

Being generally grounded within four-field anthropology, lithic studies have drawn extensively on most of the other subdisciplines, though most evidently on cultural anthropology. This situation is especially true of the last 40 years, when most of archaeology, including lithic studies, was inspired by the perspective of cultural materialism. In terms of lithics in particular, the goal has been to understand how lithic technology functioned within an ongoing cultural system in the past. In fact, it is fair to say that the majority of such studies fall under the rubric of "technological organization" (Nelson 1991), which emphasizes the design, maintenance, and function of lithic technology within the context of the landscape. These studies entail considerations of group mobility (Carr 1994; Shott 1986), raw material procurement (Bamforth 1990; Binford 1980; Dib-

ble et al. 1995; Montet-White and Holen 1991; Roth and Dibble 1998), reuse and recycling (Dibble 1995a; Frison 1968; McPherron 1995, 2000), and other factors (Dibble et al. 1997). In addition, lithics have also been used to address questions of language (Davidson and Noble 1993; Dibble 1989; Holloway 1981), symbolism (Gibson and Ingold 1993; Gowlett 1984), cognition (Mithen 1995; Wynn 1985, 1991), trade and exchange (Ammerman 1979; Tankersley 1991), craft specialization (Mallory 1984), and linkages between lithic technology and biological evolution. Thus, virtually every aspect of four-field anthropology is addressed, at least to some degree.

It would be possible to use the preceding paragraphs as an introduction to a paper on why lithic archaeology needs to be allied with anthropology, and arguments to that effect would be valid. However, many methods and middle-range theories in lithic analysis do not depend heavily, if at all, on cultural theory or any other area of anthropology, yet they pertain to some of the most fundamental processes that underlie lithic assemblage variability. An equally valid argument could be made that until our basic understanding of lithic variability increases considerably, any attention to the higher levels of cultural explanation is essentially a waste of time.

We are fortunate that stone was used

MODIFICATION

Non-retouched   **Retouched**

LEVALLOIS   NON-LEVALLOIS   DEBITAGE

Typical Levallois Flake   Pesudo-Levallois point   Cores
Atypical Levallois flake   Naturally backed knife   Normal flakes
Levallois point   Shatter and debris

RETOUCH TYPE

Notching   **Burin**   **Borer**   **Core-like**   **Other**
Notch   Typical burin   Typical borer   Chopper   Mousterian tranchet
End-notched flake   Atypical burin   Atypical borer   Chopping tool   Pseudo-microburin
Notched triangle   Inverse chopper   Pieces w/ abrupt &
Alternate retouched beak   Rabot   alternating retouch
Denticulate   Stemmed point
Tayac point   Stemmed tool
                                                     Continuous   Miscellaneous

RETOUCHED SURFACE

Interior   **Alternate**   **Exterior**   **Bifacial Retouch**
Scraper on interior surface Scraper with thinned back   Scraper with bifacial retouch
                            Alternate scraper   Bifacial foliate
                                                                            Bifacially retouched piece
                                                                            Hachoir
                                                                            Truncated-faceted piece

LOCATION OF RETOUCHED EDGES

Parallel Edges   Single Lateral Edge   **Convergent Edges**   **Distal/Proximal**
Double straight scraper   Retouched Levallois point   Straight transverse scraper
Double straight-convex scraper   Mousterian point   Convex transverse scraper
Double straight-concave scraper   Elongated Mousterian point   Concave transverse scraper
Double convex scraper   Limace   Typical endscraper
Double convex-concave scraper   Straight convergent scraper Atypical endscraper
Double concave scraper   Convex convergent scraper   Truncation
                                             Concave convergent scraper
                                             Déjeté scraper

EDGE ANGLE

Non-abrupt   **Abrupt**
Single straight scraper   Abrupt scraper
Single convex scraper   Typical backed knife
Single concave scraper   Atypical backed knife
                                  Raclette

FIGURE 6.1. An attribute-based flowchart of Bordes's (1961) typology of Lower and Middle Paleolithic flake tools. Although originally put forward as reflecting naturally patterned forms, this classification is essentially based on relatively few attributes, such as whether or not the object is retouched and, if so, what kind of retouch is present and on what edges. Redrawn from Debénath and Dibble 1994.

virtually throughout the evolution of hominids, for without it archaeologists would often be left with little or nothing to say about prehistoric behavior. We are also fortunate in that lithic artifacts are so pervasive that we never lack specimens to study. I calculated, for instance, that if Acheulian groups lived in Europe for 500,000 years, if there were 5,000 toolmakers living at one time, and if each of them made only ten bifaces a year, that amounts to 25 billion handaxes that are potentially available for study (Debénath and Dibble 1994). Extending those numbers to a global scale, assuming that 25,000 flintknappers were living at any one time, and that the Acheulian epoch (at least in Africa) lasted some 1.5 million years, we arrive at a total of 375 billion handaxes, many trillions of retouched flake tools, and some unbelievably large number (quadrillions? quintillions?) of flakes, cores, and debris.

Having enough data, then, is not our problem, but knowing how to interpret them presents formidable difficulties. The biggest problem is that, for twenty-first century archaeologists, lithic technology is essentially alien knowledge. That is, virtually no archaeologist has grown up in a society that has relied on stone tools; consequently, our ability to make inferences based on personal experience is limited. Although ethnoarchaeological studies have contributed enormously to our understanding of lithic technology (Brandt et al. 1996; Gould et al. 1971; Gould and Saggers 1985; Hayden 1979; White and Dibble 1986; White and Thomas 1972), they are constrained because traditional methods of stone tool manufacture are disappearing rapidly. Sadly, archaeologists just missed being able to use this approach effectively. At about the time that archaeology emerged as a discipline, lithic technology was still common in parts of the Americas, and as recently as the nineteenth century, gunflint manufacture, based on the same knapping principles as Paleolithic blade manufacture, remained a major industry in Europe (Witthoft 1966). What this lost opportunity means is that archaeologists have had to draw on their own resources to reconstruct how lithic artifacts were made and used,

and they have had to create their own methods for categorizing and analyzing them. In fact, many methods and most middle-range theory for lithic analysis have developed outside of general anthropology.

The rest of this chapter is divided into two major parts. The first presents an overview of some of the methods that have been developed to study prehistoric lithic assemblages, emphasizing those that originated outside of anthropology (including ethnoarchaeology). The second part summarizes what has been learned about the basic mechanics of lithic manufacture and the effects of site formation processes on lithic assemblage variability—concerns that, again, fall outside the realm of traditional anthropological theory.

METHODS FOR THE STUDY OF LITHIC ARTIFACTS
Typological Analysis

One of the principal means of studying lithic artifact and assemblage variability is through typology. In the current literature, there is a great deal of debate regarding how lithic typologies should be constructed, what their meaning is in terms of past behaviors and native classifications, and what their usefulness is for archaeological interpretation.

Basically, typology is the classification of lithic objects according to various criteria, most often morphological ones. In other words, objects that look alike or are otherwise related to each other in some way (e.g., share particular attributes) are grouped together as examples of a particular type (Figure 6.1). Of course, all scientific inquiry is based on some degree of classification: it provides a means of organizing the phenomena under study and provides the analytical framework for investigating and explaining variability (Ramenofsky and Steffen 1998a). To a large extent, lithic typology parallels concepts developed in biology for organizing and studying organisms, and the traditional use of typology in archaeological research is due, in part, to the shared natural historical background of archaeology and biology.

In biology, four concepts relate directly to lithic typology. First, there is the concept of systematics, which is defined by Simpson (1961) as "the scientific study of the kinds and diversity of organisms and any and all relationships among them." In turn, systematics consists of three parts. The first of these is taxonomy, which is the theoretical study of how classifications are made. The second is classification, or the definition of groups and the assignment of individual cases, or individuals, to them. The third part is nomenclature, which deals with the naming of those groups. Specific lithic typologies, such as Bordes's (1961) typology for the Lower and Middle Paleolithic (Figure 6.1) or Ritchie's (1961) typology of New York projectile points, are examples of classifications. Types are defined as constellations of specific attribute states, and objects are categorized, or classified, according to the features that they exhibit. It is fair to say that most classic lithic typologies have focused more on the morphological variability of retouched pieces than other classes of objects or attributes.

Taxonomy has been an issue in archaeology for many years, reflected especially in the classic debate between Ford (1954) and Spaulding (1953; see also Lyman et al. 1997) on whether archaeological typologies should reflect native classification schemes (or at least inherent patterning of the material) or whether they can be somewhat artificial constructs developed to solve particular archaeological problems. Spaulding himself advocated the former position and was a pioneer in the development and application of statistical techniques designed to isolate and describe inherent patterning.

The use of morphological criteria is, indeed, one of the major questions being debated in current lithic taxonomy. Many lithic analysts argue, for example, that lithic reduction involves several different processes, and in some cases different processes may lead to similar morphologies—a problem known as equifinality (see Chapters 2, 8, and 9, this volume). For this reason, many French lithic analysts now feel that classificatory frameworks should be based on technological criteria, which emphasize process, rather than morphological ones. Advocates of this approach—called *chaîne opératoire*—often contrast their emphasis on

technology with one based on typology, even though their approach is still typological in nature because it rests on the classification of objects. The difference is in the kind of criteria used: technological vs. morphological (see Dibble and Bar-Yosef 1995).

Regardless of the criteria used—morphology or process—and regardless of whether or not the typology is based on statistical patterning, the fundamental issue reflected in the Ford/Spaulding debate is still with us. Although not often explicitly stated, there are still many who believe that the ideal typology is one that accurately reflects original native classifications, and others who feel that it is more important to develop typologies based on whatever criteria would be useful for addressing particular archaeological questions. While it may be interesting to know how prehistoric flintknappers organized their material, the fact remains that it is nearly impossible to test whether or not a particular lithic typology is an accurate reflection of ancient intentions. In other words, we are unsure of the validity of these units (Ramenofsky and Steffen 1998b) in terms of their representing native categories, regardless of whether those categories are based on stylistic or functional criteria. Furthermore, even if we were able to reconstruct a native classification, it is not at all certain that it alone would provide sufficient analytical potential to allow us to address a range of anthropological questions. This uncertainty occurs because the fit between the two is not the sole criterion for judging the usefulness of the typology, whether the typology was designed for descriptive or analytical purposes. No matter what the intended purpose of a typology is, there is still the need to understand how different factors give rise to variability; otherwise, typological differences are not interpretable.

The classification of lithic artifacts involves the definition of lithic types and the assignment of objects to those types. Perhaps the principal issue in most lithic classifications concerns their reliability (Adams and Adams 1991; Ramenofsky and Steffen 1998a). Low reliability is a serious concern because it means that different people arrived at different results even

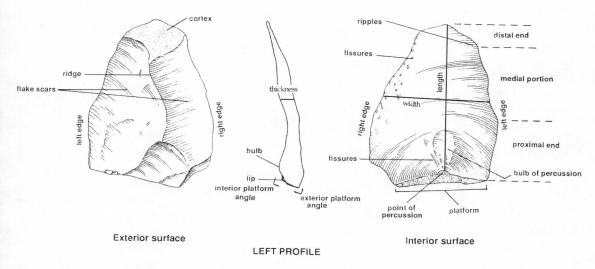

FIGURE 6.2. Some basic flake attributes. Most of the discrete attributes shown here can be broken down into finer classifications, such as different kinds of platform preparation, the overall amount of cortex present on the exterior surface, the orientation of the flake scars, and so on. In essence, lithic attributes represent classifications in themselves and thus face the same issues that occur in any typological system. Redrawn from Debénath and Dibble 1994.

though the body of material under investigation is the same (see Dibble 1984, 1995b). Unfortunately, many lithic typologies are vague or subjective and are therefore not very reliable. There is also a degree of inconsistency in applying particular typologies, no matter how rigorously the types are defined.

In lithic studies, nomenclature has not received the attention that it has in biology, and there are virtually no conventions for assigning names to various types. In Paleolithic archaeology, for example, types are often given names that correspond to presumed functions, such as knives, axes, scrapers, or points. For novices, the biggest trap to avoid is thinking that the "names" given to types, such as "Mousterian Point" or "scraper," reflect their actual functions. In many cases, the functions of pieces are not known, but only surmised. Other types are named after similar-looking vegetation, such as Solutrean "laurel leaves"; animals, such as *limaces* or slugs; or after various sites, towns, or regions.

It is fair to say that typology is the primary way of analyzing lithic assemblages and will undoubtedly remain so for some time. While there have been numerous debates among an-

thropological archaeologists over various issues, the typological approach in lithic analysis is fundamentally based on biological systematics and not on anthropological theory.

Attribute Analysis

Generally speaking, a type usually represents a particular configuration of various attributes. Another way to look at lithic variability is to analyze differences among individual attributes, which is often called attribute analysis. Lithic attributes (Figure 6.2) can be recorded as discrete or nominal scale variables (e.g., different kinds of platform preparation), ranked or ordinal scale variables (e.g., the degree of retouch intensity, as in "light," "medium," or "heavy"), or interval or ratio scale variables (e.g., measurements of artifact length). To some extent, attribute analyses have often been used to create typologies, especially when approached through various numerical taxonomic methods. The analysis of individual attributes can have many other goals, however, and such an approach can be used in conjunction with, or independent of, other typologies (see Sullivan and Rozen 1985).

Actually, most attribute coding schemes

themselves represent typologies and carry with them all of the issues associated with any typology. One issue concerns the definition of attributes and attribute states (or values) and how attribute observations are made. Obviously, if observations are not recorded in the same way, replicability of results is difficult to achieve and reliability is compromised.

There is also the issue of the meaning of individual attributes; that is, knowing exactly what they reflect in terms of the many factors that contribute to lithic variability. It is easy to compare different assemblages on the basis of several attributes, but the differences among assemblages are not going to be interpretable unless the variation inherent in the attributes is understood. One of the most promising lines of current lithic research involves the study of variability in individual attributes, either through experiments or analysis of archaeological specimens.

Use-Wear and Residue Analysis
Since the pioneering work of Semenov (1964) in the early 1960s, the study of artifact function by means of macroscopic and microscopic analyses has developed enormously and currently receives considerable attention. Among the first techniques to have been developed was the investigation of patterns of breakage and striations along the edges of artifacts, visible either macroscopically or under low-power magnification (Odell and Odell-Vereecken 1980; Tringham et al. 1974). Many of these patterns have been interpreted as reflecting different actions (e.g., cutting, shaving, sawing). Under high-power magnification, certain polishes are visible on lithic artifacts that are attributable to their use on different materials, such as bone, wood, and hide (Anderson 1980; Anderson-Gerfaud 1990; Keeley 1980). Certain residues, especially blood, have been identified on lithics and are accompanied by claims that species-specific hemoglobins and DNA can be determined (Custer et al. 1988; Eisele et al. 1995; Federicksen 1986; Fiedel 1996; Loy 1983, 1994; Loy and Hardy 1992). These techniques are mainly employed to infer the uses of specific artifacts, to investi-

gate the relationship between particular types and their functions, and to identify specific resources that were exploited with lithics. To a more limited extent, they can also aid in identifying post-depositional disturbances.

The development of these techniques involved rigorous scientific methodology that arose entirely outside of anthropology. Most of the matching of different wear patterns with specific functions or materials has been based on extensive experiments, and interpretations of artifact functions have been evaluated through blind tests (Newcomer and Keeley 1979; Newcomer et al. 1986; see also Bamforth 1988; Hurcombe 1988). In fact, it is fair to say that use-wear studies in general have been subjected to some of the most extensive scrutiny in the history of lithic research (Moss 1987). These evaluations indicate that while many of the techniques hold a high degree of potential, there are problems both with reliability and accuracy of their interpretations, which are commonly attributed to the effects of post-depositional alteration or contamination.

Refitting Analysis
By reassembling the by-products of lithic reduction to their original form, refitting studies, although exceedingly time-consuming, provide a powerful method for understanding prehistoric lithic technology. One of the earliest and most famous examples of refitting was that of Worthington-Smith at the English site of Caddington, where he rejoined flakes that were taken off a biface, and from this reconstruction was able to make a plaster cast of the missing biface itself.

Currently, core refitting is the most common application. Because it is possible to see the exact sequence of flake removals, this technique has been used to reconstruct technological reduction sequences with a degree of accuracy that is unobtainable through either experimentation or analysis of individual pieces. Core refits have also been used to assess the degree of disturbance at a site and the degree to which items have been exported from a site.

Tool refits are not as common as core refits principally because of the scale of the problem: the numerous flakes removed through retouching can be very small, which decreases the chances of their recovery and makes the refits more difficult to achieve. The pioneering work in tool refits was that of Frison (1968) at a Paleo-Indian site in Wyoming. By refitting flakes to tools and conjoining broken pieces of tools, Frison was able to demonstrate conclusively that tool shape changed because of resharpening. Through both tool and core refits it is also possible to reconstruct movement of lithic material within a site and thus identify specific activity loci (Cahen et al. 1979; de Bie and Caspar 2000; Hietala 1984). There is one example of an inter-site refit (Allard 1993), which is extraordinary given the very low probability of such an occurrence.

The degree to which refits can be performed depends on several factors. First, the size of the assemblage to be refitted affects the amount of time that can be devoted to the effort. Second, because related lithic elements can be scattered over large areas, the scale of an excavation for a given occupation surface can become a constraint of the scope of refitting studies. Third, the success of a refitting study depends on the bulk of related elements not having been removed from an occupation surface by either purposeful exportation or by natural agencies.

Experiments

Experimental approaches to understanding function, technology, and other factors underlying artifact and assemblage variability have enjoyed a long history in lithic archaeology because they provide direct insights into how stone tools were made and used. As previously stated, one of the big problems facing archaeologists studying lithic materials is that virtually none of them have been raised in societies that employ lithic technology. In addition, because chipped stone technology is so fundamentally dissimilar to other traditional technologies, such as ceramics and metallurgy, analogies are limited. On the other hand, while scientific approaches do not necessarily depend on personal experience, experiments provide an important means of generating relevant hypotheses that can then be tested against archaeological assemblages.

Experiments also allow archaeologists to investigate sources of variability. With rigorous experimental design, it is possible to control for the effects of several independent variables in order to focus on the effects produced by one. Because archaeological assemblages reflect the consequences of a multitude of competing factors, the isolation of causal relationships is challenging and requires many experiments. However, three kinds of experiments dominate lithic research: replicative, controlled, and actualistic.

Replicative Experiments

Flintknapping—using what are believed to be traditional techniques and methods for producing stone tools—is by far the most common experimental approach in lithic studies. Because most flintknapping experiments are undertaken to try to reproduce or replicate particular prehistoric technologies and their end products, they are termed "replicative" experiments. By replicating certain forms, it is possible to better understand the technical processes required in their manufacture.

First performed during the nineteenth century, lithic replicative experiments were fundamental in demonstrating human antiquity by showing that the lithic objects found in association with extinct animals were indeed of human origin, rather than pieces accidentally produced through natural agencies. In the 1960s, replicative experiments started to gain widespread popularity, due mostly to the work of Don Crabtree in North America (Crabtree 1967, 1968, 1970; Crabtree and Butler 1964) and François Bordes in France (Figure 6.3), each of whom influenced a large number of later flintknappers. In fact, these two figures first met at a conference held in Les Eyzies, France, in 1964, which marked a real milestone in bringing together both Old and New World lithic researchers (Bordes and Crabtree 1969). Today, replicative experiments form an essential component of technological analysis

FIGURE 6.3. François Bordes flintknapping at his home in Carsac, France.

because they help reveal the behavioral basis of patterned variation in lithic artifacts.

Controlled Experiments

In order to quantify various mechanical aspects of flake production, researchers have designed highly controlled experiments, often using shaped cores and mechanical strikers. This approach allows one to control nearly all aspects of flaking, from the angle and force of the blow and type of hammer to aspects of core surface and platform morphology. In this way, it is possible to study the effects of particular independent variables (such as how the core is shaped and struck) on flake morphology. Such experiments are called "controlled" experiments because their common goal is to control as many variables involved with flintknapping as possible in order to isolate the effects of any single variable. Although such experiments are often criticized because the products do not resemble actual lithic artifacts, the degree of control is much higher than in normal replicative experiments, and the relationships can be quantified to a greater extent. Other controlled experiments have been undertaken to determine more precisely the effects of post-depositional processes on lithic assemblage formation (Schick 1986).

Actualistic Experiments

In these experiments, lithic artifact replicas are subjected to use under more or less natural conditions. By far, the greatest number of these experiments has been focused on isolating patterns of use-wear that result from working different materials with different motions. In particular, projectile points have been the subject of a number of trial experiments that involved driving them into (usually) dead animals or other targets, both to assess the kinds of damage brought about by impact and to investigate patterns of breakage and subsequent reworking (Dockall 1997; Flenniken and Raymond 1986; Frison 1979, 1988; Huckell 1979; Odell and Cowan 1986).

Discussion

In reviewing these methods, it is clear that virtually all were developed outside of anthropology, and, in fact, many of the pioneers of these approaches were Old World researchers who had no anthropological training. To be fair, the collection of data—no matter what the discipline—has to be appropriate to the materials being studied. Lithic data are no exception, but this fact does not necessarily mean that those data cannot be interpreted in terms of anthropological theory. Indeed, this is the goal of virtually every anthropological archaeologist, even though we are still far from being able to achieve it. Nonetheless, based largely on the methods described in the preceding section, a significant amount has been learned about the major processes underlying lithic artifact and assemblage variability. The two examples offered below reflect some of my own experiences in lithic research. What they have in common is that none are tied in any significant way to traditional anthropological method or theory, though, of course, the ultimate goal is to use them to explain past behavior.

THE MECHANICS OF FLAKE PRODUCTION

Flakes are removed from a nodule by striking it with a hammer (percussion technique) or by applying pressure against an edge (pressure technique). Applied force initiates a fracture that cleaves through the material until it intersects an exterior surface, producing a flake. Such flaking is central to all aspects of chipped stone technology, from platform preparation (which often involves removing small flakes, or facets, from the platform surface), to core surface preparation (where flakes are removed to shape the surface or to set up certain patterns of ridges), to the production of flakes intended for use. Even the manufacture and maintenance of tools involve the removal of flakes, generally along the edge of a flake, through a process called retouching. Thus, understanding chipped stone technology is necessarily based on an understanding of the processes of flake production. This understanding comes from three sources: replicative experiments based on actual flintknapping, controlled experiments in which mechanical devices are constructed to imitate flake production under specific conditions, and fracture mechanics theory.

Of these sources, the most important, both from a practical standpoint and in terms of direct archaeological application, is the work of experimental flintknappers. Modern flintknappers have been successful in replicating forms found in the archaeological record, and to a large extent this success demonstrates their ability to control the mechanical factors underlying flake production. Acquiring such control is not particularly easy; part of the difficulty of learning flintknapping stems from the high degree of hand-eye coordination involved, and significant practice is required before one can consistently strike a particular spot on a core with sufficient accuracy and force. Even more important is the fact that a number of variables must be controlled, and a successful flintknapper must understand, either consciously or subconsciously, what they are and how to manipulate them (Mewhinney 1957; Waldorf 1984; Whittaker 1994). A successful flintknapper, therefore, may be able to achieve consistent results without really knowing, at least on a conscious level, exactly which key variables are being manipulated or what their exact effects will be.

It is also difficult to isolate and quantify the effects of a single variable with replicative experiments because so many variables interact at the same time. When a flintknapper changes one thing (e.g., the type of hammer), other things may change as well (e.g., type of platform, angle of the blow). For this reason, much of the emphasis in replicative experimentation is on core preparation and sequences of reduction, and not on identifying the processes underlying the production and morphology of individual flakes (however, see Bordes 1947; Hayden and Hutchings 1989; Ohnuma and Bergman 1988). Thus, while lithic archaeology has benefited greatly from replicative experiments, they are less relevant to understanding the details of flake production.

The physical mechanics of flaking has received sustained attention for many years. One of the earliest works on physical properties of flaked stone is that of Pond (1930), followed by Goodman (1944) and Bourdier (1963). Kerkhof and Müller-Beck (1969) were the first to discuss concepts of Hertzian fracture and

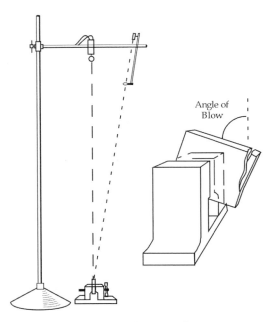

Angle of
Blow

FIGURE 6.4. Schematic drawing of an apparatus used in controlled flaking experiments. Redrawn from Dibble and Whittaker 1980.

their application to stone tools. Since these initial studies, there has been a virtual explosion of interest in the subject (e.g., Bertouille 1989; Bonnichsen 1977; Cotterell and Kamminga 1979, 1986, 1987, 1990; Cotterell et al. 1985; Dibble 1997; Dibble and Pelcin 1995; Dibble and Whittaker 1981; Faulkner 1972; Pelcin 1997a, b; Speth 1972, 1974, 1975, 1981; Tsirk 1974).

Most of this research on the physics of flintknapping draws on a very specialized, though relatively extensive, literature dealing with fracture mechanics. Fortunately, much of this work has been based on glass, which has properties like the most common flaked stones, so results potentially have considerable relevance to archaeological lithics. On the other hand, even though some basic aspects of fracture mechanics are generally well known among archaeologists, the application of fracture-mechanic theory has not yet achieved a high level of success in interpreting lithic assemblages, for several reasons. First, as is true in any science, there is considerable controversy within the field of fracture mechanics itself, and this controversy has carried

over to the archaeological literature. Thus, little agreement exists among the works just cited in terms of which models are most relevant for lithic analysis, which puts many archaeologists at a disadvantage because they are not very well equipped themselves to evaluate the relative merits of one theoretical physical model over another. Second, basic research in physics has not focused on problems that are relevant to archaeology. What archaeologists want to know is how the various aspects of the application of force (e.g., type of hammer, how the blow is delivered) interact with platform and core morphology to produce the more significant (in a behavioral sense) aspects of variability in flake size and shape. The physicists specializing in fracture mechanics, on the other hand, have traditionally been concerned with investigating the strength of materials, especially the conditions surrounding their failures. It is not hard to imagine a situation when an archaeologist approaches a physicist to find out about broken rocks, and the physicist says, "Well, don't hit them and they won't break!" From the physicist's point of view, this is the surest way to prevent the "failure," but, of course, it is not what the archaeologist needs to know.

Another more empirical and more quantifiable approach has involved controlled experiments employing mechanical devices for detaching flakes from pieces of glass. Because glass can be shaped either by cutting or molding, the shape of the glass cores can be varied in a controlled fashion. In the simplest kinds of experiments a steel ball-bearing is dropped from an electromagnet suspended over the core (Figure 6.4). Force can then be varied by either changing the drop height or changing the ball size and weight. Different angles of blow can be delivered by varying the tilt of the core's platform surface. In order to use hammers of different materials, some devices utilize either a hinged or sliding mechanism to which different hammers can be attached. In some tests, static and tensile loads may be applied.

Although they are highly quantifiable, one major problem with controlled experiments is that the experimental designs have not allowed for the production of very realistic-looking flakes. For example, in one series of experiments (Dibble and Pelcin 1995; Dibble and Whittaker 1981), flakes were removed along the sides of plate-glass cores. The flakes themselves more closely resembled burin spalls than normal archaeological flakes or blades, and platform width and flake width were always constant (equaling the thickness of the plate glass).

In spite of the artificial conditions and atypical nature of the products, controlled experiments do have the advantage of allowing us to overcome the subjectivity that is a part of replicative flintknapping, and they can be designed to focus on particular problems that are relevant to archaeology. For example, I (Dibble 1997) suggested that flintknappers could affect flake properties by adopting one of the following strategies: (1) maximizing both exterior platform angle and platform area, (2) minimizing platform area with higher exterior platform angles, or (3) maximizing platform area with smaller exterior platform angles. If flakes are made bigger by increasing the size of their platforms, then there is a general decrease in flake dimensions relative to platform size. Adjusting the exterior platform angle shows the opposite association: flake dimensions in relation to platform size increase with higher exterior platform angles. Thus, increasing the exterior platform angle results in larger flakes relative to their platform areas.

These relationships have several important implications. First, by producing larger flakes with larger platforms, more of the edge is removed as the striking platform for a given flake area. If the exterior platform angles are increased instead, then the striking platform of a core is conserved longer, thereby extending the usefulness of the core in relation to the size of the flakes taken from it. Second, platform area represents, for most purposes, wasted material on a flake blank: it provides no cutting edge, is rarely retouched, and its overall size may constrain hafting. By producing flakes through the use of higher exterior platform angles, however, a flintknapper can increase flake dimensions while simultaneously holding down the size of both the platform

and bulb. This strategy, in turn, helps to maintain core striking platforms and at the same time produce more efficient flake blanks.

Certain aspects of platform variability described here also have implications for recent discussions on flake size/shape and group mobility (Kuhn 1994, 1996). At the Middle Paleolithic site of Combe-Capelle, for example, flakes imported into the site exhibit higher surface area to weight ratios than those that were manufactured from immediately available material and left behind (Roth and Dibble 1998). Furthermore, such flakes were produced through changes in their platform morphology.

It should be noted, however, that knowing the effects of various platform characteristics on flake morphology is only one aspect of the problem. It is also important to understand and recognize different options for controlling them: there are probably many different ways to change platform angles, and, likewise, platform shape can vary because of many different actions. Moreover, there is an obvious need to understand more of the effects of core surface morphology on flake variation, especially the degree of both lateral and longitudinal convexity.

To a large degree, the archaeological theory of lithic fracture mechanics was built on "internal" experimentation, with some input from the field of physics. In itself, it represents a field that is quite distinct from other areas of anthropology. Again, the goal of this research is not just to learn how flintknapping occurs on a physical level. Rather, the long-term objective is to apply that theory to anthropological questions involving past behavior and adaptation.

ASSESSING THE TAPHONOMIC HISTORY
OF A LITHIC ASSEMBLAGE

Anthropological archaeologists want to interpret a site in terms of the particular activities carried out by particular groups of people, but it is essential to bear in mind that many natural agents can alter both the position and morphology of the artifacts, as well as the composition of the overall assemblage. It is for this reason that studying processes underlying the formation of archaeological sites (Schiffer 1972) has become a major concern of archaeologists (Goldberg, this volume). The problem is to separate the behavioral component underlying site formation from other natural agencies because there are many such agencies that, if not recognized, can be mistakenly interpreted as reflecting human behavior alone. In a general sense, these considerations are the focus of taphonomy.

The term *taphonomy* originally referred to the transition of paleontological material from the "biosphere" to the "lithosphere" (Efremov 1940); strictly speaking, anything that happens between the death of an animal and the arrival of its bones in the laboratory is the subject of taphonomy (Brain 1981; Gifford 1981; Gifford and Behrensmeyer 1977; Isaac 1984; Lyman 1994:3–5, 12-40; Sterud et al. 1980). However, my colleagues and I (Dibble et al. 1997) use *taphonomy* to refer to a wide range of natural processes that may distort the content of an archaeological assemblage, including lithics and fauna, both during and subsequent to its deposition. In fact, lithic assemblages are affected in many ways by many natural processes, and therefore any interpretation of a lithic assemblage must take them into account. An important corollary is that the study of lithic assemblages can provide an assessment of the degree to which an archaeological assemblage has been affected by such processes. For instance, at the Acheulian site of Cagny-l'Epinette, the original excavator (Tuffreau 1988; Tuffreau et al. 1985; Tuffreau et al. 1993) thought that the lower levels represented a relatively undisturbed "living floor." Our work (Dibble et al. 1997), which was designed specifically to test this interpretation, revealed that the site consisted of unrelated fauna and lithics that had been redeposited by stream action.

Recent work at the Tayacian site of Fontéchevade was also designed to investigate similar taphonomic agencies, but this time in a cave setting. Previous excavations (Henri-Martin 1957) in the middle of the last century suggested that Fontéchevade was an occupation site, and the Tayacian industry found there became a reference for similar industries throughout the Old World (Rolland 1986). Recent excavations, along with a full analysis of the original collections, show that most of the lithics are natural "frost-fractures," and the few actual artifacts were washed in from the overlying plateau through a chimney in the back of the cave (Dibble et al. 2006). In fact, the site appears to be more of a carnivore den, at least in the lower levels, which is the only "occupation" that can be seen.

DAMAGE

Geological processes that can displace artifacts do not always result in damage to the pieces. An example of an often nondestructive process is aeolian deflation, where the lighter sedimentary matrix is removed through wind action, leaving the once vertically dispersed heavier artifacts and other coarse material on a common surface. In this case, the damage to lithic artifacts is minimal, but the effects on stratigraphic context can be significant. However, many other processes—such as mass soil movements (e.g., solifluction and cryoturbation), water action (e.g., stream or slopewash), and trampling—usually do leave obvious traces on lithic artifacts, ranging from small nicks and other kinds of damage along the sharp edges to a high degree of fragmentation of the artifacts. The extent to which such damage is apparent, therefore, can give some indication of the amount of disturbance.

In any high-energy environment, lithic artifacts will be subjected to stress as stones come into contact. Because artifact edges are so thin, such contact creates a problem in distinguishing natural damage from intentional retouch. Under conditions of sediment folding or convoluting, it is likely that the damage will occur on both sides of the piece as either alternating (on the exterior and interior surface along the same edge) or alternate (on two opposite edges) damage.

If the water flow is sufficient to transport lithics, then significant damage can also occur. Most edge damage that is attributable to water action is quite abrupt and is often alternate or alternating due to the rolling of the piece along the streambed or down the slope. This movement can also result in significant abrasion, and heavily rolled lithic artifacts can exhibit extreme roundedness and smoothing of their edges. Depending on the chemical composition of the water, some lithics will become heavily patinated or polished. Spring polish, for example, is very characteristic of carbonate-charged spring deposits in limestone regions. Taken alone, however, patina or polish is not a good indication of movement.

Aeolian processes can also affect lithic artifacts when exposed surfaces are subjected to abrasion by airborne dust particles. This form of alteration can result in a kind of polish forming on the surface or, if of sufficient duration and intensity, a rounding of the higher ridges between flake scars (Keeley 1980; Knutsson and Lindé 1990; Mansur-Franchomme 1990).

Thanks to numerous experiments, the effects of trampling on lithic artifacts have been known for many years (e.g., Flenniken and Haggerty 1979; McBrearty et al. 1998; Nielsen 1991; Shea and Klenck 1993). The principal effects are, of course, edge damage and breakage. Unlike rolling, trampling tends to produce more unifacial damage, usually brought about by contact with underlying particles as the artifact is stepped on. Thus, trampling often produces pseudo-tools because the damage itself can resemble deliberate retouch.

It is generally acknowledged (Bordes and Bourgon 1951:17; Bordes 1953; Dibble and Holdaway 1993; McBrearty et al. 1998; Verjux 1988) that post-depositional artifact damage can alter an assemblage in ways that resemble behavioral modifications. For example, edge damage can be difficult to differentiate from macroscopic use-wear and can also be easily mistaken for retouch. In some cases, therefore, "types" have nothing to do with human behavior or the production of desired end products (Figure 6.5). This problem is especially acute in the case of Bordes's typology for the Lower and Middle Paleolithic, in which several of his types (including four types of abrupt and alternating pieces, so-called Tayac points, and other notched and denticulated types [Bordes and Bourgon 1951:17]) are probably best interpreted as being due to natural damage. Obviously, the identification of damage can be subjective, and it is clearly not an unambiguous indicator of post-depositional disturbance. Use of an artifact will result in both microscopic (Semenov 1964; Tringham et al. 1974) and macroscopic edge damage, ridges can suffer from abrasion because of hafting, and flakes and tools are broken both during production and use.

SIZE DISTRIBUTIONS

In the course of flintknapping, a wide range of object sizes is produced, from large flakes, tools, and cores, through smaller retouch or preparation flakes, down to microscopic particles. Thanks to a number of quantitative replicative experiments, such as the pioneering work of Newcomer (1971), we have some understanding of the expected distribution of flake size, which is log-normal in shape with smaller sizes represented in increasing frequency. Although the upper size range may vary, the general shape of the distribution seems to hold despite differing technologies or degree of core reduction. With this type of distribution, one would therefore expect to find many more small flakes than large ones.

However, natural processes, especially water action, will differentially move small flakes. As stream flow increases (or as the slope gradient increases), water is capable of transporting increasingly heavier sediment loads. Consequently, as the flow increases, increasingly larger flakes will be winnowed from an assemblage and redeposited downstream as the flow energy diminishes. In a well designed and carefully controlled experiment, Schick (1986) was able to quantify many of the effects of stream action on lithic assemblage content. These experiments—conducted with a flume that precisely controlled the flow of water across experimentally produced lithic assemblages—have direct implications for the interpretation of archaeological assemblages. If smaller flakes have been winnowed by stream action, leaving only the larger size classes, the size distribution of the lithic artifacts should match the size distribution of the surrounding sediments, which were presumably deposited at the same time. Applying these principles at the Acheulian site of

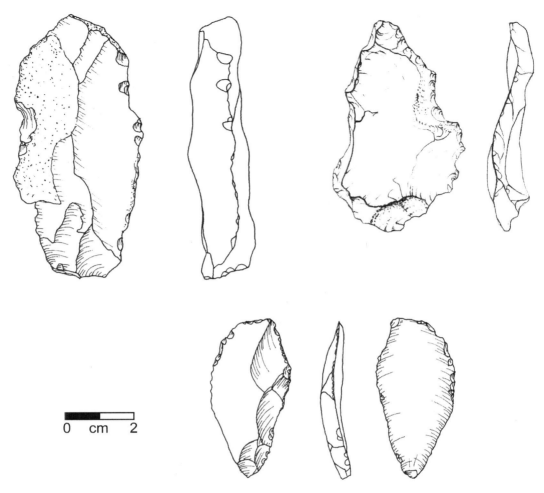

FIGURE 6.5. Examples of edge-damaged pieces from the site of Fontéchevade, France (excavations by McPherron and Dibble). In this case, the damage was a result of artifacts washing into the cave through a natural chimney in the rear.

Cagny-l'Epinette, which was deposited in alluvial sediments (Figure 6.6), size distribution analysis ruled out the possibility that humans imported only larger pieces to the site.

Although shape will affect the degree to which lithic objects are transported, it is possible to obtain a reasonably accurate picture of the size distribution by using only weight or length. For such analyses, it is important to include all categories of the lithic assemblage: flakes, cores, tools, and debris. A major consideration, however, is that care be taken during excavation to systematically recover small pieces. All excavators employ some minimal size cutoff for proveniencing their finds. In

European Paleolithic archaeology, for example, it is typical to piece plot all lithics greater than 2–3 cm in maximum dimension and to bag smaller pieces by level. Because small flakes can be easily missed (especially in wet or clayey sediments), it is advisable to screen all, or a controlled sample, of the sediment to verify the density of the small fraction.

ARTIFACT ORIENTATIONS

Relatively new to archaeological taphonomic studies, but well known in geological research, are analyses based on the distribution of both horizontal (declination) and vertical (inclination) orientations of artifacts (Dibble

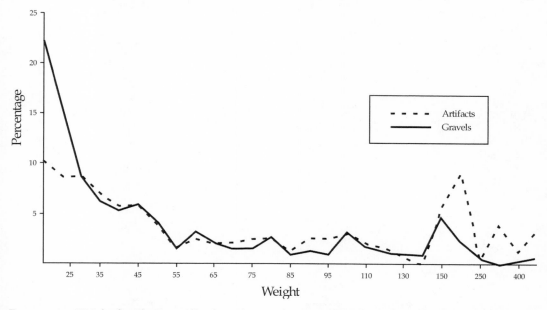

FIGURE 6.6. Weight distributions of both artifacts and natural clasts from the site of Cagny-l'Epinette, France (redrawn from Dibble et al. 1996). The fact that both natural and artifactual material are represented by virtually identical distributions argues strongly that both were brought into the site via the same process—in this case, stream flow.

et al. 1997; Kluskens 1995; McPherron 2005; Rick 1976). Normally artifacts that fall to the ground will orient themselves horizontally in a random pattern and vertically in alignment with the existing surface. However, various natural agencies, primarily water action and mass soil movement, will alter these patterns, leaving telltale signatures that they have affected the lithic assemblage.

Streams and slopewash have a pronounced effect on both horizontal and vertical artifact orientations. As water flows over elongated artifacts, they tend to align themselves parallel to the current (as a way of decreasing their resistance to the flow) or, especially when the flow is strong, perpendicular to it (which makes it easier for them to roll with the rest of the bed load). Thus, a unimodal or bimodal distribution of artifact strikes at angles parallel and perpendicular to the flow will indicate some reaction to water action. Also, once an artifact comes to rest in a streambed, the flow of water tends to scour sediment from its upstream end, eventually causing the stone to dip down (imbricate) at that point, resulting in imbrication angles that range from 10 to 30

degrees or more from the slope of the streambed (Kluskens 1995; Schick 1986).

One of the more common mass movements of material in periglacial environments is solifluction, which occurs as sediments slide down a slope. Solifluction can affect both the strike and dip orientations of elongated artifacts. In this situation, elongated pieces tend to be realigned parallel to the flow, especially those that are within the solifluctuated sediment (as opposed to lying on the surface). Likewise, solifluction tends to imbricate the upslope end of artifacts up to 30–55 degrees from the slope angle (French 1971; Kluskens 1995), though whenever there is significant churning of sediments there may be a wide dispersion of dip angles. A complex folding or churning of sediments often characterizes solifluction and related processes, such as debris flow and cryoturbation, and results in dispersed dip-angle distributions (Figure 6.7).

CONCLUSIONS

It should be clear from the preceding examples that there are many fundamental aspects of lithic assemblages that need to be understood

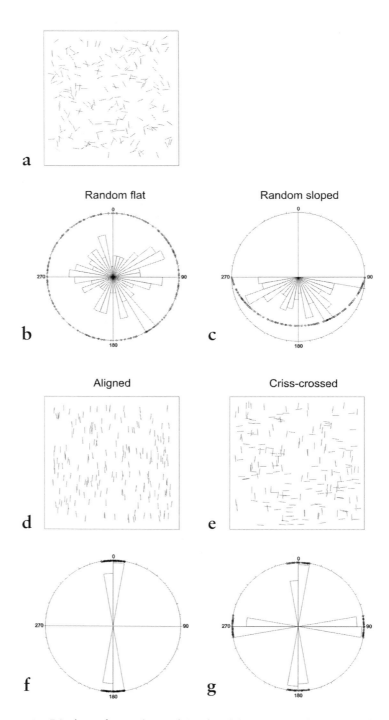

FIGURE 6.7. Displays of several sets of simulated data (200 artifacts each) illustrating how artifacts can show alignments: (*a*) plan view of artifacts randomly oriented on a flat surface and (*b*) Schmidt diagram of these same data; (*c*) Schmidt diagram of randomly oriented data lying on a sloping surface; (*d*) plan view of aligned artifacts lying on a nearly flat surface and (*e*) Schmidt diagram of these artifacts; (*f*) plan view of artifacts aligned on perpendicular axes and (*g*) Schmidt diagram of these artifacts. Reprinted from McPherron 2005, with permission of the author.

before we can apply them to infer past human behavior. Undoubtedly, most of those applications will be situated in the context of modern anthropological theory. But much of what we have to learn first about the nature of our evidence will come through the development of middle-range theory and methods that are largely irrelevant to other aspects of anthropology.

Would I conclude, therefore, that lithic studies could or should exist independent of culture theory? My answer would be no. Examples of the kind that I have outlined here can be drawn from physical anthropology just as easily: an understanding of variation in skeletal morphology, for example, draws heavily on biology, anatomy, genetics, and even taphonomy, which are completely independent of anthropological theory. What separates physical anthropology from those fields is the explanation of skeletal morphology as a reflection of the interplay between biology and culture. For those purposes, at least, we need anthropological theory. Similarly, we should continue to develop methods that are pertinent to the study of our material, lithic artifacts and assemblages, bearing in mind that the ultimate goal is to explain variability in terms of human behavior.

REFERENCES

Adams, William Y., and Ernest W. Adams
1991   Archaeological Typology and Practical Reality: A Dialectical Approach to Artifact Classification and Sorting. Cambridge University Press, Cambridge.

Allard, Michel
1993   Remontage Lithique Exceptionnel dans le Solutreen Inferieur des Peyrugues (Orniac, Lot). Paléo 5:179–192.

Ammerman, Albert J.
1979   A Study of Obsidian Exchange Networks in Calabria. World Archaeology 19:95–110.

Anderson, Patricia
1980   A Testimony of Prehistoric Tasks: Diagnostic Residues on Stone Tool Working Edges. World Archaeology 12:181–194.

Anderson-Gerfaud, Patricia
1990   Aspects of Behaviour in the Middle Palaeolithic: Functional Analysis of Stone Tools from Southwest France. In The Emergence of Modern Humans: An Archaeological Perspective, edited by Paul Mellars, pp. 389–418. Cornell University Press, Ithaca.

Bamforth, Douglas B.
1988   Investigating Microwear Polishes with Blind Tests: The Institute Results in Context. Journal of Archaeological Science 15: 11–23.

1990   Settlement, Raw Material, and Lithic Procurement in the Central Mojave Desert. Journal of Anthropological Archaeology 9: 70–104.

Bertouille, Horace
1989   Théories Physiques et Mathématiques de la Taille des Outils Préhistoriques. L'Anthropologie 88:131–132.

Binford, Lewis
1980   Willow Smoke and Dogs' Tails: Hunter-Gatherer Settlement Systems and Archaeological Site Formation. American Antiquity 45:4–20.

Bonnichsen, Robson
1977   Models for Discovering Cultural Information from Stone Tools. Archaeological Survey of Canada Paper No. 60. National Museum of Canada, Ottawa.

Bordes, François
1947   Étude Comparative des Différentes Techniques de Taille du Silex et des Roches Dures. L'Anthropologie 51:1–29.

1953   Le Dernier Interglacier et la Place du Micoquien et du Tayacien. L'Anthropologie 57: 172–177.

1961   Typologie du Paléolithique Ancien et Moyen. Publications de l'Institut de Préhistoire de l'Université de Bordeaux, Mémoire No. 1. Delmas.

Bordes, François, and Maurice Bourgon
1951   Le Complexe Mousterien: Mousterien, Levalloisien et Tayacien. L'Anthropologie 55: 1–23.

Bordes, François, and Don Crabtree
1969   The Corbiac Blade Technique and Other Experiments. Tebiwa 12:1–21.

Bourdier, F.
1963   Sur la Genèse et la Morphologie de l'éclat Préhistorique. Comptes Rendus de l'Acadamie des Sciences (Paris) 257:3975–3978.

Brain, Charles K.
1981 *The Hunters or the Hunted?* University of Chicago Press, Chicago.

Brandt, Steven A., Kathryn J. Weedman, and Girma Hundie
1996 Gurage Hide Working Stone Tool Use and Social Identity: An Ethnoarchaeological Perspective. In *Essays on Gurage Language and Culture*, edited by Grover Hudson, pp. 35–51. Harrassowitz, Wiesbaden.

Cahen, Daniel, Lawrence H. Keeley, and Van F. Noten
1979 Stone Tools, Toolkits, and Human Behavior in Prehistory. *Current Anthropology* 20: 661–686.

Carr, Philip J.
1994 Technological Organization and Prehistoric Hunter-Gatherer Mobility: Examination of the Hayes Site. In *The Organization of North American Prehistoric Chipped Stone Tool Technologies*, edited by Philip J. Carr, pp. 35–44. International Monographs in Prehistory, Ann Arbor.

Cotterell, Brian, and Johan Kamminga
1979 The Mechanics of Flaking. In *Lithic Use-Wear Analysis*, edited by Brian Hayden, pp. 97–112. Academic Press, New York.
1986 Finials on Stone Flakes. *Journal of Archaeological Science* 13:451–461.
1987 The Formation of Flakes. *American Antiquity* 52:675–708.
1990 *Mechanics of Pre-Industrial Technology.* Cambridge University Press, Cambridge.

Cotterell, Brian, Johan Kamminga, and Frank P. Dickson
1985 The Essential Mechanics of Conchoidal Flaking. *International Journal of Fracture* 20:205–221.

Crabtree, Don E.
1967 Notes on Experiments on Flintknapping 3: The Flintknapper's Raw Materials. *Tebiwa* 23:8–25.
1968 Mesoamerican Polyhedral Cores and Prismatic Blades. *American Antiquity* 33:446–478.
1970 Flaking Stone with Wooden Implements. *Science* 169:146–153.

Crabtree, Don E., and B. Robert Butler
1964 Notes on Experiments in Flint Knapping: Heat Treatment of Silica Materials. *Tebiwa* 7:1–6.

Custer, Jay F., John Ilgenfritz, and Keith R. Doms
1988 A Cautionary Note on the Use of Chemstrips for Detection of Blood Residues on Prehistoric Stone Tools. *Journal of Archaeological Science* 15:343–345.

Davidson, Iain, and William Noble
1993 Tools and Language in Human Evolution. In *Tools, Language and Cognition in Human Evolution*, edited by Kathleen Gibson and Tim Ingold, pp. 363–388. Cambridge University Press, Cambridge.

Debénath, André, and Harold L. Dibble
1994 *The Handbook of Paleolithic Typology.* Vol. 1, *The Lower and Middle Paleolithic of Europe.* University Museum Press, Philadelphia.

de Bie, Marc, and Jean-Paul Caspar
2000 *Rekem: A Federmesser Camp on the Meuse River Bank.* Vol. 1. Leuven University Press, Leuven.

Dibble, Harold L.
1984 The Mousterian Industry from Bisitun Cave (Iran). *Paléorient* 10:23–34.
1989 The Implications of Stone Tool Types for the Presence of Language during the Middle Paleolithic. In *The Human Revolution: Behavioural and Biological Perspectives on the Origins of Modern Humans*, edited by Paul Mellars and Christopher B. Stringer, pp. 415–432. Edinburgh University Press, Edinburgh.
1995a Middle Paleolithic Scraper Reduction: Background, Clarification, and Review of Evidence to Date. *Journal of Archaeological Method and Theory* 2:299–368.
1995b Biache-Saint-Vaast, Level IIa: A Comparison of Approaches. In *The Definition and Interpretation of Levallois Variability*, edited by Harold L. Dibble and Ofer Bar-Yosef, pp. 93–116. Prehistory Press, Madison.
1997 Platform Variability and Flake Morphology: A Comparison of Experimental and Archaeological Data and Implications for Interpreting Prehistoric Lithic Technological Strategies. *Lithic Technology* 22:150–170.

Dibble, Harold L., and Ofer Bar-Yosef (eds.)
1995 *The Definition and Interpretation of Levallois Variability.* Prehistory Press, Madison.

Dibble, Harold L., Philip G. Chase, Shannon P. McPherron, and Alain Tuffreau
1997 Testing the Reality of a "Living Floor" with Archaeological Data. *American Antiquity* 62:629–651.

Dibble, Harold L., and Simon Holdaway
1993 The Middle Paleolithic of Warwasi Rockshelter. In *The Paleolithic Prehistory of the*

Zagros, edited by Deborah Olszewski and Harold L. Dibble, pp. 75–99. University Museum Press, Philadelphia.

Dibble, Harold L., Shannon P. McPherron, Philip G. Chase, William A. Farrand, and A. Debénath
2006 Taphonomy and the Concept of Paleolithic Cultures: The Case of the Tayacian from Fontéchevade. *PaleoAnthropology* 2006:1–21.

Dibble, Harold L., and Andrew W. Pelcin
1995 The Effect of Hammer Mass and Velocity on Flake Mass. *Journal of Archaeological Science* 22:429–439.

Dibble, Harold L., Barbara J. Roth, and Michel Lenoir
1995 The Use of Raw Materials at Combe-Capelle Bas. In *The Middle Paleolithic Site of Combe-Capelle Bas (France)*, edited by Harold L. Dibble and Michel Lenoir, pp. 259–287. University Museum Press, Philadelphia.

Dibble, Harold L., and John C. Whittaker
1981 New Experimental Evidence on the Relation between Percussion Flaking and Flake Variation. *Journal of Archaeological Science* 8:283–296.

Dockall, John E.
1997 Wear Traces and Projectile Impact: A Review of the Experimental and Archaeological Evidence. *Journal of Field Archaeology* 24:321–331.

Efremov, Ivan
1940 Taphonomy: A New Branch of Paleontology. *Pan-American Geologist* 74:81–93.

Eisele, J. A., D. D. Fowler, G. Haynes, and R. A. Lewis
1995 Survival and Detection of Blood Residues on Stone Tools. *Antiquity* 69:36–46.

Faulkner, Alaric
1972 *Mechanical Principles of Flintworking*. PhD dissertation, Department of Anthropology, Washington State University, Pullman. University Microfilms, Ann Arbor.

Federicksen, C.
1986 The Detection of Blood on Prehistoric Flake Tools. *New Zealand Archaeological Association Newsletter* 28:155–164.

Fiedel, Stuart J.
1996 Blood from Stones? Some Methodological and Interpretive Problems in Blood Residue Analysis. *Journal of Archaeological Science* 23:139–147.

Flenniken, J. Jeffrey, and J. C. Haggerty
1979 Trampling as an Agency in the Formation of Edge Damage: An Experiment in Lithic Technology. *Northwest Anthropological Research Notes* 13:208–14.

Flenniken, J. Jeffrey, and Anan W. Raymond
1986 Morphological Projectile Point Typology: Replication Experimentation and Technological Analysis. *American Antiquity* 51:603–614.

Ford, James A.
1954 Comment on A. C. Spaulding, "Statistical Techniques for the Discovery of Artifact Types." *American Antiquity* 19:390–391.

French, Hugh M.
1971 Slope Asymmetry of the Beaufort Plain, Northwest Banks Island, N.W.T., Canada. *Canadian Journal of Earth Sciences* 8:717–731.

Frison, George C.
1968 A Functional Analysis of Certain Chipped Stone Tools. *American Antiquity* 33:149–155.
1979 Observations on the Use of Stone Tools: Dulling of Working Edges of Some Chipped Stone Tools in Bison Butchering. In *Lithic Use-Wear Analysis*, edited by Brian Hayden, pp. 259–268. Academic Press, New York.
1988 Experimental Use of Clovis Weaponry and Tools on African Elephants. *American Antiquity* 54:766–784.

Gibson, Kathleen R., and Tim Ingold (eds.)
1993 *Tools, Language and Cognition in Human Evolution*. Cambridge University Press, Cambridge.

Gifford, Diane
1981 Taphonomy and Paleoecology: A Critical Review of Archaeology's Sister Disciplines. In *Advances in Archaeological Method and Theory*, edited by Michael B. Schiffer, Vol. 4, pp. 365–438. Academic Press, New York.

Gifford, Diane, and Anna K. Behrensmeyer
1977 Observed Formation and Burial of a Recent Occupation Site. *Quaternary Research* 8:245–266.

Goodman, Mary Ellen
1944 The Physical Properties of Stone Tool Materials. *American Antiquity* 9:415–433.

Gould, Richard A., Dorothy A. Koster, and Ann H. Sontz
1971 The Lithic Assemblage of the Western Desert Aborigines of Australia. *American Antiquity* 36:149–169.

Gould, Richard A., and Sherry Saggers
1985 Lithic Procurement in Central Australia: A

Closer Look at Binford's Idea of Embeddedness in Archaeology. *American Antiquity* 50:117–135.

Gowlett, John A. J.

1984 Mental Abilities of Early Man: A Look at Some Hard Evidence. In *Hominid Evolution and Community Ecology: Prehistoric Human Adaptation in Biological Perspective*, edited by Robert A. Foley, pp. 167–192. Academic Press, London.

Hayden, Brian

1979 *Paleolithic Reflections: Lithic Technology and Ethnographic Excavation among the Australian Aborigines*. Humanities Press, New Jersey.

Hayden, Brian, and W. Karl Hutchings

1989 Whither the Billet Flake? In *Experiments in Lithic Technology*, edited by Daniel S. Amick and Raymond P. Mauldin, pp. 235–258. British Archaeological Reports, Oxford.

Henri-Martin, Germaine

1957 *La Grotte de Fontechevade. Première Partie: Historique, Fouilles, Stratigraphie, Archéologie*. Archives de l'Institut de Paléontologie Humaine 28. Masson et Compagnie, Paris.

Hietala, Harold J. (ed.)

1984 *Intrasite Spatial Analysis in Archaeology*. Cambridge University Press, Cambridge.

Holloway, Ralph L.

1981 Culture, Symbols, and Human Brain Evolution. *Dialectical Anthropology* 5:287–303.

Huckell, Bruce B.

1979 Of Chipped Stone Tools, Elephants, and the Clovis Hunters: An Experiment. *Plains Anthropologist* 24:177–188.

Hurcombe, Linda

1988 Some Criticisms and Suggestions in Response to Newcomer *et al.* (1986). *Journal of Archaeological Science* 15:1–10.

Isaac, Glynn

1984 The Archaeology of Human Origins: Studies of the Lower Pleistocene in East Africa, 1971–1981. In *Advances in World Archaeology*, edited by Fred Wendorf, pp. 1–87. Academic Press, Orlando.

Keeley, Lawrence H.

1980 *Experimental Determination of Stone Tool Uses: A Microwear Analysis*. University of Chicago Press, Chicago.

Kerkhof, F., and Hans Müller-Beck

1969 Zur Bruchmechanischen Deutung der Schlagmarken an Steingeräten. *Glastechnische Berichte* 42:439–448.

Kluskens, Stephen L.

1995 Archaeological Taphonomy of Combe-Capelle Bas from Artifact Orientation and Density Analysis. In *The Middle Paleolithic Site of Combe-Capelle Bas (France)*, edited by Harold L. Dibble and Michel Lenoir, pp. 199–243. University Museum Press, Philadelphia.

Knutsson, Kjel, and K. Lindé

1990 Post-Depositional Alterations of Wear Marks on Quartz Tools: Preliminary Observations on an Experiment with Aeolian Abrasion. In *Le Silex de sa Genèse à l'Outil*, Tome II, edited by M. R. Séronie-Vivien and Michel Lenoir, pp. 607–621. Cahiers du Quaternaire No. 17. CNRS, Paris.

Kuhn, Steven L.

1994 A Formal Approach to the Design and Assembly of Mobile Toolkits. *American Antiquity* 59:426–442.

1996 The Trouble with Ham Steaks: A Reply to Morrow. *American Antiquity* 61:591–596.

Loy, Thomas H.

1983 Prehistoric Blood Residues: Detection on Tool Surfaces and Identification of Species of Origin. *Science* 220:1269–1271.

1994 Identifying Species of Origin from Prehistoric Blood Residues. *Science* 266:298–300.

Loy, Thomas H., and Bruce L. Hardy

1992 Blood Residue Analysis of 90,000-year-old Stone Tools from Tabun Cave, Israel. *Antiquity* 66:24–35.

Lyman, R. Lee

1994 *Vertebrate Taphonomy*. Cambridge University Press, London.

Lyman, R. Lee, Michael J. O'Brien, and Robert C. Dunnell

1997 *The Rise and Fall of Culture History*. Plenum Press, New York and London.

McBrearty, Sally, Laura Bishop, Thomas Plummer, Robert Dewar, and Nicholas J. Conard

1998 Tools Underfoot: Human Trampling as an Agent of Lithic Artifact Edge Modification. *American Antiquity* 63:108–129.

McPherron, Shannon P.

1995 A Re-examination of the British Biface Data. *Lithics* 16:47–63.

2000 Handaxes as a Measure of the Mental Capabilities of Early Hominids. *Journal of Archaeological Science* 27:655–664.

2005 Artifact Orientations and Site Forma-

tion Processes from Total Station Proveniences. *Journal of Archaeological Science*
32:1003–1014.

Mallory, John K., III
1984   *Late Classic Maya Economic Specialization: Evidence from the Copan Obsidian
Assemblage.* PhD dissertation, Department of Anthropology, Pennsylvania State
University. Microfilms, Ann Arbor.

Mansur-Franchomme, M.
1990   Quelques Observations sur les Altéra-
tions Naturelles des Microtraces d'usage
des Outillages Lithiques. In *Le Silex de sa
Genèse à l'Outil,* Tome II, edited by M.-R.
Séronie-Vivien and Michel Lenoir, pp.629–
634. *Cahiers du Quaternaire* no. 17, CNRS,
Paris.

Mewhinney, Hubert
1957   *Manual for Neanderthals.* University of
Texas Press, Austin.

Mithen, Steven
1995   Palaeolithic Archaeology and the Evolution of Mind. *Journal of Archaeological
Research* 3:305–332.

Montet-White, Anta, and Steve Holen (eds.)
1991   *Raw Material Economies among Prehistoric Hunter-Gatherers.* Publications in
Anthropology No. 19. University of Kansas, Lawrence.

Moss, Emily
1987   A Review of "Investigating Microwear Polishes with Blind Tests." *Journal of Archaeological Science* 14:473–481.

Nelson, Margaret C.
1991   The Study of Technological Organization.
In *Advances in Archaeological Method
and Theory,* Vol. 3, edited by Michael B.
Schiffer, pp. 57–100. University of Arizona
Press, Tucson.

Newcomer, Mark
1971   Some Quantitative Experiments in Hand-
axe Manufacture. *World Archaeology* 3:
85–94.

Newcomer, Mark, Roger Grace, and Romana
Unger-Hamilton
1986   Investigating Microwear Polishes with
Blind Tests. *Journal of Archaeological Science* 13:203–217.

Newcomer, Mark, and Lawrence H. Keeley
1979   Testing a Method of Microwear Anal-
ysis with Experimental Flint Tools. In
Lithic Use-Wear Analysis, edited by Brian
Hayden, pp. 195–205. Academic Press,
New York.

Nielsen, Axel E.
1991   Trampling the Archaeological Record: An
Experimental Study. *American Antiquity*
56:483–503.

Odell, George H., and Frank L. Cowan
1986   Experiments with Spears and Arrows on
Animal Targets. *Journal of Field Archaeology* 13:195–212.

Odell, George H., and Frieda Odell-Vereecken
1980   Verifying the Relationships of Lithic Use
Wear Assessments by "Blind Tests": The
Low-Power Approach. *Journal of Field Archaeology* 7:87–120.

Ohnuma, Katsuhiko, and Chris Bergman
1988   Experimental Studies in the Determination of Flaking Mode. In *Ksar Akil, Leba-
non,* Vol. III: Levels XXV–XIV, edited by
Katsuhiko Ohnuma, Chris Bergman, and
Mark Newcomer, pp. 329–350. British Archaeological Reports, Oxford.

Pelcin, Andrew
1997a The Effect of Indentor Type on Flake Attributes: Evidence from a Controlled Experiment. *Journal of Archaeological Science*
24:613–621.

1997b The Formation of Flakes: The Role of Platform Thickness and Exterior Platform Angle in the Production of Flake Initiations
and Terminations. *Journal of Archaeological Science* 24:1107–1113.

Pond, Alfonso
1930   Primitive Methods of Working Stone,
Based on Experiments of Halvor L. Skav-
lem. *Logan Museum Bulletin* 2(1). Beloit
College, Beloit, Wisconsin.

Ramenofsky, Ann F., and Anastasia Steffen (eds.)
1998a *Unit Issues in Archaeology: Measuring
Time, Space, and Material.* University of
Utah Press, Salt Lake City.

Ramenofsky, Ann F., and Anastasia Steffen
1998b Units as Tools of Measurement. *In Unit
Issues in Archaeology: Measuring Time,
Space, and Material,* edited by Ann F. Ra-
menofsky and Anastasia Steffen, pp. 3–17.
University of Utah Press, Salt Lake City.

Rick, John W.
1976   Downslope Movement and Archaeological
Intrasite Spatial Analysis. *American Antiquity* 41:133–144.

Ritchie, William A.
1961   *A Typology and Nomenclature for New
York Projectile Points.* New York State Museum and Science Service Bulletin Number
384. Albany.

Rolland, Nicolas

1986   Recent Findings from La Micoque and Other Sites in Southwestern and Mediterranean France: Their Bearing on the "Tayacian" Problem and Middle Paleolithic Emergence. In *Stone Age Prehistory: Studies in Memory of Charles McBurney*, edited by Geoffrey N. Bailey and Paul Callow, pp. 121–151. Cambridge University Press, Cambridge.

Roth, Barbara J., and Harold L. Dibble

1998   The Production and Transport of Blanks and Tools at the French Middle Paleolithic Site of Combe-Capelle Bas. *American Antiquity* 63:47–62.

Schick, Kathy D.

1986   *Stone Age Sites in the Making: Experiments in the Formation and Transformation of Archaeological Occurrences*. British Archaeological Reports International Series 319, Oxford.

Schiffer, Michael B.

1972   Archaeological Context and Systemic Context. *American Antiquity* 37:156–165.

Semenov, Sergei A.

1964   *Prehistoric Technology: An Experimental Study of the Oldest Tools and Artefacts from Traces of Manufacture and Wear*. Cory, Adams, and Mackey, London.

Shea, John J., and Joel D. Klenck

1993   An Experimental Investigation of the Effects of Trampling on the Results of Lithic Microwear Analysis. *Journal of Archaeological Science* 20:175–194.

Shott, Michael J.

1986   Technological Organization and Settlement Mobility: An Ethnographic Examination. *Journal of Anthropological Research* 42:15–51.

Simpson, George G.

1961   *Principles of Animal Taxonomy*. Columbia University Press, New York.

Spaulding, Albert C.

1953   Statistical Techniques for the Discovery of Artifact Types. *American Antiquity* 18:305–313.

Speth, John D.

1972   The Mechanical Basis of Percussion Flaking. *American Antiquity* 37:34–60.

1974   Experimental Investigations of Hard-Hammer Percussion Flaking. *Tebiwa* 17:7–36.

1975   Miscellaneous Studies in Hard-Hammer Percussion Flaking: The Effects of Oblique Impact. *American Antiquity* 40:203–207.

1981   The Role of Platform Angle and Core Size in Hard-Hammer Percussion Flaking. *Lithic Technology* 10:16–21.

Sterud, Eugene, Lawrence G. Straus, and Katherine Abramovitz

1980   Recent Developments in Old World Archaeology. *American Antiquity* 45:740–758.

Sullivan, Alan P., III, and Kenneth C. Rozen

1985   Debitage Analysis and Archaeological Interpretation. *American Antiquity* 50:755–779.

Tankersley, Kenneth B.

1991   A Geoarchaeological Investigation of Distribution and Exchange in the Raw Material Economies of Clovis Groups in Eastern N. America. In *Raw Material Economies among Prehistoric Hunter-Gatherers*, edited by Anta Montet-White and Steven Holen, pp. 285–304. University of Kansas, Lawrence.

Tringham, Ruth, Glenn Cooper, George H. Odell, Barbara Voytek, and Anne Whitman

1974   Experimentation in the Formation of Edge Damage: A New Approach to Lithic Analysis. *Journal of Field Archaeology* 1:171–196.

Tsirk, Are

1974   Mechanical Basis of Percussion Flaking: Some Comments. *American Antiquity* 39:122–130.

Tuffreau, Alain

1988   Les Habitats du Paléolithique Inférieur et Moyen dans le Nord de la France (Nord, Pas-de-Caliais, Somme). In *Cultures et Industries Lithiques en Milieu Loessique*, edited by Alain Tuffreau, pp. 91–104. Revue Arch. de Picardi.

Tuffreau, Alain, Pierre Antoine, Philip G. Chase, Harold L. Dibble, Brooks Ellwood, Thijs van Kolfschoten, Agnès Lamotte, Michel Laurent, Shannon P. McPherron, Anne-Marie Moigne, and André V. Munaut

1993   Le Gisement Acheuléen de Cagny-l'Epinette (Somme). *Bulletin de la Société Préhistorique Française* 92:169–191.

Tuffreau, Alain, Jean-Paul Bouchet, Anne-Marie Moigne, and André V. Munaut

1985   Les Niveaux Acheuleens de la Moyenne Terasse du Bassin de la Somme a Cagny-l'Epinette. *L'Anthropologie* 90:9–27.

Verjux, C.

1988   Les Denticulés Moustériens. In *L'Homme de Neandertal*, Vol. 4, *La Technique*, edited by Lewis R. Binford and Jean-Philippe Rigaud, pp. 197–204. University of Liege, Liège.

Waldorf, D. C.

1984   *The Art of Flintknapping.* 3rd ed. Mound Builder Arts and Trading Co., Branson, Missouri.

White, J. Peter, and Harold L. Dibble

1986   Stone Tools: Small-scale Variability. In *Stone Age Prehistory: Studies in Memory of Charles McBurney*, edited by Geoffrey N. Bailey and Paul Callow, pp. 47–53. Cambridge University Press, Cambridge.

White, J. Peter, and David H. Thomas

1972   What Mean These Stones? Ethno-Taxonomic Models and Archaeological Interpretation in the New Guinea Highlands. In *Models in Archaeology*, edited by David L. Clarke, pp. 275–308. Methuen, London.

Whittaker, John

1994   *Flintknapping: Making and Understanding Stone Tools.* University of Texas Press, Austin.

Witthoft, John

1966   A History of Gunflints. *Pennsylvania Archaeologist* 36:12–49.

Wynn, Thomas

1985   Piaget, Stone Tools, and the Evolution of Human Intelligence. *World Archaeology* 17:32–42.

1991   Archaeological Evidence for Modern Intelligence. In *The Origins of Human Behavior*, edited by Robert A. Foley, pp. 52–66. Unwin Hyman, London.

7

Exploring the Historical Foundations and Interpretive Potential of Provenience

JULIE K. STEIN

It may well be asked whether the meaning of the artifacts for the culture of Pecos is
thought to lie in their form and classification of form, or whether it lies in their relations
to one another and to the broad cultural and natural environment of Pecos. If it is true,
as Kidder says (1932:12), that provenience "would be of interest to a very limited number
of persons," then this is the most damning criticism of Americanist archaeology
that has appeared in print to date!

WALTER W. TAYLOR

Contemporary archaeologists study the cultural past as it is revealed by objects, left in and on the ground, whose contexts and stratigraphic relations can be documented in terms of their provenience. The concept of *provenience*—which refers to methods for registering the vertical locations or relative positions (thereby yielding information relevant to dating) of objects with respect to their horizontal associations on surfaces (thereby yielding information relevant to inferring human behavior)—evolved independently of theoretical developments in sociocultural anthropology. Provenience is such a basic concept in archaeology, and is used so routinely today, that few have stopped to think about the circumstances that led to its origin and introduction into archaeological practice. Moreover, provenience itself has undergone profound changes in application and, importantly, spawned a theoretical framework for conceptualizing how inferences about the cultural past can be developed by examining the positions of objects in stratigraphic contexts. Provenience methods—each designed to increase the precision of relational information among artifacts, deposits, and

surfaces—have varied from simple trait comparisons, to locating excavation units according to grid coordinates, to grouping objects extracted from separate stratigraphic levels, to fixing the three-dimensional locations for individual objects with laser transits (Goldberg, this volume). As archaeologists slowly began to recognize that objects and their locations could directly address questions about human evolution and social change, proveniences were measured at higher resolutions, which resulted in concerns about how sites are created and how objects come to rest together. In this chapter, I discuss definitions of provenience, context, and stratigraphy, and trace the pathways that have influenced archaeologists to refine provenience concepts, thereby increasing the interpretive potential of objects and their recovery contexts.

PROVENIENCE: A SHORT HISTORY

The word *provenience* comes from the Latin verb *proveniens*, which means "to come forth." English usage commonly refers to the origin, source, or place where something is found or produced. In art history, provenience refers to

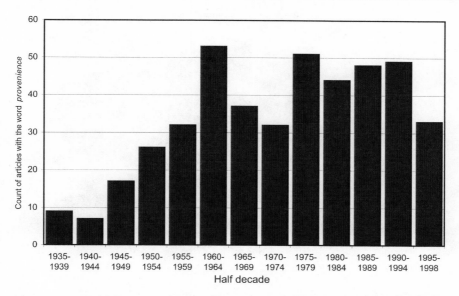

FIGURE 7.1. The number of articles in the journal *American Antiquity* that contain the word *provenience* (grouped in half-decade increments) are displayed for years 1935 to 1999. The numbers increase from less than 10 to over 50. Note that the last half decade, from 1995 to 1998, includes only four, rather than five, years. The data were obtained from the JSTOR library database, which includes scanned articles up to 1999 only.

documentation regarding the history and origin of an object.[1] In archaeology, provenience is most frequently used to denote the location of an object as determined by its horizontal and vertical position in relation to a coordinate system.

As a technical term in archaeology, *provenience* appeared as early as 1884, when Percy Gardner used it in an article published in *The Journal of Hellenic Studies* (based on JSTOR key word search; Gardner 1884). However, the Oxford English Dictionary gives the credit to Arthur J. Evans, whose 1892–1893 article "A Mykenaean Treasure from Aegina" also appeared in *The Journal of Hellenic Studies*. Writing at roughly the same time in the late nineteenth century, General Augustus Lane Fox Pitt-Rivers (Fagan 2005:92–94) urged all archaeologists to record the locations of artifacts when they excavated.

To investigate the appearance and use of the term *provenience* in anthropological archaeology, as distinct from classical archaeology and art history, I undertook a historical analysis of the journal *American Antiquity* from 1935 to 1998. A JSTOR search on *provenience* resulted in 457 articles that contained the term at least once (Figure 7.1). To correct for changing sizes of issues over the decades (which may have influenced the number of articles containing the word *provenience*), I calculated the total number of articles published in each half-decade period and compared them (Figure 7.2), then combined these two figures (number of articles mentioning provenience and the number of articles published each half decade) to obtain the ratio displayed in Figure 7.3.

Inspection of these three figures reveals a clear trend. Few articles contained the word *provenience* in the half decade of 1935–1939. The first article in which the word appears is Frederica de Laguna's 1936 paper entitled "Archaeological Reconnaissance of the Middle and Lower Yukon Valley, Alaska," in which she reports that "no specimens of proved provenience have been found which are indubitable works of human hands" (de Laguna 1936: 7). Thereafter, the number of articles that used *provenience* decreased during World War II (1940–1944) but then steadily increased, reaching a peak during 1960–1964.

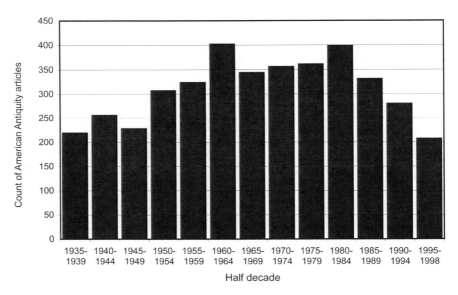

FIGURE 7.2. The total number of articles in the journal *American Antiquity* (grouped in half decade increments) are displayed for years 1935 to 1999. The numbers increase from 225 to over 400. Note that the last half decade from 1995 to 1998 includes only four years. The data were obtained from the JSTOR library database.

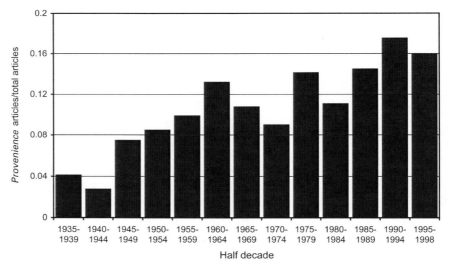

FIGURE 7.3. The ratio of the number of articles in the journal *American Antiquity* that contain the word *provenience* (grouped in half decade increments), divided by the total number of articles per half decade, are displayed for years 1935 to 1998. Note that the last half decade, from 1995 to 1998, includes only four years. The data were obtained from JSTOR library database.

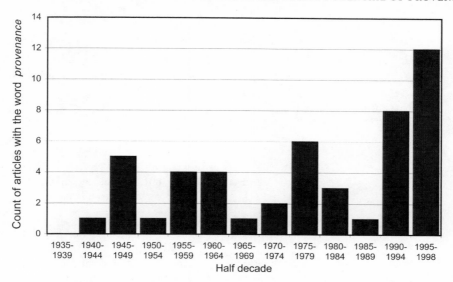

FIGURE 7.4. The number of articles in the journal *American Antiquity* that contain the word *provenance* (grouped in half-decade increments) are displayed for the years 1935 to 1998. The data were obtained from JSTOR library database.

Although the term is used more frequently during 1960–1969, it refers simply to an "exact location in space" or to a "find spot." A sample of the 53 articles from 1960 to 1969 in which *provenience* is used includes phrases such as "provenience unknown," "provenience data," "original provenience is uncertain," and "provenience" as a header in a table, as well as "surface provenience," "provenience data will be supplied," "their provenience noted," and "unknown provenience." All of these phrases indicate that archaeologists were focusing on find-spots of artifacts to a greater extent than ever before.

In the half decade 1975—1979, a new connotation for *provenience* appeared: "archaeological provenience." This time period corresponds to the pinnacle of New Archaeology, whose practitioners frequently used the concept of provenience in their analyses. Phrases such as "one or more provenience units," "differentiated provenience units or levels," and "early provenience of arrow points" suggest an expansion of the concept of provenience as archaeologists methodically investigated the properties of and alterations to the archaeological record itself (e.g., effects of plowing).

The decrease in articles using *provenience* in the half decade from 1980 to 1984 is difficult to explain. Perhaps it reflects a greater concern with social theory, and less interest in artifact-specific data analysis. But following that half decade, the use of the term seems to level off (the last half decade is only four years long because the 1999 volume of *American Antiquity* had not yet been scanned at time of writing and hence was not included in the JSTOR sample).

Lastly, a similar analysis was conducted for the word *provenance* and the results are displayed in Figure 7.4. Clearly, archaeologists who published in *American Antiquity* between 1935 and 1998 did not consider *provenance* a key term, as demonstrated by the small number and scattered distribution of its appearances through the decades. The use of *provenience* in archaeology during the twentieth century, to the virtual exclusion of *provenance*, may be attributable to the influence of geoscientists who encouraged archaeologists to note associations of artifacts with biological and geological remains, and to consider depositional history and artifact movements in their interpretations.

TABLE 7.1. Introductory texts with definitions of *provenience*

Date	Author(s)	Definition
1913	Webster's Dictionary	Origin; source; place where found or produced; provenance; used especially in fine arts and archaeology.
1971	Oxford English Dictionary	Preferred to *provenance* by those who object to the French form of the latter. Dates to 1882. First archaeological usage by A. J. Evans in 1895.
1976	Schiffer	Usually thought of as the spatial location of archaeological remains. In a sense, every item present in the archaeological structure has a unique provenience defined in terms of Euclidean three-dimensional space (p. 133).
1978	Fladmark	The horizontal and/or vertical position of an object in relation to a set of spatial coordinates (p. 159).
1981	Dancey	A precise term for *location* and is preferred because of the multiple, differing meanings of the more common term location (p. 75).
1986	Bower	Exact location in space (p. 200).
1987	Schiffer	The archaeological find-spot of an artifact (p. 17).
1991	Thomas	In general, where an artifact came from. In the context of a specific site, it refers to the horizontal and vertical position of an object in relation to the established coordinate system (p. 281).
1991	Renfrew and Bahn	Horizontal and vertical position within the matrix (p. 42).
1993	Sharer and Ashmore	Refers to a three-dimensional location—the horizontal and vertical position on or within the matrix—at which the archaeologist finds data (p. 125).
1993	Webster, Evans, and Sanders	The exact location in three-dimensional space of any material in its archaeological context (p. 121).
1996	Ashmore and Sharer	The three-dimensional location of archaeological data within or on the matrix (p. 241).
1997	Hester, Shafer, and Feder	The exact measurement of the horizontal and vertical locations of these *in situ* items (p. 116).
1998	Thomas	The location in which something was found. In archaeological excavation, most recovered artifacts and ecofacts are assigned a provenience within a three-dimensional reference system. The horizontal coordinates are assigned by a grid system, the vertical dimension by a datum point (p. 170).
1998	Rapp and Hill	The precise location at which an artifact was recovered (from survey or excavation) (p. 134).
1999	Wenke	Objects and features found can be given precise three-dimensional coordinates, the "provenience" (p. 62).
2002	McDowell-Loudan	The exact horizontal and vertical location of an artifact, archaeological feature, or set of artifacts (p. 101).

TABLE 7.2. Introductory texts with no definition of *provenience*

DATE	AUTHOR	REFERENCE
1952	Kenyon, K. M.	*Beginning in Archaeology.* Praeger, New York.
1954	Woolley, L	*Digging up the Past* (2nd ed.). Penguin, Baltimore.
1956	Childe, V. G.	*A Short Introduction to Archaeology.* Collier, New York.
1956	Wheeler, M.	*Archaeology from the Earth.* Penguin, Baltimore.
1958	Heizer, R. F.	*A Guide to Archaeological Field Methods.* National Press, Palo Alto.
1958	Willey, G. R., and P. Phillips	*Method and Theory in American Archaeology.* University of Chicago Press, Chicago.
1959	Piggott, S.	*Approaches to Archaeology.* A & C Black, London.
1965	Hole, F., and R. F. Heizer	*An Introduction to Prehistoric Archaeology.* Holt, Rinehart, and Winston, New York.
1966	Meighan, C. W.	*Archaeology: An Introduction.* Chandler Publishing, San Francisco.
1966	Bass, G. F.	*Archaeology Under Water.* Praeger, New York.
1967	Deetz, J.	*An Invitation to Archaeology.* Natural History Press, New York.
1967	de Paor, L.	*Archaeology: An Illustrated Introduction.* Penguin, Baltimore.
1968	Clarke, D. L.	*Analytical Archaeology.* Methuen, London.
1970	Alexander, J.	*The Directing of Archaeological Excavations.* John Baker, London.
1972	Petrie, W. M. F.	*Methods and Aims in Archaeology.* Benjamin Blom, New York.
1973	Brennan, L. A.	*A Beginner's Guide to Archaeology.* Stackpole, Harrisburg.
1976	Newlands, D. L., and C. Breede	*An Introduction to Canadian Archaeology.* McGraw-Hill Ryerson, Toronto.
1980	Joukowsky, M. A.	*A Complete Manual of Field Archaeology.* Prentice-Hall, Englewood Cliffs, NJ.

The patterns described above are also reflected in textbooks (Table 7.1). These data support the supposition that *provenience* was being used according to its common English definition until the late 1970s and early 1980s. Evidently, only after the term took on the additional meaning of cultural context, a concept propagated by Taylor (1948) and practitioners of the New Archaeology, did it begin to appear routinely in introductory texts (Table 7.2).

CONTEXT

In archaeology, *context* refers to the characteristics of archaeological data that emerge from the analysis of documented associations among artifact assemblage variation, matrix composition, and provenience. Consid-

erations of context became prominent in archaeology when archaeologists began to view artifacts as the material relics of social and cultural behavior, and used them to elucidate functions of the material remains within those behavioral contexts. Context in this sense is the "full associational setting of any archaeological object or feature, its position on or in the ground, and its positional relationships to other objects and features" (Willey and Sabloff 1993:156).

The concept of context is so important in archaeology that it has been traditionally divided into two categories. *Primary context* is used when artifact assemblage 'composition, matrix properties, and provenience relationships have not been disturbed since archaeological materials were deposited. *Secondary context* refers to those situations where the provenience, association, and matrix have been wholly or partially altered since archaeological materials were deposited. Importantly, these two types of contexts refer to the positions of artifacts, not to the depositional history of the stratigraphic unit or layer. A group of objects (or sedimentary grains) forming the layer came together only in the last depositional event, whereas an individual object (or grain) will carry information about previous depositional events or contexts. Primary and secondary contexts, therefore, can be determined only for individual artifacts within layers. The information those individual objects contain is either different from or similar to the information contained in the whole layer. If the object's behavioral history is different from the layer's depositional history (behavioral or geological), then the object is in secondary context. If the two histories are the same, then the object is in primary context.

In the mid-twentieth century, Walter W. Taylor (1948) urged archaeologists to integrate their data into cultural contexts by employing the "conjunctive approach," which required that all affinities among different data classes be documented and analyzed, particularly in terms of their provenience relations (Taylor 1983:193). He emphasized interdisciplinary research, particularly input from the biological and geological sciences, to appreciate the factors that contribute to variation among cultural contexts. Although archaeologists were slow to rise to Taylor's challenge (see Watson 1983 for a discussion), context eventually became a key interpretive concept. For instance, Michael B. Schiffer (1972, 1983, 1987) used "systemic context" to refer to "artifacts when they are participating in a behavioral system," and "archaeological context" to refer to "artifacts that interact only with the natural environment" in order to model the complexities of archaeological inference. These terms are similar to *primary* and *secondary context*, and involve sorting out depositional histories by examining individual artifacts and comparing them to the attributes of all the objects and sedimentary grains within a layer.

STRATIGRAPHY

Archaeological stratigraphy is "the archaeological evaluation of the significance of stratification to determine the temporal sequence of data within stratified deposits by using both the law of superposition and context evaluations" (Sharer and Ashmore 1993:621; see also Joukowsky 1980:159). *Stratigraphy* is defined in geoscience as "the science dealing with the description of all rock bodies forming the Earth's crust—sedimentary, igneous, and metamorphic—and their organization into distinctive, useful, mappable units based on their inherent properties or attributes" (Salvador 1994:137).

The difference between these two definitions has subtle but significant consequences. The archaeological definition does not include formally describing, naming, and classifying strata. Rather, the archaeological definition indicates that the primary purpose of stratigraphy is to date deposits by considering their provenience relations and content differences. The geoscientific definition focuses on the description, classification, and interpretation of lithologic units. The purpose of stratigraphic research for geoscientists is to establish the relationship of strata in space and their succession in time. The reason for this disparity is that geoscience and archaeology operate at different spatial scales (Stein 2000). Unlike geoscientists, archaeologists do not routinely correlate depositional units across sites, sometimes not even across trenches, and are not concerned with features as large as drainage basins, oceans, or subduction zones (Stein and Linse 1993).

Historians of archaeology (e.g., Daniel 1950) commonly divide the discipline into periods before and after the time when stratigraphic excavation was introduced, which initiated a significant shift in the centrality of provenience and context. Referred to as the "stratigraphic revolution" (Willey and Sabloff 1993:97), this period began around 1911 when archaeologists (especially Americanist archaeologists) embraced stratigraphy as the method by which they could record the locations of artifacts more precisely (Woodbury 1960a, 1960b). The revolution did not occur quickly but rather in stages (Browman and Givens 1996) as archaeologists shifted their efforts from merely extracting objects from the ground to noting the strata from which they were removed, to recording the locations of each object in three-dimensional space. Nonetheless, if context is based on a consideration of stratigraphy, and stratigraphy implies methods of interpreting site formation processes (i.e., the origins of the sedimentary matrix within which artifacts are enclosed and the surfaces upon which they repose), then at the heart of context and stratigraphy is the concept of provenience. The historical analysis that follows illustrates how provenience became the most fundamental, original concept in archaeology.

GLOBAL APPLICATIONS OF ARCHAEOLOGICAL PROVENIENCE

European Prehistory

The beginnings of prehistoric archaeology in Europe are intimately tied to the pivotal contributions of Steno, Hutton, Smith, and Lyell (Stein 2000). Prehistorians and naturalists developed the laws of superposition and uniformitarianism, establishing through context and associations the antiquity of fossils and humans (Daniel 1976). Stratigraphy was essential to these early efforts, but provenience, as we conceive of it today, was not. Archaeologists, geologists, and paleontologists in the mid-nineteenth century were committed to supporting the theory of evolution, but associations were recorded only at the grossest level (Grayson 1983). Archaeologists sought cave sequences that could be interpreted in much the same manner as rock sequences (Winchester 2001). Consequently, they noted only the most minimal information concerning the relative position of artifacts to each other, to surfaces, and to other remains.

As geologists increased their knowledge of fossils and of correlations among fossils and rock sequences across Europe (Conkin and Conkin 1984; Dean 1992; Faul and Faul 1983; Phillips 1978 [1844]; Schneer 1969), guided by stratigraphic protocols (Hedberg 1976; Salvador 1994; Stein 1987, 1990, 1993), the continent's historical geology emerged. Prehis-

toric archaeologists who excavated caves and sites associated with glacial or other Pleistocene deposits followed the same methods that had been codified in the stratigraphic guides (Bishop 1978; Farrand 1993; Jacobsen and Farrand 1987; Laville et al. 1980; L. Leakey 1967; M. Leakey 1978). Hence, prehistorians paid attention to differentiating units based on their content variation by noting changes in faunal and floral remains, artifacts, and oxygen isotopes. In addition, these archaeologists increased the resolution of their proveniences by reducing the sizes of grids and the thicknesses of excavation levels. Throughout the twentieth century, however, the goals of European prehistorians moved away from the goals of geoscientists and began to focus on questions concerning the evolution of human behavior. Not surprisingly, therefore, in the first half of the twentieth century, many American archaeologists went to Europe to study with these prehistorians, and some of them were actually trained as geologists (Willey and Sabloff 1993:98–108).

Paleo-Indian Archaeology

Archaeologists investigating the antiquity of Native American cultures at first used the morphology of objects to suggest great time depth for the human occupation of the New World (Meltzer 1983). They compared the forms of objects found in North America to those recovered in the Lower Paleolithic strata of Europe. This comparative, morphological method was replaced by the use of stratigraphic criteria to evaluate the age of a site. For instance, Ales Hrdlicka, a physical anthropologist, suggested the following protocols:

> In order to demonstrate that human bones were geologically ancient, one had to prove 1) that the specimens were found in geologically ancient deposits, 2) that the age of the deposits was confirmed by paleontological remains, 3) that the bones presented evidence of organic as well as inorganic alterations, 4) that the bones showed morphological characteristics referable to an earlier type, and 5) that the human remains were not introduced in later times. (Hrdlicka 1912:2)

Hence, each case was to be evaluated according to its provenience, context, associations, and stratigraphy. Hrdlicka pushed those archaeologists looking for Paleo-Indian sites into adopting provenience and context far earlier than these concepts and techniques were embraced by most other Americanist archaeologists (Jackson and Thacker 1992).

Hrdlicka might have strongly advocated the use of provenience because he was influenced by geologists (e.g., Kirk Bryan and Ernst Antevs) who worked at putatively early sites. Geologists and archaeologists at the Smithsonian Institution, other natural history museums, and universities were collaborating to find fossils and artifacts. In America, many of the first practitioners of the new discipline called geoarchaeology were, in fact, these geologists or archaeologists who worked so closely together on common problems (Holliday 1997).

Paleoanthropology

Paleoanthropology is the study of human origins (Wolpoff 1980). This field of study is challenging because establishing proveniences of specimens, rare as they are, is problematic (Behrensmeyer and Hill 1980; Isaac 1967). Stern (1993) summarizes the situation best when she suggests that most views concerning human origins fail to consider a critical implication of provenience. According to Stern (1993:202), paleoanthropologists had used associations of tools and fossils to signify short "slices of time" that, in fact, represented rather long periods of formation: "Pleistocene sediments contain palimpsests of debris that accumulated over time spans ranging from 1,000 to 100,000 years." Implied by these considerations is the idea of a *palimpsest*, which in archaeology refers to the deposition of artifacts from sequential activities or occupations on one surface (Enloe, this volume). Stiner et al. (1996:279) quote an anonymous archaeologist who said in 1981 that "for all we know, the archaeological record is just one big palimpsest, incompletely effaced." Clearly, consideration of palimpsests in paleoanthropology and archaeology (e.g., Binford 1981:197; Ferring 1986:265) during the last 20 years re-

flects an increased interest in provenience and an effort to understand the past at an appropriate temporal resolution (Bailey 2007).

European Historic Archaeology

Early in the twentieth century, archaeologists excavating ancient cities in England, Rome, Egypt, Greece, and the Near East began to explore the connections between archaeological remains and historical texts, languages, and classical period civilizations (Trigger 1989). Interacting with ancient historians, linguists, classicists, and art historians, these archaeologists invented methods of excavation independently of the prehistorians working nearby. Their method of excavation was to open a room, expose the foundation, collect artifacts from within the walls, and search for clues written in texts. Because it was presumed that the texts spoke greater volumes than utilitarian artifacts, the proveniences of artifacts and the relative positions of strata were largely ignored.

Many of these "urban" archaeologists drew plans of architecture and profiles of trench walls but, according to later experts, did not pay attention to layers while excavating. Sir Mortimer Wheeler (1954:43), for example, states that "we may be grateful to Schliemann for plunging his spade into Troy, Tiryns, and Mycenae in the seventies of the last century, because he showed us what a splendid book had in fact been buried there; but he tore it to pieces in snatching it from the earth, and it took us upwards of three-quarters of a century to stick it more or less together again and to read it aright." Wheeler's point is that, for European urban archaeologists at the end of the nineteenth century and in the first part of the twentieth century, considerations of provenience, stratigraphy, and superposition in archaeological excavation were not crucial. Instead, archaeologists of this era relied on historical texts, inscriptions, and known relationships to Egypt and other Near Eastern civilizations to interpret their sites and place them in time. For instance, Dame Kathleen Kenyon, noting in her text *Beginning in Archaeology* the manner by which urban sites occupied during the last 3,000 years could be dated, provides insight into the relative unimportance of provenience half a century ago:

> As the city states and then kingdoms increased in complexity of organization the need for some chronological basis for records became apparent, and also some method for calculating the seasons.... Therefore a system based on observation of the stars was worked out, and on this system was based the records of the reigns of the kings. Modern scholars have been able to correlate these records with our present calendar within a small margin of error. (Kenyon 1953:23)

From this passage, it is clear that Kenyon believes that dating urban sites from this period was based on the King List of ancient Egypt. To be fair, however, Kenyon was aware of the different dating challenges that confronted Paleolithic archaeologists, on the one hand, and the excavators of Bronze Age and Iron Age sites on the other:

> [F]or the earlier periods, including the whole of the Paleolithic and Mesolithic periods, such methods clearly cannot be employed since at this time there was no contemporary historical record with which stages of development could be correlated. For these periods, largely geological evidence has to be employed. Geologists and geochronologists have been able to provide a broad chronological framework for the advance and retreat of the ice-cap during the glacial period. (Kenyon 1953:24)

This is not to say that these archaeologists were completely oblivious to provenience and superposition. They did appreciate, for example, the temporal significance of finding the tablets attributable to one king's reign below inscriptions recorded during a later king's reign. The archaeologists even described strata observed in the profile, but according to Browman and Givens (1996:83), these archaeologists did not excavate layers or collect artifacts within strata separately. Clearly, although stratification was sometimes described, stratigraphic excavation that included a consideration for provenience was not practiced. Because artifacts were the primary targets of these late nineteenth and early twentieth century archaeological investigations, excavators did not consider how useful context and provenience could be in reconstructing the lives of the former inhabitants of these sites because, it was thought, those circumstances were securely known from texts.

The beginning of interest in provenience among these archaeologists can be traced to Sir Mortimer Wheeler, who wrote that "the archaeologist must know his dates and how to use them: recorded dates where they are valid, and unwritten dates where geological or physical or chemical or botanical science can win them from the earth" (Wheeler 1954:24). His emphasis on stratigraphy is not only for placing a site in a regional chronology, but also for determining the length of time it took for a layer to form or a house to be built. Wheeler (1954:44) asks: "What is the time-value of archaeological strata? How long did it take, say four feet of stratified deposit to accumulate? A very searching and important question, well worthy of the most careful consideration: if we could always answer it, half our battle would be won."

Kenyon and Wheeler were among the first historical archaeologists to change the method and scale of excavation because they were influenced by prehistorians and other archaeologists who were calling for "digging up people rather than mere things" (Wheeler 1954:246). They asked, for the first time, that archaeologists not just find the events recorded in texts, but use the archaeological record to expand upon them. This new focus called for observations to be made about construction sequences and artifact associations: provenience had become a central concern.

The next major shift in provenience studies came when Edward C. Harris developed a dynamic method to record strata that were exposed in historical excavations (Harris 1975, 1977, 1979, 1989). Frustrated by having only two-dimensional sections to guide the reconstruction of complex arrangements of historic walls, floors, and features in Winchester, England, Harris created a graphical method—the Harris Matrix—to represent the relations of strata to one another in three dimensions. The Harris matrix revolutionized how archaeologists registered the context and association of objects extracted from various strata. Instead of looking only at sections, archaeologists number each wall, trench, and floor, and describe them in the field. Each layer is represented by a rectangle of equal size and the placement of the rectangles relative to each other corresponds to the temporal ordering of their deposition (Figure 7.5). With the Harris Matrix, one must pay attention to contacts and deposits that are encountered during excavation, and make temporal inferences as excavation progresses.[2]

New World Developments

In the Americas, archaeologists embraced provenience when seriation, a relative dating technique (O'Brien and Lyman 1999), began to be applied to a wide variety of contexts. Developed in the first half of the twentieth century, seriation could be based on material from non-stratified contexts, such as artifacts found with burials or in pits, artifacts extracted from arbitrary levels, or surface assemblages (Rowe 1961). American archaeologists established chronologies using frequencies of projectile points or ceramic types (Marquardt 1978) that could then be used to date sites and landforms.

Seriation is based on concepts of style and function embedded in early to mid-twentieth century American cultural anthropology (Dunnell 1978); consequently, those American archaeologists who employed seriation often were influenced by cultural anthropologists in selecting traits and assigning meaning to them. However, cultural anthropology did not influence the methods of seriation as a provenience-based technique. For instance, consider the approach developed by Phillips, Ford, and Griffin for their work in the Lower Mississippi Valley:

> It frequently happens, as we shall show, that a homogeneous deposit, without observable soil stratification, may be made to yield a stratigraphic record of the utmost value. Obviously, such an unstratified deposit will have to be excavated by arbitrary levels, to which method the term "metrical stratigraphy" has sometimes been applied in derogation, as opposed to "natural stratigraphy" obtained by peeling stratified layers.... Village site deposits in the Alluvial Valley rarely exceed 1 to 2 meters in total depth. Ten centimeters was therefore chosen as a unit of depth, convenient for seriating, without presenting serious difficulties in excavating. (Phillips et al. 1951: 240–241)

Because no stratification of the non-artifactual sediments was perceptible to them, Phillips, Ford, and Griffin could not differentiate levels on the basis of sedimentological characteristics. Yet, they did not want to miss stylistic changes that might be expressed by artifact assemblages that had been deposited in successive layers. Although they knew that using arbitrary levels to group artifacts was not an aspect of conventional archaeo-stratigraphic practice, they did presume, however, that chronological information might be conveyed by documenting variation among layers. I suggest that both methods are stratigraphic: one is based on non-anthropogenically deposited lithology and the other on anthropogenically deposited artifacts (Stein 1987, 1990). In many respects, the contribution of these American archaeologists to building the foundation of provenience studies was realized with the introduction of arbitrary levels to create assemblages.

From the efforts of Phillips, Ford, and Griffin in the Lower Mississippi Valley came many of the basic excavation strategies, terms, methods, and techniques that are integral to and distinctive of American archaeology (Willey and Phillips 1958). Henceforth, American archaeologists who used seriation focused squarely on assemblages of artifacts collected in certain proveniences, and the inferences drawn from such analyses primarily concerned chronological correlation.

Seriation allowed archaeologists to "tell time" without reference to fossils or King Lists. To create a seriation, one had to collect certain artifacts in particular ways, group them into

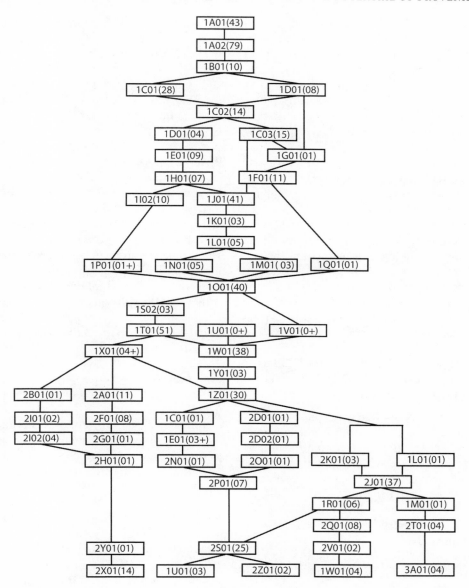

FIGURE 7.5. An example of a Harris diagram from Unit 308/300 of the English Camp shell midden, San Juan Island, Washington. The rectangles represent facies (small litho-stratigraphic units). The text in the rectangles notes the name of the facies and number of 8 liter buckets (modified from Stein 1992b:141).

assemblages to achieve requisite sample sizes, and arrange those assemblages with regard to superposition and provenience relationships. An interesting historical note is that, although questions eventually shifted from a focus on time to a concern with behavior, the methods for examining contexts and for extracting ob-jects and creating assemblages have remained largely unchanged (e.g., Fanning and Hold-away 2001; Holdaway et al. 2002). In fact, as seriation gained prominence, archaeologi-cal focus on artifacts and assemblages intensi-fied. Consequently, the interpretive potential of *matrix*—defined as "the physical material

that surrounds, holds, and supports an artifact" (Sharer and Ashmore 1993:616)—was
disregarded. Actually, because matrix cannot
be seriated in the same way that artifacts can,
it was considered, until recently, disposable
material and unimportant with regard to provenience—a situation that was not corrected
until the late twentieth century (Goldberg,
this volume).

As the "New Archaeology" (Gibbon 1989)
gained traction in the last quarter of the twentieth century, provenience became a rallying
point with those who were curious about the
nature of the archaeological record and what
its variation meant in behavioral and organizational terms (e.g., Ascher 1968). Behavioral archaeologists, in particular, preached
that archaeologists had to consider both the
"cultural" and the natural "processes" that
affect artifacts and the circumstances surrounding their recovery (Stein 2001). As part
of the Cache River Archeological Project, for
example, Michael B. Schiffer and J. Jefferson
Reid proposed a system for designating be-
haviorally significant provenience units:

> In this research design we argue that mean-
> ingful analyses of materials for the purpose
> of reconstructing past human behavior
> must take place within analytic units de-
> fined in terms of the formation processes of
> the archaeological record. This view leads
> to a consideration of how provenience des-
> ignation can serve to identify and opera-
> tionalize the minimal depositional units
> out of which composite analytic units at
> various levels can be constructed. (Schiffer
> and Reid 1975:253)

Rather than simply register the locations of
artifacts with respect to one another and to
surfaces, provenience was to be employed,
in Schiffer and Reid's research program, as a
basic unit of analysis for understanding the
origins of the archaeological record and for
inferring human behavior.

SUMMARY

Provenience is so basic to the discipline today
that few archaeologists realize that the term
did not routinely appear in introductory texts
until the 1980s. Although it was used in publications as early as 1880, it carried only the
English meaning of "noting an object's origin."
After the term crept into the archaeological
discipline, it infiltrated its methods and practices, and influenced its theories. As conclusions about the cultural past were criticized as
being insufficient on theoretical and methodological grounds (e.g., Binford 1968; Clarke
1968; Taylor 1948), they were replaced by inferences that necessitated a consideration of
all the processes—cultural and natural—that
influence an object's provenience (Stein 2001;
Wood and Johnson 1978).

Today, innovations in total station and
GPS technology make possible ever greater
accuracy in determining and recording provenience. These developments have been inspired by—and have inspired—new dimensions of spatial analyses of archaeological
materials (e.g., McPherron et al. 2005). Despite the current emphasis on spatial data in
archaeology, few archaeologists realize their
dependence on the concept of provenience, or
how it developed as the standard for evaluating fieldwork and inference.

NOTES

1. Art historians primarily use the word *provenance*, which was replaced by *provenience* by
those who objected to the French form of the
word (Oxford English Dictionary 1971).
2. By 1983, excavation strategies among many European urban and historic archaeologists had
become so idiosyncratic and non-comparable
that a *Guide to Archaeostratigraphic Classification and Terminology* was published to correct the situation. The guide was followed by a

roundtable discussion at the University of Gh-
ent in 1983 called the "Workshop for Archaeo-
stratigraphic Classification and Terminology."
Subsequently, a short-lived journal, *Stratigraphica Archaeologica*, was published in
1984 and 1987 that contained further clarifications about types of stratigraphic units. The
guide and the two-issue journal generated a
controversy as to whether archaeological stratigraphy differs from geological stratigraphy
(Cremeens and Hart 1995; Farrand 1984a,

1984b; Stein 1987, 1990, 1992a, 1996, 2000). One side of the argument is best expressed by Brown and Harris (1993:15), who state that "we do not think that these geological methods can be extended to a majority of archaeological sites, which are those stratigraphically fabricated as a by-product of human society. Nor do we think that the theory underlying those methods can be suitably applied to the discipline of archaeological stratigraphy." The other side of the controversy, which is unresolved, suggests that the laws and methods underlying geological stratigraphy can be applied to archaeological stratigraphy and, in fact, are already in use (Stein 2000).

ACKNOWLEDGMENTS

I want to thank all participants of the University of Utah–sponsored roundtable at Snowbird, Utah. Without a doubt, the person to influence me most strongly in this research is Patty Jo Watson, who pointed me toward the classical works of Wheeler and Taylor. Her comments on this chapter were numerous, and I wish to thank her for her continued interest in geoarchaeology. I also would like to thank Michael Deal, who provided definitions of provenience from many introductory texts. Phoebe Anderson obtained and counted JSTOR articles and page numbers. She and Amanda Taylor also listened to my ramblings and assisted my thinking on the entire matter.

REFERENCES CITED

Ascher, Robert
1968   Time's Arrow and the Archaeology of a Contemporary Community. In *Settlement Archaeology*, edited by K. C. Chang, pp. 43–52. National Press Books, Palo Alto, California.

Ashmore, Wendy, and Robert J. Sharer
1996   *Discovering Our Past: A Brief Introduction to Archaeology.* Mayfield Publishing, Mountain View, California.

Bailey, Geoff
2007   Time Perspectives, Palimpsests, and the Archaeology of Time. *Journal of Anthropological Archaeology* 26:198–223.

Behrensmeyer, Anna K., and Andrew P. Hill
1980   *Fossils in the Making: Vertebrate Taphonomy and Paleoecology.* University of Chicago Press, Chicago.

Binford, Lewis R.
1968   Archaeological Perspectives. In *New Perspectives in Archaeology*, edited by Sally R. Binford and Lewis R. Binford, pp. 5–32. Aldine, Chicago.
1981   Behavioral Archaeology and the "Pompeii Premise." *Journal of Anthropological Research* 37:195–208.

Bishop, Walter W.
1978   *Geological Background to Fossil Man.* Scottish Academic Press, Edinburgh.

Bower, John.
1986   *In Search of the Past: An Introduction to Archaeology.* Dorsey Press, Chicago.

Browman, David L., and Douglas R. Givens
1996   Stratigraphic Excavation: The First "New Archaeology." *American Anthropologist* 98:80–95.

Brown, Marley R., III, and Edward C. Harris
1993   Interfaces in Archaeological Stratigraphy. In *Practices of Archaeological Stratigraphy*, edited by Edward C. Harris, Marley R. Brown III, and Gregory J. Brown, pp. 7–20. Academic Press, New York.

Clarke, David L.
1968   *Analytical Archaeology.* Methuen, London.

Conkin, Barbara M., and James E. Conkin
1984   *Stratigraphy: Foundations and Concepts.* Van Nostrand Reinhold, New York.

Cremeens, David L., and John P. Hart
1995   On Chronostratigraphy, Pedostratigraphy, and Archaeological Context. In *Pedological Perspectives in Archaeological Research*, edited by Mary E. Collins, Brian J. Carter, Bruce G. Gladfelter, and Randal J. Southard, pp. 15–33. Soil Science Society of America, Special Publication 44. Madison, Wisconsin.

Dancey, William S.
1981   Archaeological Field Methods: An Introduction. Burgess Publishing, Minneapolis.

Daniel, Glyn E.
1950   *A Hundred Years of Archaeology.* Duckworth, London.
1976   *A Hundred and Fifty Years of Archaeology.* 2nd ed. Harvard University Press, Cambridge, Massachusetts.

Dean, Dennis R.
1992   *James Hutton and the History of Geology.* Cornell University Press, Ithaca, New York.

de Laguna, Frederica
1936   An Archaeological Reconnaissance of the Middle and Lower Yukon Valley, Alaska. *American Antiquity* 2:6–12.

Dunnell, Robert C.
1978   Style and Function: A Fundamental Dichotomy. *American Antiquity* 43:192–202.

Evans, Arthur J.
1892 A Mykênæan Treasure from Ægina. *The Journal of Hellenic Studies* 13:195–226.

Fagan, Brian M.
2005 *A Brief History of Archaeology: Classical Times to the Twenty-First Century.* Pearson/Prentice Hall, Saddle River, New Jersey.

Fanning, Patricia, and Simon Holdaway
2001 Stone Artifact Scatters in Western NSW, Australia: Geomorphic Controls on Artifact Size and Distribution. *Geoarchaeology: An International Journal* 16:667–686.

Farrand, William R.
1984a Stratigraphic Classification: Living within the Law. *Quarterly Review of Archaeology* 5:1.
1984b More on Stratigraphic Practice. *Quarterly Review of Archaeology* 5:3.
1993 Discontinuity in the Stratigraphic Record: Snapshots from Franchthi Cave. In *Formation Processes in Archaeological Context*, edited by Paul Goldberg, David T. Nash, and Michael D. Petraglia, pp. 85–96. Prehistory Press, Madison, Wisconsin.

Faul, Henry, and Carol Faul
1983 *It Began with a Stone: A History of Geology from the Stone Age to the Age of Plate Tectonics.* John Wiley and Sons, New York.

Ferring, C. Reid
1986 Rates of Fluvial Sedimentation: Implications for Archaeological Variability. *Geoarchaeology: An International Journal* 1:259–274.

Fladmark, Knut
1978 A Guide to Basic Archaeological Field Procedures. Department of Archaeology, Simon Fraser University, Burnaby, British Columbia.

Gardner, Percy
1884 A Sepulchral Relief from Tarentum. *The Journal of Hellenic Studies* 5:105–142.

Gibbon, Guy
1989 *Explanation in Archaeology.* Basil Blackwell, Oxford, UK.

Grayson, Donald K.
1983 *The Establishment of Human Antiquity.* Academic Press, New York.

Harris, Edward C.
1975 The Stratigraphic Sequence: A Question of Time. *World Archaeology* 7:109–121.
1977 Units of Archaeological Stratification. *Norwegian Archaeological Review* 10:84–94.

1979 *Principles of Archaeological Stratigraphy.* Academic Press, London.
1989 *Principles of Archaeological Stratigraphy.* 2nd ed. Academic Press, London.

Hedberg, Hollis D.
1976 *International Stratigraphic Guide: A Guide to Stratigraphic Classifications, Terminology and Procedure.* Wiley, New York.

Hester, Thomas R., Harry J. Shafer, and Kenneth L. Feder
1997 *Field Methods in Archaeology.* Mayfield Publishing, Mountain View, California.

Holdaway, Simon J., Patricia C. Fanning, Martin Jones, Justin Shiner, Dan C. Witter, and Geoff Nicholls
2002 Variability in the Chronology of Late Holocene Aboriginal Occupation on the Arid Margin of Southeastern Australia. *Journal of Archaeological Science* 29:351–363.

Holliday, Vance T.
1997 *Paleoindian Geoarchaeology of the Southern High Plains.* University of Texas Press, Austin.

Hrdlicka, Ales
1912 *Early Man in South America.* Bureau of American Ethnology Bulletin No. 52. Smithsonian Institution, Washington, D.C.

Isaac, Glynn L.
1967 Towards the Interpretation of Occupation Debris: Some Experiments and Observations. *Kroeber Anthropological Society Papers* 37:31–57.

Jackson, L. J., and Paul T. Thacker
1992 Harold J. Cooke and Jesse D. Figgins: A New Perspective on the Folsom Discovery. In *Rediscovering Our Past: Essays on the History of American Archaeology*, edited by Jonathan E. Reyman, pp. 217–240. Avebury, Aldershot.

Jacobsen, T. W., and William R. Farrand
1987 *Franchthi Cave and Paralia: Maps, Plans, and Sections (Fascicle 1).* Indiana University Press, Bloomington.

Joukowsky, Martha
1980 *A Complete Manual of Field Archaeology: Tools and Techniques of Field Work for Archaeologists.* Prentice-Hall, Englewood Cliffs, New Jersey.

Kenyon, Kathleen M.
1953 *Beginning in Archaeology.* 2nd ed. Phoenix House, London.

Kidder, Alfred V.
1924 *An Introduction to the Study of Southwestern Archaeology.* Yale University Press, New Haven.

1932   *The Artifacts of Pecos*. Papers of the Southwestern Expedition No. 6. Yale University Press, New Haven.

Laville, Henri, Jean P. Rigaud, and James Sackett.

1980   *Rock Shelters of the Perigord: Geological Stratigraphy and Archaeological Succession*. Academic Press, New York.

Leakey, Louis S. B.

1967   *Olduvai Gorge: 1951–1961*. Cambridge University Press, Cambridge.

Leakey, Mary D.

1978   Olduvai Gorge 1911–75: A History of the Investigations. In *Geological Background to Fossil Man: Recent Research in the Gregory Rift Valley, East Africa*, edited by Walter W. Bishop, pp. 157–170. Scottish Academic Press, Edinburgh.

Mandel, Rolfe D.

2000   *Geoarchaeology in the Great Plains*. University of Oklahoma Press, Norman.

Marquardt, William H.

1978   Advances in Archaeological Seriation. In *Advances in Archaeological Method and Theory*, Vol. 1, edited by Michael B. Schiffer, pp. 257–314. Academic Press, New York.

McDowell-Loudan, Ellis E.

2002   *Archaeology: Introductory Guide for Classroom and Field*. Prentice Hall, Upper Saddle River, New Jersey.

McPherron, Shannon J., Harold L. Dibble, and Paul Goldberg

2005   Z. *Geoarchaeology: An International Journal* 20:243–262.

Meltzer, David J.

1983   The Antiquity of Man and the Development of American Archaeology. In *Advances in Archaeological Method and Theory*, Vol. 8, edited by Michael B. Schiffer, pp. 1–51. Academic Press, New York.

O'Brien, Michael J., and R. Lee Lyman

1999   *Seriation, Stratigraphy, and Index Fossils: The Backbone of Archaeological Dating*. Kluwer Academic/Plenum, New York.

Oxford English Dictionary

1971   *The Compact Edition of the Oxford English Dictionary*. Oxford University Press, London.

Phillips, John

1978   [1844] *Memoirs of William Smith*. Arno Press, New York.

Phillips, Philip, James A. Ford, and James B. Griffin

1951   *Archaeological Survey in the Lower Mississippi Valley, 1940–1947*. Papers of the

Peabody Museum of Archeology and Ethnology No. 25. Harvard University, Cambridge.

Rapp, George (Rip), Jr., and Christopher L. Hill

1998   *Geoarchaeology: The Earth-Science Approach to Archaeological Interpretation*. Yale University Press, New Haven.

Renfrew, Colin, and Paul Bahn

1991   *Archaeology: Theories, Methods, and Practice*. Thames and Hudson, New York.

Rowe, John H.

1961   Stratigraphy and Seriation. *American Antiquity* 26:324–330.

Salvador, Amos

1994   *International Stratigraphic Guide: A Guide to Stratigraphic Classification, Terminology, and Procedure*. 2nd ed. Geological Society of America, Boulder.

Schiffer, Michael B.

1972   Archaeological Context and Systemic Context. *American Antiquity* 37:156–165.

1976   Behavioral Archaeology. Academic Press, New York.

1983   Toward the Identification of Formation Processes. *American Antiquity* 48:675–706.

1987   *Formation Processes of the Archaeological Record*. University of New Mexico Press, Albuquerque.

Schiffer, Michael B., and J. Jefferson Reid

1975   A System for Designating Behaviorally-Significant Proveniences. In *The Cache River Archeological Project: An Experiment in Contract Archeology*, edited by Michael B. Schiffer and John H. House, pp. 253–255. Arkansas Archeological Survey, Research Series No. 8. Fayetteville.

Schneer, Cecil J.

1969   *Toward a History of Geology*. Massachusetts Institute of Technology Press, Cambridge.

Sharer, Robert J., and Wendy Ashmore

1993   *Archaeology: Discovering Our Past*. Mayfield, Mountain View, California.

Stein, Julie K.

1987   Deposits for Archaeologists. In *Advances in Archaeological Methods and Theory*, Vol. 11, edited by Michael B. Schiffer, pp. 337–395. Academic Press, Orlando.

1990   Archaeological Stratigraphy. In *Archaeological Geology of North America*, edited by Norman P. Lasca and Jack Donahue, pp. 513–523. Geological Society of America, Centennial Special Volume 4. Boulder.

1992a   Interpreting Stratification of a Shell Midden. In *Deciphering a Shell Midden*, edited by Julie K. Stein, pp. 71–93. Academic Press, San Diego.

1992b   Sediment Analysis of the British Camp Shell Midden. In *Deciphering a Shell Midden*, edited by Julie K. Stein, pp. 135–162. Academic Press, San Diego.

1993   Scale in Archaeology, Geosciences, and Geoarchaeology. In *Effects of Scale on Archaeological and Geoscientific Perspectives*, edited by Julie K. Stein and Angela R. Linse, pp. 1–10. Geological Society of America, Special Paper 283. Boulder.

1996   Geoarchaeology and Archaeostratigraphy: View from a Northwest Coast Shell Midden. In *Case Studies in Environmental Archaeology*, edited by Elizabeth J. Reitz, Lee A. Newson, and Syliva J. Scudder, pp. 35–54. Plenum Press, New York.

2000   Stratigraphy and Archaeological Dating. In *It's About Time: A History of Archaeological Dating in North America*, edited by Stephen E. Nash, pp. 14–40. University of Utah Press, Salt Lake City.

2001   A Review of Site Formation Processes and Their Relevance to Geoarchaeology. In *Earth Sciences and Archaeology*, edited by Paul Goldberg, Vance T. Holliday, and C. Reid Ferring, pp. 37–51. Kluwer Academic/Plenum, New York.

Stein, Julie K., and Angela R. Linse

1993   Scale in Archaeology, Geosciences, and Geoarchaeology. In *Effects of Scale on Archaeological and Geoscientific Perspectives*, edited by Julie K. Stein and Angela R. Linse, pp. 1–10. Geological Society of America, Special Paper 283. Boulder.

Stern, Nicola

1993   The Structure of the Lower Pleistocene Archaeological Record: A Case Study from the Koobi Formation. *Current Anthropology* 34:201–225.

Stiner, Mary C., Güven Arsebuk, and F. Clark Howell

1996   Cave Bears and Paleolithic Artifacts in Yarimburgaz Cave, Turkey: Dissecting a Palimpsest. *Geoarchaeology* 11:279–327.

Taylor, Walter W.

1948   *A Study of Archaeology.* American Anthropological Association, Memoir 69. Washington, D.C.

1983   [1948] *A Study of Archeology.* Reprinted. Southern Illinois University Press, Carbondale.

Thomas, David Hurst

1991   *Archaeology: Down to Earth.* Harcourt Brace Jovanovich, Fort Worth.

1998   *Archaeology.* Harcourt Brace College Publishers, Fort Worth.

Trigger, Bruce G.

1989   *A History of Archaeological Thought.* Cambridge University Press, New York.

Watson, Patty Jo

1983   Foreword to *A Study of Archeology*, by Walter W. Taylor, pp. ix–xvi. Southern Illinois University Press, Carbondale.

Webster, David, Susan Toby Evans, and William T. Sanders

1993   *Out of the Past: An Introduction to Archaeology.* Mayfield Publishing, Mountain View, California.

Wenke, Robert J.

1999   *Patterns in Prehistory: Humankind's First Three Million Years.* Oxford University Press, New York.

Wheeler, Sir Robert E. M.

1954   *Archaeology from the Earth.* Oxford University Press, London.

Willey, Gordon R., and Philip Phillips

1958   *Method and Theory in American Archaeology.* University of Chicago Press, Chicago.

Willey, Gordon R., and Jeremy A. Sabloff

1993   *A History of American Archaeology.* 3rd ed. W. H. Freeman, New York.

Winchester, Simon

2001   *The Map That Changed the World: William Smith and the Birth of Modern Geology.* Harper Collins, New York.

Wolpoff, Milford H.

1980   *Paleoanthropology.* Knopf, New York.

Wood, W. Raymond, and Donald L. Johnson

1978   A Survey of Disturbance Processes in Archaeological Site Formation. In *Advances in Archaeological Method and Theory*, Vol. 1, edited by Michael B. Schiffer, pp. 315–381. Academic Press, New York.

Woodbury, Richard B.

1960a   Nels C. Nelson and Chronological Archaeology. *American Antiquity* 25:400–401.

1960b   Nelson's Stratigraphy. *American Antiquity* 26:98–99.

8

Theory, Method, and the Archaeological Study of Occupation Surfaces and Activities

JAMES G. ENLOE

In exploring the prospect of building a science of archaeology that is not dependent on cultural anthropology for theory, concepts, or units of analysis, I had planned to advocate the proposition that archaeology is anthropology or it is nothing. In my opinion, our best theories are indeed anthropological, keeping in mind that "anthropological" does include us archaeologists. Although sociocultural anthropologists and archaeologists alike may be considered cultural anthropologists, each group investigates many of the same questions with largely different data sets. One could contend that ethnologists are constrained because they cannot observe long-term processes of change, cannot see all of the dynamic cause-and-effect relationships that might enlighten them about profound questions concerning cultural behavior. The fact that they cannot answer all anthropological questions does not make them any less anthropologists. Similarly, alleged limitations in our data do not render us necessarily any less anthropological in perspective. I disagree, therefore, with the contention that ethnological data are dynamic and that archaeological data are mute associations of matter, such that the research questions and "strategies for knowing" are worlds apart (Wylie 2002). Ideas behind the observations chosen to be described or the techniques developed for making observations have at least some implicit theoretical conceptions about the nature of the cultural world or the processes or mechanisms of change behind them. If, however, we wish to investigate dynamic cause-and-effect relationships, archaeologists need to be even more keenly aware of the differences in the nature of ethnological and archaeological data.

In contrast to our ethnologist colleagues, we can neither directly interview nor observe informants. We have only the archaeological record to observe. But the archaeological record is not the past: it is a contemporary phenomenon, an accumulation of materials from myriad events and processes, beginning with past human behavior and continuing until we investigate it (Sullivan, this volume). We cannot know the past directly; we must infer it or aspects about it from our contemporary observations. Our problem is to interpret or read the record correctly, to derive from it information relevant to some theoretical questions we might have. The development of methods for making inferences about the past from contemporary material remains constitutes the science of archaeology, which Binford (1977) called middle range theory, an unfortunate nomenclature perhaps that created some confusion between theory and methodology. Much of the confusion arises between (1) how the archaeological record comes into being and how we can read that record to infer past behavior vs. (2) the importance of such behaviors with regard to evaluating a theoretical construct.

Stephen H. Lekson, a Southwestern archaeologist, once said that the difference between a scientist and a humanist is that "A scientist has an insight and develops a method for its evaluation or demonstration; a humanist can have an insight and go straight to press" (1996:887). Here he has centered the question: science is about the evaluation of ideas, and methodology is the key to evaluating those ideas. Theories can come from anywhere, but their origin has no bearing on their utility. What really matters is their applicability, on two counts. First, do they address an important issue? And second, can we find archaeological evidence to evaluate the theory? Not all ideas or theories that have originated within sociocultural anthropology can be investigated using the archaeological record. Nor can ethnology give us directly testable theories about such processes as the beginning and subsequent evolution of hominid cultural behavior. In my view, it is not theory that separates us from much of the ethnological bloc of the discipline but methodology—that is, the ways that we use the archeological record to explore theories.

One could argue, however, that we do not have an invariable need to look to ethnology for theory. We must recall the unique position of archaeology within anthropology, at least in the United States (Killick, this volume), to answer "Big Questions," such as the origins of culture, the adoption of agriculture, or the rise of state-level societies. Ethnological theorists have thought about and expounded on such questions, generally using some sort of modern ethnographic analogy to project their ideas back into the past. In hunter/gatherer studies, Steward (1955), Sahlins (1972), and Lee and Devore (1968), among others, have posited original forms and lifeways for human ancestors and have laid out evolutionary scenarios to account for changes in social organization since that supposed pristine original form. Modern ethnographic, archaeological, and paleoanthropological studies have rarely been kind to those theorists. Nonetheless, the privileged position of archaeology to address long-term change raises important issues about our relationship with

particular ethnographic records, and about what constitutes an appropriate application of an ethnographic analogy for the interpretation of a specific archaeological case. We should not be looking for an analogy to a specific ethnographic case—an exemplification of Wobst's (1978) concerns regarding ethnographic tyranny—but for clues to understanding aspects of a wide range of past economic, technological, and social behaviors. It is not the identity of the people that is important, "those folks were like these modern ones," but rather how specific activities were conditioned by their spatial, economic, and social constructs. If equifinality is a persistent problem (Deal, this volume), recognizing signature patterns would not be useful unless we understand how combinations of heterogeneous activities might structure the spatial nature of the archaeological record. Cautionary tales from examples of equifinality should not deter us from looking for other cases where the signatures might be more explicitly recognized as being attributable to a particular set of circumstances. When we can recognize certain kinds of activities or spatial relationships among classes of archaeological data, we can begin to read the archaeological record in ways that are productive for evaluating theories (Enloe 2004).

Theories, which may be inspired by poetry, navel gazing, dreams, ethnographic observation, or ethnological comparison, posit causal relationships among variables thought to be of interest. They are ideas to be tested and evaluated through the examination of data. But data and theory might be seen to occupy polar ends of a scientific triumvirate: theory, methodology, and data. Methodology interpolates between the needs of the theory and the reality of potentially observable data. We choose which data to observe and how to record them; we give them meaning through the methodologies we employ.

If the primary differences between ethnological and archaeological anthropology are the data available for observation, these differences are most visibly exhibited in the choices we make in our observations. The investigation of occupation surfaces and activities illustrates the point that methodologies only become relevant in the context of a well-defined theoretical question in which there is a necessity for seeing certain patterns in the data. The recognition of activities and occupation surfaces needs to be more than enriched description. We can use spatial patterning on occupation surfaces to address specific questions and, as theoretically oriented scientific archaeologists, develop and use methodologies to investigate appropriate data sets that will shed light on theoretical issues. The theories that we choose to investigate must have firmly grounded methodologies for interpreting the material remains that will make some real contribution to theory. It is primarily on methodological bases that my research has been directed at studies of occupation surfaces and activities, which the following case illustrates.

THEORY, METHODOLOGY, AND DATA: AN ARCHAEOLOGICAL CASE

The study of occupation surfaces and activities has not been exclusively archaeological; for example, Wiessner (1982a) examined the structure of modern campsite organization as it relates to issues of food sharing. But for the most part the development of techniques has been most fully explored in recent archaeological research. Activities that occur on occupation surfaces are inherently and directly related to the kinds of human behavior that are observable in an ethnographic context. They are best perceived as short-term phenomena. In fact, our ability to see them depends on that aspect. While we may learn something about the scale or tempo of long-term accumulations of activities on surfaces, the very nature of palimpsests makes it difficult to discern and interpret the potential multitude of varied activities that are responsible for their deposition. The most productive research on occupation surfaces and the activities that occurred upon them will require the least distorted archaeological record—an example of the oft-cited Pompeii Premise (Ascher 1961; Binford 1981a). I argue that this requirement may be one of the most productive archaeological research pursuits in terms of addressing anthropological problems. In this case I am interested in variability in food sharing among hunter/gatherers and in the potential for food sharing to have played a fundamental role in causing important social and economic changes in the prehistoric past.

Theory

A number of theories of anthropological interest concern the role of food sharing in modern human organization and in the process of human biological and cultural evolution. These range from theories about the behavior of the earliest hominids, such as Lovejoy's (1981) arguments for the central role of food sharing in bipedalism and hominid origins or Isaac's (1978a, 1978b) arguments about the archaeological evidence for base camps, human social organization, and mate bonding, to theories about culturally specific ideologies (Bird-David 1990; Wiessner 1982a, 1982b), to theories about the origins of complex or hierarchically stratified societies (Mellars 1985; Testart 1982). My particular theories involve the organization of mobility and subsistence among late Upper Paleolithic hunter/gatherers and their implications for evolutionary processes.

A fundamental issue in Paleolithic archaeology concerns subsistence organization of prehistoric hunter/gatherers, the social organization that integrates members of groups through basic economic activities. Binford (1980) has described subsistence and social organization as ranging along an axis from foraging to logistical collecting. In the former, consumers are moved to resource acquisition locations, while in the latter, resources are acquired one place and returned to another location for consumption. This organization is often structured by the nature of resource availability, determining whether consumption of food will be immediate or delayed (Woodburn 1982), whether food sharing is an important mechanism for social integration, or whether storage of food by individual households takes precedence over distribution of food. Although it is clear that food sharing is practiced by most if not all modern hunter/gatherers, the antiquity of that practice has more often been assumed than demonstrated. Food sharing has been proposed as an element of the pattern of adaptation of our earliest hominid ancestors and is a core research topic in Paleolithic archaeology (Isaac 1978a, 1978b; Lovejoy 1981). The distinction between food sharing and food storage is integral to understanding the evolutionary significance of the organizational differences between foraging and logistical collecting. The advent of logistical collecting has been theorized to have played a fundamental role in the evolutionary success of anatomically modern humans versus the disappearance of Neanderthals (Binford 1982; Mellars 1973, 1989, 1994; Olsen 1987; Simek 1987).

A review of modern hunter/gatherer food-sharing practices suggests that meat is shared more extensively than plant foods because of its larger mean *package size* and because of a reduction in *synchronic acquisition*, that is, when all hunters are not successful at the same time (Kaplan and Hill 1985), which contrasts with a situation, such as a mass kill during reindeer migration, when all hunters are successful simultaneously. Among modern hunter/gatherers, the primary social and economic relationships are defined by kinship. The closest family ties are exhibited in the daily provisioning and consumption of food in the immediate family. There are, however, other important social relationships in subsistence organization that are most often expressed in terms of food sharing. For instance, cooperative hunting of seals during the winter by the Netsilik Eskimo involves a set of hunting partners who have reciprocity obligations of sharing prey when only one or a few hunters have been successful (Balikci 1970). Among the tropical forest-dwelling Ache, meat brought into the camp is shared with everyone (Kaplan and Hill 1985). Among the Nunamiut Eskimo, who subsist largely on stored caribou meat during the winter, sharing of stored meat is very limited because all hunters had virtually equal access to migrating caribou. Fresh meat, usually of Dall sheep, brought into camp during the winter is much more widely shared, distributed along the lines of the kinship network (Binford 1978a).

The organization of space used by humans can be viewed as a reflection of social organization, indicating degrees of economic and social interactions. For example, in the organization of camps of prehistoric hunters and gatherers, the spatial placement of family or commensal groups and the distribution of food may be a veritable map of social relationships. This spatial manifestation of social organization has been noted in the ethnographic literature for the !Kung (Whitelaw 1983), Alywara (O'Connell 1987), Pintupi (Gargett and Hayden 1991), and others (Whitelaw 1991). Differential degrees of food sharing between occupants of the camps can demonstrate aspects of social organization in terms of economic interaction, such as immediate family provisioning, obligations to more distant kin or hunting partners, communal cooperation, or general reciprocity. These differences in spatial structure should be discernible in the archaeological remains of prehistoric hunter/gatherer campsites.

Methodology

It has been argued that firmly grounded methodology exists for two realms of data: faunal and spatial analyses. Binford (1977:8) asks whether there are "classes of data available to us for which a more reliable set of conditions might be projected into the past than for projections of human behavior per se?" He suggests three domains of archaeologically recoverable data that can be used to evaluate past human behavior in light of comparisons to ethnographically documented modern behavior. The first domain is ethology and ecology of other species, referring to such aspects as their known distributions, abundance, or seasonality. The second domain is the anatomy and economic utility of such species, as exploited by humans under a variety of conditions, referring, for example, to use, transport, and abandonment of animal body parts. These two domains are most often represented in the archaeological record by faunal remains. The third domain is that of space use: "The way in which this behavior is organized must be conditioned by certain relationships between the properties of alternative spatial organizations and the labor and social pressures operative during periods of organized behavior" (Binford 1977:9). Binford advocated moving beyond the formal or content categories of tool types or frequencies to help understand the structure of behavior. These categories have guided the development of my research programs. I have been searching for the content and configuration of archaeological remains that can be reliably read as indicating specific human behaviors or, perhaps more accurately, specific structures in the organization of human activities.

The most essential aspect of this research has been in the development of methodology to recognize and give meaning to such patterning in content and configuration, in which spatial and faunal data can be combined to contribute to understanding the subsistence organization of prehistoric hunter/gatherers in archaeological cases. In this case, methodological development centered on finding a means to identify bones in an archaeological assemblage that had come from each individual prey carcass. This method might be considered somewhat analogous to the refitting of flakes and blades to identify the individual original flint nodules from which the lithic assemblage was derived (Dibble, this volume). Refitting of bones from individual animals is the primary mechanism used to investigate the distribution of body parts and food sharing across social or commensal units on an archaeological site. Following the work of Todd (1987) on bison, the refitting procedure used in these analyses is based on measurements from modern control samples of reindeer and caribou skeletons. Certain measurements with high internal consistency ($r = 0.99$) within the skeleton of any given individual were identified in the modern control sample and were used to guide the search for dispersed elements of individual reindeer carcasses in the archaeological case.

For example, inferences about the economic and social organization of prehistoric hunter/gatherers can be drawn from the patterns of food distribution and sharing. On an occupation surface with more than one campfire, if parts of the same animal were found with or adjacent to more than one fire, it would imply the practice of food sharing, a risk reduction strategy found today in many of the remaining hunters and gatherers from arctic to tropical settings. If all of the parts of each individual were found only with separate hearths, it would imply that the carcasses were not shared and that each household stored food for its individual consumption.

Data

A certain level of depositional integrity and an appropriate data set are required to employ this methodology. Dibble et al. (1997) convincingly demonstrated, for example, the geological origins of Lower Paleolithic "sites" in the valley of the Somme by using a carefully documented record of the spatial structure of the deposit, rather than by presuming a priori that a site was disturbed or intact. Villa (1982), as well, used skeletal refits within the deep, stratified deposits at Tautavel Cave (France) to demonstrate the jumbled nature of those deposits.

At Pincevent, a late Magdalenian site ($12,600 \pm 200$; $12,100 \pm 120$ radiocarbon years BP [uncalibrated], or Dryas II) that is located downstream of the confluence of the Yonne and the Seine rivers about 60 km upstream and southeast of Paris (Figure 8.1), Leroi-Gourhan (1984; Leroi-Gourhan and Brézillon 1966, 1972) pioneered and refined the practice of *décapage* of an open air site. This broad horizontal exposure of "living floors" makes observable a "*paléoethnographie*" of artifacts and associational structure. The provenience control at this site is extraordinary because all of the material—tools, debitage, bones, fragments—was photographically mapped, providing precise horizontal control. Such precision allows detailed analyses of site structure (Binford 1984; Enloe 1983; Johnson 1984; Leroi-Gourhan and Brézillon 1966, 1972; Simek 1984; Simek and Larick 1983) during the Magdalenian (18,000–11,000 BP), a period that has been proposed as having been characterized by the greatest degree of logistical organization (Straus 1983).

Even more important for the goals of this study are the nature of the remains and their

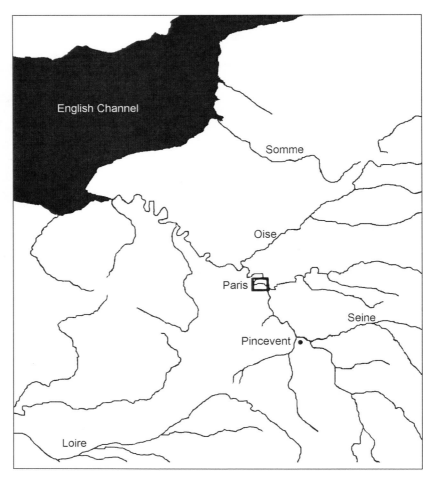

FIGURE 8.1. Location of Pincevent in France.

preservation at Pincevent. First of all, the site was preserved by its almost immediate burial by low-energy fluvial action that did not significantly disturb the horizontal distribution of materials on the former surface. Size sorting does not appear to have occurred, as tiny retouch flakes are spatially associated with hearth stones and cores that are much larger. Refitting of cores and hearth stones indicates that the distributions of debitage and fire-cracked rock have not been disturbed by post-depositional geologic activity (Julien et al. 1992). Orientation of elongated objects also suggests integrity of the content and configuration of the material (Bertran and Texier 1995; Enloe 2006). Second, the fauna at Pincevent is dominated by reindeer (David 1972, 1994;

David and Enloe 1992, 1993). The variability in *Rangifer* ethology and human exploitation patterns can be used to advantage in the search for the contrast between foragers and collectors. Finally, this archaeological site is characterized by multiple hearths on the same level, documented as a single occupation surface (Baffier et al. 1982; Orliac 1991). At least seven major hearths on that surface are identified as domestic occupation units or households (Leroi-Gourhan and Brézillon 1972). Each consists of a redundant module of a slab-lined basin hearth surrounded by structured spatial organization of debris. On one side of the hearth there is an area of cleaned or maintained sleeping space; tool and food preparation debris is located immediately adjacent to the hearth on that same side; on the other side of the hearth there are trash dumps and ash dumps; technical annexes for specific activities are clustered around those areas. Distances between domestic units range from 7 m to 30 m. Each hearth-centered unit had extraordinary preservation and was excavated with such precision that there are very accurate maps of where each bone or fragment was found around or between the hearths.

The question of contemporaneity for these domestic units is a critical issue. Numerous sites thought to represent "living floors" of short-term occupations have been argued to represent long-term accumulations of temporally dispersed, unrelated events (Ascher 1961; Binford 1981a). This question has been specifically addressed at Pincevent by a number of studies. Geologically, 15 occupation levels are included in as much as 3 m of an extremely fine-grained accumulation of varve-like alluvial sediments, each generally less than 1 cm thick. Innovative use of latex peels on stratigraphic profiles in widely dispersed test pits allowed identification of the major occupation surfaces at distances of over 100 m (Orliac 1975, 1991). These relationships were confirmed by contiguous excavation linking surfaces identified in test pits (Baffier et al. 1982), revealing an integrated occupation surface of over 4,500 m² for Level IV-20. Refits of fire-cracked rock among the stone-lined hearths and trash dumps reinforce the idea of internal integrity of the occupation surface (Julien et al. 1992).

Even more detailed are the flint-refitting studies, which indicate contemporaneity of the hearths and their debris across the occupation surface of Level IV-20 (Bodu 1991, 1994, 1996, 2004). An extremely long history of refitting analyses by successive generations of archaeologists at Pincevent has resulted in the reassembly of as much as 90 percent of the flint pieces > 1 cm (Bodu, pers. comm., 2005). Their differing degrees of technical skills and idiosyncratic motor habits have made it possible to identify the work of several individual Paleolithic flintknappers (Ploux 1989). Refitting of debitage and cores has traced not only the movement of raw materials within local-

ized domestic units, often used alternately by knappers of different skill levels, but also movement of the same core between domestic units, with removals and transformations of blades into tools by the same knapper (Bodu 1996: 68). Other instances document flint pieces acquired from five different domestic units. Bodu argues that while refitting of pieces from one domestic hearth to another does not indicate strict contemporaneity—one piece could have been taken from an occupation unit after its abandonment—distribution of pieces in both directions between two units shows synchronous function of both units during a common time period. He concludes that "there is a question of whether or not the entirety of the hearths present on the whole 4,500 sq m of the same flood level were effectively used at the same time. By extending the refitting study to about 50,000 pieces discovered on this level, it has been possible to demonstrate that all the features were contemporaneous" (Bodu 1996:69). Such bidirectional exchanges and closed loops of interaction among multiple hearths and domestic units of Level IV-20 can be seen in Figure 8.2. Additionally, and perhaps more convincingly, refitting of reindeer carcasses, discussed in more detail below, offers a more fine-grained evaluation of contemporaneity. While hearth slabs or flint cores or blades might have long re-use careers, ranging from a day or weeks to years or millennia, meat and marrow have much shorter use-lives. Some animal products, including bone and antler, have technological utility that can be recognized by final products and debris from manufacture, but the vast majority are nutritional and subject to rapid decay. Widely distributed pieces of the same individual animal carcass clearly indicate contemporaneous use of that space over a much shorter time span (Enloe and David 1989, 1992).

In order to test hypotheses about the practices of food sharing and storage, with significant theoretical implications for the identification of foraging vs. logistical collecting in the mobility and subsistence strategies in the late Upper Paleolithic, the carcass-refitting methodology was applied to the reindeer bones at Pincevent. Those key measurements,

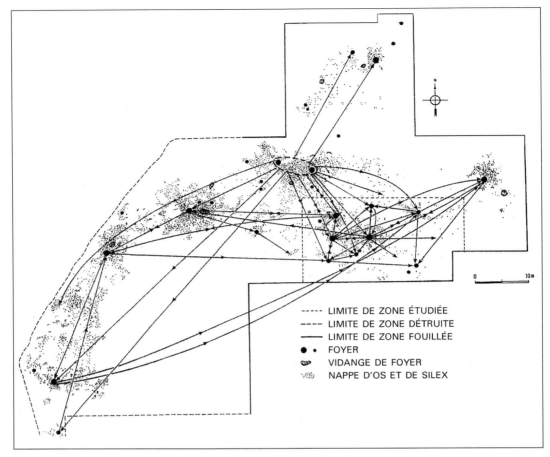

FIGURE 8.2. Distribution of flint refits across the occupation surface of Level IV-20 at Pincevent. Multi-directional interactions among the domestic units at the major hearths demonstrate strict contemporaneity among their occupations.

in turn, were used to predict potential matches to identify the scattered components of individual carcasses. These predicted matches that consisted of left and right pairs based on the bilateral symmetry of ungulate skeletons, and of adjacent elements of articulated joints, were then subjected to a verification procedure that confirmed them by means of examination of individual morphological details (Enloe 1991; Enloe and David 1989, 1992).

Archaeological Interpretations

The results of the refitting analysis show clear and, to me, surprising patterning. My expectations for food storage characteristic of logistical collectors in the late Upper Paleolithic were not totally met. Although seasonality de-

terminations clearly demonstrated that all of the reindeer were killed in a very short time period, during the fall migration, the prey was not stored for individual household consumption. Although hunters probably had equal success in acquiring game at this time, and would in principle not have needed to share food at that time, substantial sharing was indicated by the distribution of reindeer carcasses across the campsite.

Carcasses were transported only a short distance from a kill site, as indicated by a conspicuous lack of vertebrae but by almost complete representation of appendicular skeletal elements. The final stages of processing involve further disarticulation of the transported carcasses for distribution to consumers

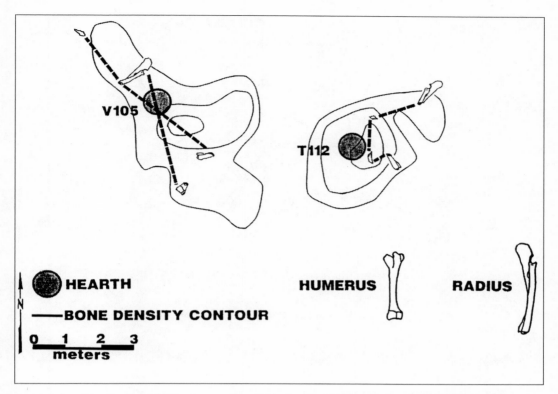

FIGURE 8.3. Distribution of refitted upper fore-limb elements from a single reindeer individual at Section 36 of Pincevent IV-20. The left limb is associated with Hearth T112, while the right limb is associated with Hearth V105.

and for preparation for cooking and eating. The spatial distribution of refitted elements of individual reindeer carcasses exhibited interesting contrasts in distribution and consumption. This contrast can be seen between the meat-rich elements of the upper fore-limb and the meat-poor, but marrow-rich elements of the lower fore- and hind-limbs.

At Pincevent, paired and articulated distal humerus and proximal radiocubitus elements often indicate that the left and right forelimbs of a single individual were shared between domestic households, such as this individual shared between hearths V105 and T112 (Figure 8.3). When we examine this pattern of meat distribution at the level of the large excavated surface with numerous indicators of contemporaneous occupation, we can see long-distance refits of up to 63 meters (Figure 8.4), indicating a high degree of economic and social integration among the site's inhabitants.

The greatest amount of interaction and food sharing occurred between the closest neighbors, a pattern that frequently indicates close kinship among modern hunter/gatherers.

The paired distal metacarpals and metatarsals, which have no meat but are rich marrow sources, yielded another pattern, however. Paired elements from the same individual carcass were almost always associated with the same hearth, rather than shared domestic units, as we can see in Figure 8.5 at Hearths V105 and T112.

When we examine this distribution at the campsite level, we can see that only three of the domestic hearths that participated in long-distance meat sharing are locations of concentration of the marrow-rich metapodials (Figure 8.6). These areas might be interpreted as the locations of the hunters' households, who are distributing meat but not marrow among their kin and neighbors. This marrow

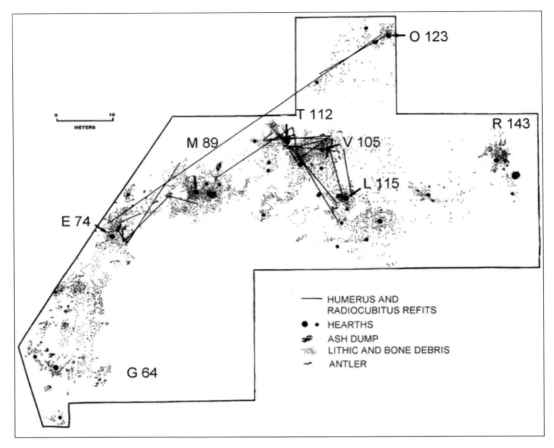

FIGURE 8.4. Distribution of refits of meat-bearing upper fore-limb elements across the occupation surface of Level IV-20 at Pincevent. Note long-distance interactions between most hearth-centered households.

consumption pattern is frequent among hunters from tropical to arctic environments, often occurring at kill sites from which meat is transported to other consumers.

Could other behaviors have resulted in these patterns of archaeological deposition? Archaeologists' growing awareness of the complicated histories of site formation processes and taphonomic entanglement of various geological, biological, and cultural agents are implicated in considerations of the effects of equifinality for site content and configuration (Binford 1981b; Behrensmeyer and Hill 1980; Brain 1981; Isaac 1967; Schick 1986; Schiffer 1972, 1983) and thus require evaluation of alternate pathways for the creation of the archaeological record. In the case of Pincevent, it entails an evaluation of whether

the occupation of all of the domestic units of Level IV-20 began and ended at the same times, and in general whether hunter/gatherers establish, utilize, and abandon their encampments in lock-step fashion, all arriving, setting up shop, and departing at the same time. One could argue, as did Binford (1978b) for another occupation level of Pincevent, that the distribution of remains linking one residential unit to another in Level IV-20 was simply a function of "tossing" remains over the shoulder into a hearth abandoned the day before. His analyses of the Mask site demonstrated the combination of place, drop, and toss behaviors that could account for the patterns of accumulation on the earlier Habitation N° 1 level. Leroi-Gourhan's (1972) subsequent models for the modular nature of

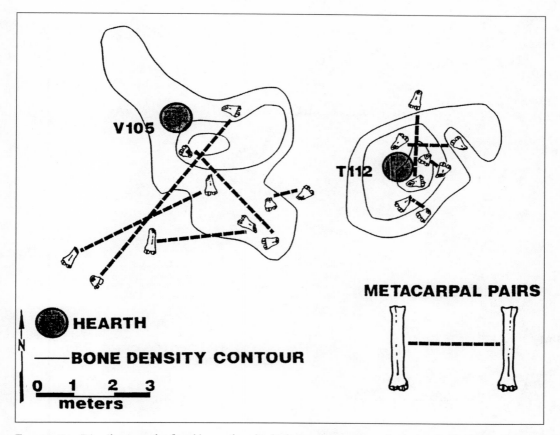

FIGURE 8.5. Distribution of refitted lower fore-limb elements from several reindeer individuals at Section 36 of Pincevent IV-20. Pairs of left and right distal metacarpals from some individuals are associated with Hearth T112, while other pairs are associated with Hearth V105. Marrow-bearing metapodials do not appear to have been shared between hearths.

each of the residential units of Level IV-20 include the different disposal modes to which Binford referred. These modes can be seen in the analysis of the internal organization of the faunal remains of one of the residential units, M89, with a combination of placement disposal in the maintained area between the sleeping area and the hearth, drop disposal of small metapodial diaphysis fragment from marrow extraction in the heterogeneous work area adjacent to the hearth, and toss disposal of larger, more cumbersome skeletal elements in a dump across the hearth from the sleeping area (Enloe et al. 1994).

I have previously argued that not only are the residential units of Level IV-20 similar in content and configuration, but that they are all similarly aligned, perhaps to prevailing wind direction (Enloe 1983), which would run counter to an argument for change in wind direction, which was the reorganizing factor for the Mask site. The fact that each residential module of Level IV-20 is essentially redundant in content and configuration would necessitate similar "lock-step" transformations throughout their occupations, a seemingly unnecessary complication. Further, while Units T112 and V105 are separated by a short distance, for which one could argue tossing disposal, the consistent pattern of longer-distance refits of meat-bearing elements between them and the other residential units contrasting with the shorter distant refits of marrow elements within the residential units argues for intentionality of the different patterns; the refits of up to 63 m would require a substantial leap

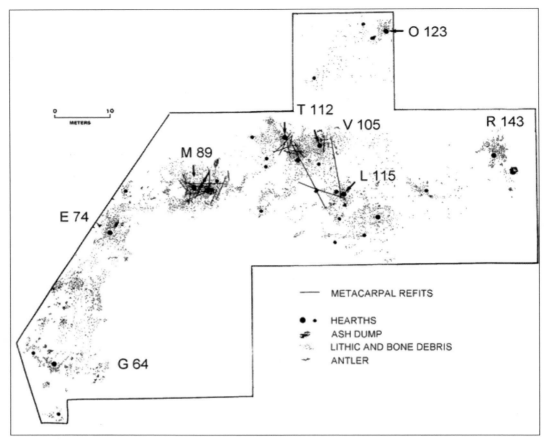

FIGURE 8.6. Distribution of refits of marrow-bearing lower fore-limb elements across the occupation surface of Level IV-20 at Pincevent. Note the virtual lack of long-distance interactions between households.

of faith (and a strong arm) for a toss disposal explanation. In summary, while other behavioral arguments might still be mounted to account for the archaeological patterning on Level IV-20 at Pincevent, the most parsimonious and powerful explanation for much of the spatial distribution information can be seen in food-sharing behavior.

CONCLUSIONS AND IMPLICATIONS FOR ARCHAEOLOGICAL THEORY

Reindeer hunting is clearly the focus of subsistence activities for many of the Magdalenian sites in the Paris Basin for which we have substantial faunal preservation. Sites such as Pincevent exhibit redundant patterning in seasonality and carcass processing, indicating that fall migration interception was a

strategic choice for the acquisition of significant quantities of food for the entire year. A large portion of their economic systems was based on the planned exploitation of this single species. Food-sharing patterns between occupants of Magdalenian campsites indicate close economic, social, and probably kinship ties among these Magdalenians.

My original hypotheses about individual acquisition and storage of reindeer carcasses in lieu of exchange and sharing between hunters, based on ethnographic analogies and contrasting cases, were not supported. Do these results mean that ethnologically based theories about food sharing are inappropriately exploited by archaeologists? Of course it does not. It means that archaeological research is proceeding correctly, using well-grounded methodologies for seeing significant patterns in the archaeological record to test those theoretical ideas. Hypotheses and theories are meant to be evaluated, falsified, or refined. The use of theory is not incorrect; the failure of results to support hypotheses just means that our theories were too simplistic and still need to be reformulated in anthropologically significant ways. We have seen new, interesting, and unanticipated patterns in the organization and interactions of Magdalenians at Pincevent. We have a much richer and more complex picture of the nature of acquisition and exchange, which has opened the way for the proposition of newer, more refined hypotheses to be tested, both at this site and others.

In the larger picture, this study demonstrates how anthropological theory regarding hunter-gatherer adaptation inspired the de-velopment of methodologies for acquiring evidence from the archaeological record about the evolutionary significance of food sharing. Those methodologies were grounded, on one hand, in mammalian osteology and, on the other, in ethnoarchaeology. Neither could have been derived directly and exclusively from archaeological observations. Their applications to an archaeological case allow us to see additional examples or cases in the spectrum of human behavior, particularly in the realm of food sharing as it is embedded in social and economic relationships of hunter-gatherers. Moreover, this approach broadens our understanding of variability among modern hunter-gatherer societies and shows us a path for evaluating food sharing's role in initiating profound evolutionary change.

ACKNOWLEDGMENTS

I would like to express my appreciation to all of the participants at the Snowbird conference for the lively intellectual exchange. I also thank Jeffrey Grathwohl and the University of Utah Press for hosting the event and for making this publication possible. I am indebted to anonymous reviewers for pointing out where clarifications needed to be made in previous drafts of this chapter.

REFERENCES CITED

Ascher, Robert
1961   Analogy in Archaeological Interpretation. *Southwestern Journal of Anthropology* 17: 317–325.

Baffier, D., Francine David, G. Gaucher, M. Julien, D. Karlin, A. Leroi-Gourhan, and M. Orliac
1982   Les Occupations Magdaléniennes de Pincevent: Problèmes de Durée. In *Les Habitats du Paléolithique Supérieur: Actes du Colloque en Hommage au Professeur André Leroi-Gourhan*, Vol. 2, Roanne-Villerest, 22–24 Juin 1982:243–271.

Balikci, Asen
1970   *The Netsilik Eskimo.* Natural History Press, New York.

Behrensmeyer, Anna K., and Andrew P. Hill (editors)
1980   *Fossils in the Making: Vertebrate Taphonomy and Paleoecology.* University of Chicago Press, Chicago.

Bertran, Pascal, and Jean-Pierre Texier
1995   Fabric Analysis: Application to Palaeolithic Sites. *Journal of Archaeological Science* 22:521–535.

Binford, Lewis R.
1977   General Introduction. In *For Theory Building in Archaeology: Essays on Faunal Remains, Aquatic Resources, Spatial Analysis, and Systemic Modeling,* edited by Lewis R. Binford, pp. 1–10. Academic Press, New York.

1978a   *Nunamiut Ethnoarchaeology.* Academic Press, New York.

1978b   Dimensional Analysis of Behavior and Site Structure: Learning from an Eskimo Hunting Stand. *American Antiquity* 43:330–361.

1980   Willow Smoke and Dogs' Tails: Hunter-Gatherer Settlement Systems and Archaeological Site Formation. *American Antiquity* 45:4–20.

1981a   Behavioral Archaeology and the "Pompeii Premise." *Journal of Anthropological Research* 37:195–208.

1981b   *Bones: Ancient Men and Modern Myths.* Academic Press, New York.

1982   The Archaeology of Place. *Journal of Anthropological Archaeology* 1:5–31.

1984   Butchering, Sharing, and the Archaeological Record. *Journal of Anthropological Archaeology* 3:235–257.

Bird-David, Nurit

1990 The Giving Environment: Another Perspective on the Economic System of Gatherer-Hunters. *Current Anthropology* 31:189–196.

Bodu, Pierre

1991 Pincevent, Site Magdalénien. In *Les Premiers Chasseurs dans la Vallée de la Seine*, pp. 60–67. Les Dossiers d'Archéologie 164.

1994 *Analyse Typo-Technologique du Matériel Lithique de Quelques Unités du Site Magdalénien de Pincevent (Seine-et-Marne): Applications Spatiales, Économiques et Sociales.* Thèse de Nouveau Doctorat, Université de Paris I, Sorbonne, 3:1267.

1996 The Magdalenian Hunters of Pincevent, Aspects of Their Behavior. *Lithic Technology* 21:48–70.

2004 Paléolithique Supérieur et Habitat: Réflexions sur un Fossile-Directeur Potentiel. In *La Préhistoire en France, 100 ans de Découvertes*, pp. 14–24. Société Préhistorique Française, Dossiers d'Archéologie 296.

Brain, Charles K.

1981 *The Hunters or the Hunted? An Introduction to African Cave Taphonomy.* University of Chicago Press, Chicago.

David, Francine

1972 Temoins Osseux. In *Fouilles de Pincevent: Essai d'analyse Ethnographique d'un Habitat Magdalénien (la Section 36)*, pp. 295–320. VIIe Supplément à Gallia Préhistoire, Paris.

1994 La Faune de Pincevent et Verberie. In *Environnements et Habitats Magdaléniens dans le Centre du Bassin Parisien*, edited by Y. Taborin, pp. 105–110. Documents d'Archéologie Française 43, Paris.

David, Francine, and James G. Enloe

1992 Chasse Saisonnière des Magdaléniens du Bassin Parisien. *Bulletin et Mémoire de la Société d'Anthropologie de Paris* 4(3–4):167–174.

1993 L'exploitation des Animaux Sauvages de la Fin du Paléolithique Moyen au Magdalénien. In *Exploitation des Animaux Sauvages à travers le Temps*, edited by J. Desse and F. Audouin, pp. 29–47. Juan-les-Pins, Éditions APDCA.

Dibble, Harold L., Philip G. Chase, Shannon P. McPherron, and Alain Tuffreau

1997 Testing the Reality of a "Living Floor" with Archaeological Data. *American Antiquity* 62:629–651.

Enloe, James G.

1983 Site Structure: A Methodological Approach to Analysis. *Haliksa'i: UNM Contributions to Anthropology* 2:28–39.

1991 *Subsistence Organization in the Upper Paleolithic: Carcass Refitting and Food Sharing at Pincevent.* PhD dissertation, University of New Mexico, University Microfilms, Ann Arbor.

2004 Equifinality, Assemblage Integrity, and Behavioral Inferences at Verberie. *Journal of Taphonomy* 2:147–165.

2006 Geological Processes and Site Structure: Assessing Integrity at a Late Paleolithic Open-air Site in France. *Geoarchaeology: An International Journal* 21:523–540.

Enloe, James G., and Francine David

1989 Le Remontage des os par Individus: Le Partage du Renne chez les Magdaléniens de Pincevent (La Grande Paroisse, Seine-et-Marine). *Bulletin de la Société Préhistorique Française* 86:275–281.

1992 Food Sharing in the Paleolithic: Carcass Refitting at Pincevent. In *Piecing Together the Past: Applications of Refitting Studies in Archaeology*, edited by Jack L. Hofman and James G. Enloe, pp. 296–315. British Archaeological Reports International Series 578. Oxford, UK.

Enloe, James G., Francine David, and Timothy S. Hare

1994 Patterns of Faunal Processing at Section 27 of Pincevent: The Use of Spatial Analysis and Ethnoarchaeological Data in the Interpretation of Archaeological Site Structure. *Journal of Anthropological Archaeology* 13:105–124.

Gargett, R., and B. Hayden

1991 Site Structure, Kinship, and Sharing in Aboriginal Australia: Implications for Archaeology. In *The Interpretation of Archaeological Spatial Patterning*, edited by Ellen M. Kroll and T. Douglas Price, pp. 11–32. Plenum Press, New York.

Isaac, Glynn L.

1967 Towards the Interpretation of Occupation Debris: Some Experiments and Observations. *Kroeber Anthropological Society Papers* 37:31–57.

1978a The Food Sharing Behavior of Protohuman Hominids. *Scientific American* 238:90–106.

1978b Food Sharing and Human Evolution: Archaeological Evidence from the Plio-

Pleistocene of East Africa. *Journal of Anthropological Research* 34:311–325.

Johnson, Ian

1984 Cell Frequency Recording and Analysis of Artifact Distributions. In *Intrasite Spatial Analysis in Archaeology*, edited by Harold J. Hietala and Paul A. Larson, pp. 75–96. Cambridge University Press, Cambridge.

Julien, M., C. Karlin, and B. Valentin

1992 Déchets de Silex, Déchets de Pierres Chauffées: De l'intérêt des Remontages à Pincevent (France). In *Piecing Together the Past: Applications of Refitting Studies in Archaeology*, edited by Jack L. Hofman and James G. Enloe, pp. 287–295. British Archaeological Reports International Series 578. Oxford, UK.

Kaplan, Hillary, and Kim Hill

1985 Food Sharing among Ache Foragers: Tests of Explanatory Hypotheses. *Current Anthropology* 26:223–246.

Lee, Richard B., and Irven DeVore

1968 Problems in the Study of Hunters and Gatherers. In *Man the Hunter*, edited by Richard B. Lee and Irven DeVore, pp. 3–12. Aldine, Chicago.

Lekson, Stephen H.

1996 Landscapes with Ruins: Archaeological Approaches to Built and Unbuilt Environments. *Current Anthropology* 37:886–892.

Leroi-Gourhan, André

1972 Structures Hétérogènes: Les Unités Domestiques. In *Fouilles de Pincevent: Essai d'analyse Ethnographique d'un Habitat Magdalénien (la Section 36)*, edited by André Leroi-Gourhan and Michel Brézillon, pp. 215–256. VIIe Supplément à Gallia Préhistoire.

1984 *Pincevent: Campement Magdalénien de Chasseurs de Rennes.* Guides Archéologiques de la France, Ministère de la Culture. Imprimerie Nationale, Paris.

Leroi-Gourhan, André, and Michel Brézillon

1966 L'habitation Magdalénienne No. 1 de Pincevent près Montereau (Seine-et-Marne). *Gallia Préhistoire* IX:263–385.

1972 *Fouilles de Pincevent: Essai d'analyse Ethnographique d'un Habitat Magdalénien (la Section 36).* VIIe Supplément à Gallia Préhistoire.

Lovejoy, C. Owen

1981 The Origin of Man. *Science* 211:341–350.

Mellars, Paul A.

1973 The Character of the Middle-Upper Paleolithic Transition in Southwest France. In *The Explanation of Culture Change: Models in Prehistory*, edited by Colin Renfrew, pp. 255–276. Duckworth, London.

1985 The Ecological Basis of Social Complexity in the Upper Paleolithic of Southwestern France. In *Prehistoric Hunters and Gatherers: The Emergence of Cultural Complexity*, edited by T. Douglas Price and James A. Brown, pp. 271–298. Academic Press, Orlando.

1989 Major Issues in the Emergence of Modern Humans. *Current Anthropology* 30:349–385.

1994 The Upper Paleolithic Revolution. In *The Oxford Illustrated Prehistory of Europe*, edited by Barry W. Cunliffe, pp. 42–78. Oxford University Press, Oxford.

O'Connell, James F.

1987 Alyawara Site Structure and Its Archaeological Implications. *American Antiquity* 52:74–108.

Olsen, Sandra L.

1987 Magdalenian Reindeer Exploitation at the Grotte des Eyzies, Southwestern France. *Archaeozoologia* 1:171–182.

Orliac, M.

1975 Empreintes au Latex des Coupes du Gisement Magdalénien de Pincevent: Techniques et Premiers Résultats. *Bulletin de la Société Préhistorique Française* 72:274–276.

1991 Topographie du Campement Magdalénien. In *Le Milieu Naturel des Magdaléniens du Bassin Parisien*, edited by Yvette Taborin, pp. 201–210. Documents ·d'Archéologie Française 43. Paris.

Ploux, S.

1989 Approche Archéologique de la Variabilité des Comportements Techniques Individuels: Les Tailleurs de l'unité 27-M 89 de Pincevent. Thèse de préhistoire de l'Université de Paris X—Nanterre.

Sahlins, Marshall D.

1972 *Stone Age Economics.* Aldine-Atherton, Chicago.

Schick, Kathy D.

1986 *Stone Age Sites in the Making: Experiments in the Formation and Transformation of Archaeological Occurrences.* British Archaeological Reports International Series 319. Oxford, UK.

Schiffer, Michael B.

1972 Archaeological Context and Systemic Context. *American Antiquity* 37:156–165.

1983 Toward the Identification of Site Formation Processes. *American Antiquity* 48:675–706.

Simek, Jan F.

1984 *A K-means Approach to the Analysis of Spatial Structure in Upper Paleolithic Habitation Sites: Le Flageolet I and Pincevent Section 36.* British Archaeological Reports International Series 205. Oxford, UK.

1987 Spatial Order and Behavioral Change in the French Palaeolithic. *Antiquity* 61:25–40.

Simek, Jan F., and Roy R. Larick

1983 The Recognition of Multiple Spatial Patterns: A Case Study from the French Upper Paleolithic. *Journal of Archaeological Science* 10:165–180.

Steward, Julian H.

1955 *Theory of Culture Change: The Methodology of Multilinear Evolution.* University of Illinois Press, Urbana.

Straus, Lawrence G.

1983 From Mousterian to Magdalenian: Cultural Evolution Viewed from Vasco-Cantabrian Spain and Pyrenean France. In *The Mousterian Legacy*, edited by Erik Trinkaus, pp. 73–111. British Archaeological Reports International Series 164. Oxford, UK.

Testart, Alain

1982 The Significance of Food Storage among Hunter-Gatherers: Residence Patterns, Population Densities, and Social Inequalities. *Current Anthropology* 23:523–530.

Todd, Lawrence C.

1987 Bison Bone Measurements. In *The Horner Site: The Type Site of the Cody Cultural Complex*, edited by George C. Frison and Lawrence C. Todd, pp. 371–403. Academic Press, Orlando.

Villa, Paola

1982 Conjoinable Pieces and Site Formation Processes. *American Antiquity* 47:276–290.

Whitelaw, Todd M.

1983 People and Space in Hunter-Gatherer Camps: A Generalizing Approach in Ethnoarchaeology. *Archaeological Review from Cambridge* 2:48–66.

1991 Some Dimensions of Variability in the Social Organization of Community Space among Foragers. In *Ethnoarchaeological Approaches to Mobile Campsites: Hunter-Gatherer and Pastoralist Case Studies*, edited by Clive Gamble and William A. Boismier, pp. 139–188. International Monographs in Prehistory, Ann Arbor.

Wiessner, Polly

1982a Risk, Reciprocity and Social Influences on !Kung San Economics. In *Politics and History in Band Societies*, edited by Eleanor B. Leacock and Richard B. Lee, pp. 61–84. Cambridge University Press, Cambridge.

1982b Beyond Willow Smoke and Dogs' Tails: A Comment on Binford's Analysis of Hunter-Gatherer Settlement Systems. *American Antiquity* 47:171–178.

Wobst, H. Martin

1978 The Archaeo-Ethnography of Hunter-Gatherers or the Tyranny of the Ethnographic Record in Archaeology. *American Antiquity* 43:303–309.

Woodburn, James

1982 Egalitarian Societies. *Man* 17:431–451.

Wylie, Alison

2002 *Thinking From Things: Essays in the Philosophy of Archaeology.* University of California Press, Berkeley.

9

Abandonment Patterning at Archaeological Settlements

MICHAEL DEAL

...in time, every community will become first a "ghost" town then a cube below the ground. The problem for the prehistorian is to reconstruct the community from the cube.

ROBERT ASCHER

All settlements are eventually abandoned. What concerns most archaeologists is how past abandonment practices affect their interpretations of archaeological sites. This point was brought home through a series of "cautionary tales" in the late twentieth century that exposed the simplicity of existing models of site formation (Ascher 1977; Bonnichsen 1973; Lange and Rydberg 1972; Longacre and Ayres 1968). That settlement abandonment plays a major role in the development of the archaeological record, and in the creation of primary archaeological data (Sabloff et al. 1987:203), has led to the recognition that understanding its effects must be a central goal of modern archaeology (e.g., Cameron and Tomka 1993; Inomata and Webb 2003a). In this chapter, the results of archaeological, actualistic, and historic studies are used to develop a general model of settlement abandonment behavior and material culture patterning. The basic concepts are taken from my earlier efforts to understand the development of prehistoric pottery assemblages at permanently occupied Maya settlements (Deal 1985, 1998), and they are shamelessly etic in nature (for a critique, see Martin and Russell 2000). The

original model was inspired by the writings of Michael B. Schiffer (1972, 1987) and Lewis R. Binford (1978, 1979) on site formation processes, and David L. Clarke (1973) and Marc G. Stevenson (1982) on site abandonment. My recent research has focused on the settlement and subsistence patterning of late prehistoric hunter-gatherers of the far Northeast (Deal 2002; Deal and Butt 2003).

A human settlement embodies a relationship with the landscape and reflects the technology and socioeconomic conditions of its builders (*sensu* Chang 1972:1–2). A settlement can vary in size from an overnight campsite to a sprawling city. Previous studies have indicated that the housesite (or household cluster) is the most effective unit for the study of settlement abandonment (e.g., Cameron 1991). Sanders (2003:195) even states that "The unit of abandonment is the household—the fundamental human social unit." Indeed, settlement abandonment could be viewed as the abandonment of many households, each acting independently. Even the social status of households can affect abandonment decisions (e.g., Inomata 2003; Levy 1992; Palka 2003).

The study of occupied and abandoned

housesites in the Maya region of Mexico suggests that abandonment can be viewed as a sequence of stages, beginning with behavioral processes that precondition a site for abandonment (pre-abandonment) and concluding with natural processes (post-abandonment) that further transform the material culture patterning caused by intentional abandonment (Deal 1985). In this sense, *abandonment patterning* is viewed as the disposition of material culture from specific processes operating during the life of a settlement that affect its ultimate dismantling and desertion. Individual patterns might represent the results of a specific disposal process, the effects of several processes on an individual structure, or the cumulative effects of abandonment processes on an entire settlement.

There has been some debate in the literature as to whether abandonment should be viewed as process or event. I argue that abandonment, like the concept of erosion, involves both process and event (Schiffer 2003:xi; see also Schiffer 1987:89). A process can be seen as a series of occurrences (events) that generate change. The American Geological Institute defines erosion as the "group of processes whereby earthy or rock material is loosened or dissolved and removed from any part of the earth's surface" (AGI 1976:148). The processes of erosion (i.e., weathering, solution, corrosion, and transportation) are each characterized by multiple events over a period of time. Likewise, abandonment is the group of processes (e.g., disposal, recycling, scavenging) that contributes to the archaeological composition of a dwelling or, ultimately, of a site. Most dwellings will follow a routine course of establishment, gradual abandonment, and post-abandonment, which largely operates apart from regional, social, economic, and political realities. Nelson and Schachner (2002: 171) differentiate between intrasite abandonment, which they admit may be idiosyncratic, and broadscale regional abandonment, which they characterize as "being embedded in social relationships" (see discussion below). Inomata and Webb (2003b:9) characterize this difference as the *micro* and *macro* scales of abandonment.

PRE-ABANDONMENT OF DWELLING SITES

The pre-abandonment (preconditioning) stage is characterized by various disposal processes (or "modes," according to Binford 1978:344) that are intimately connected with the internal arrangement of structures, facilities, and activity areas within a houselot (or campsite). These disposal processes include provisional discard, maintenance disposal, dumping, loss, and accidental breakage. Table 9.1 outlines the predicted variation in the refuse type, artifact condition, and feature association related to each of these disposal processes. Loss probably has a minimal impact on archaeological assemblages. In particular, large objects have a low loss potential (see Fehon and Scholtz 1978:271; Hildebrand 1978:277) and, conversely, a high rate of recovery. Breakage of items such as gardening tools and water carrying pots at activity areas will also have a minimal effect on the content variation of the archaeological record.

Provisional discard is represented by two distinctive strategies. The first strategy involves the isolated storage of material item fragments, often in difficult-to-get-at places, in anticipation of potential future repair and/ or reuse (e.g., Sullivan 1989). The second strategy involves the discrete storage, or caching, of damaged or partly damaged items. The placement of such items might occur along the outside walls of structures, in structures used for storage, or in abandoned structures (Figure 9.1). The basic difference between the two strategies is that the former is a less structured activity that features the storage of items singly, or in disordered association, rather than in tightly bounded clusters. The locations of singly stored items could soon be forgotten, whereas a cache represents a common household facility. Both forms of provisional discard have been recorded in ethnoarchaeological studies (e.g., Lindahl and Matenga 1995: 106; Reina and Hill 1978:247; Weigand 1969: 23). Hayden and Cannon (1983) have suggested that this kind of storage is related to the principle of least effort, because collecting refuse for periodic trips to dumping locations is much more efficient than making a trip to the

TABLE 9.1. Disposal processes in relation to refuse type, artifact condition, spatial patterning, and associations

	REFUSE TYPES	ARTIFACT CONDITION	SPATIAL PATTERNING (ASSOCIATED FEATURE)
Provisional Discard			
1. Single items	Secondary	Fragmented or damaged	Individual items (floors of structures)
2. Clusters of items	Secondary	Fragmented or damaged	Cluster (edge of building features)
Maintenance	Secondary	Fragmented (small size)	Cluster (work areas; drainage ditch)
Loss	de facto	Whole, fragmented, or damaged	Individual items or cluster (away from structures)
Accidental Breakage	Primary	Fragmented	Individual items (pathways, gardens)
Dumping			
1. Discrete	Secondary	Fragmented or damaged	Cluster (household toft)
2. Broadcast	Secondary	Fragmented or damaged	Individual items or cluster (household toft perimeter)
3. Tossing	Secondary	Fragmented or damaged	Individual items (toss zone)

Source: Adapted from South 1979:221.

FIGURE 9.1. Provisional discard of damaged pottery vessels and metate beside pathway of Chanal household, Chiapas.

FIGURE 9.2. Drainage ditches, such as this one at a household in Chanal, Chiapas, become artifact traps for materials carried by water from patios.

dump each time something is broken. Sommer (1990:52) makes a useful distinction among activity areas, provisional discard locations, and passive areas. Passive areas are spaces, such as sleeping areas and storage rooms, that are not normally involved in the production of refuse. Wendt (2005a) successfully used provisional discard patterning to infer structure location and layout at the Olmec site of El Remolino. He suggests that this approach may be useful in areas where building materials are scavenged for the fabrication of new structures (Wendt 2005b:464).

The immediate vicinity of a dwelling and its outbuildings is sometimes referred to as a *toft* (Lewis 1976:101). By definition, a toft includes any pathways and open spaces used for traffic and general outdoor activities associated with structures or campsites. It is the location of most activities associated with the dwelling and therefore is the principal area of domestic refuse disposal (Hurst 1971:116; Lewis 1976: 105). Toft disposal is characterized by dispersed (i.e., broadcast) refuse, sweepings accumulated along the edges of open spaces and pathways, small discrete dumping locations, and a "toss zone" (Binford 1978:345) toward its outer limits.

Maintenance disposal refers to efforts intended to keep living and working spaces clean. Places left uncleaned are likely to become artifact traps for small items (Green 1961a:91; Weigand 1969:26). Drainage ditches along structure walls also serve as artifact traps (Figure 9.2). The movement of animals, people, and rainwater can displace smaller items (that often originate initially from sweepings) into ditches, where they accumulate. Pits are often reused as dumping locations, or even refilled with refuse related to the excavation and use of the pit (see Green 1961b). If a structure was slowly being dismantled within an ongoing household, it might become a dumping location for large inorganic items, especially pottery (Deal 1985).

In all likelihood, the bulk of material items contributed to the archaeological record of sedentary communities is the direct result of the intentional dumping of refuse. This activity could involve discrete dumping locations, as well as areas of dispersed (or "broadcast") refuse. Dumping locations might include individual housesites, neighborhood or community dumps, and/or community streets. Hayden and Cannon (1983) have identified three general principles that are related to refuse disposal in terms of how refuse is sorted and where it is dumped: (1) economy of effort, (2) temporary retention of potentially reusable materials, and (3) hindrance minimization. For example, dangerous items, such as sharp lithic flakes or glass, are more likely to be deposited away from living spaces (Deal and Hayden 1987).

The vertical and, to some extent, horizontal dispersal of refuse in occupation areas is often attributed to trampling activity (e.g., Bradley and Fulford 1980; Hughs and Lampert 1977;

Nielsen 1991). Stockton (1973) has conducted experiments to determine the effects of trampling on artifact displacement, particularly how variation in surface composition affects the vertical movement of artifacts. In general, small artifacts are more likely to move downward in less compact deposits, such as sandy or loamy surfaces, whereas large objects tend to move upward. Pre-abandonment trampling is usually most intense in high traffic areas, such as house floors and pathways. Small items missed during the maintenance of these areas are likely to be kicked about and trampled into compacted surfaces. Vertical displacement of artifacts may vary seasonally, with little movement during dry seasons, when surfaces are hard, and maximum movement during the wet season, when the same surfaces are softer (Lindahl and Matenga 1995:103–104).

Another precondition to the abandonment of housesites in settlements is the reuse and renovation of individual structures (David 1971). Some structures are never completely abandoned, but are used for refuse disposal or are dismantled in order to recycle the materials in the construction of another building. During the occupation of a housesite, structures may change function as new ones are added. Alternatively, structures can retain their original function throughout their entire history and merely be renovated or rebuilt. An additional problem occurs in areas with wattle-and-daub or mud-brick structures because wall clay, which accumulates over former living floors, generally retains both the color and texture of the surrounding soil (McIntosh 1974, 1977). Also, the pits from which the clay is obtained become artifact traps and are occasionally used for refuse disposal.

Because a given structure or housesite may enter the abandonment stage at any moment, "an element of confusion" may be added to the interpretation of the archaeological situation if there has been a change in position, number, or function of structures within the compound (David 1971:123; also Stanislawski 1973:380). The size and number of structures may be in a constant state of flux because of changes in family size and economic position. Most importantly, as structures change func-

tion, there may be concomitant changes or re-orientation of activity and storage areas and dumping locations. Changes in structure location may disrupt artifact patterning in toft areas and will generally destroy artifact patterning from previous structure configurations resulting from provisional discard and loss. However, there may be little or no effect on pathway, maintenance, or dumping refuse patterning. Thus, except for possible remnants of the previous toft areas, refuse patterning should reflect the last use-configuration of structures.

ABANDONMENT OF DWELLING SITES

In a study of abandoned structures in historic mining camps, Stevenson (1982) discovered that the primary behavioral factors determining the nature of the material items (e.g., size, condition, value, location) left at a site include the rapidness of the departure and the anticipation of returning or not returning to the site at some future date. This observation allows us to treat abandonment in terms of several behavioral modes: *provisional abandonment*, involving gradual site abandonment with return anticipated; *planned abandonment*, involving gradual abandonment with return not anticipated; *temporary abandonment*, where abandonment is rapid and return anticipated; and *total abandonment*, where abandonment is rapid and return not anticipated. These behavioral modes have different effects on material cultural patterning during abandonment (Table 9.2).

Most dwellings are abandoned gradually for a number of reasons, such as improved social ranking of the family, increased wealth, or a death in the family (Figure 9.3). Decisions to abandon a group of related housesites in this way may be caused by village factionalism, religious disputes, conflicts over rights to resources or trade, health problems, or climatic degradation (e.g., Heizer 1962; Markman 1972:199; Stanislawski 1973). Studies of modern abandoned dwelling sites suggest that items of significant social or economic value, as well as items in a state of manufacture or in association with activity areas, are

TABLE 9.2. Probability of different types of material culture patterning at abandoned living sites

	PROVISIONAL ABANDONMENT	PLANNED ABANDONMENT	TEMPORARY ABANDONMENT	TOTAL ABANDONMENT
Artifacts in association with activity loci	Low	Low	Moderate	High
Artifacts in provisional discard	High	Moderate/High	High	High
Artifacts in de facto state (or due to death)	Low/Moderate	Low	Moderate/High	Moderate/High
Artifacts in manufacture	Low	Low	Moderate/High	Moderate/High
Artifacts in storage	Moderate	Low	Moderate/High	High
Artifacts of socioeconomic value	Low	Low	Moderate	Moderate

FIGURE 9.3. Recently abandoned housesite near Coapa, Chiapas. This is an isolated rural site where patio and pathway areas are intact and post-abandonment alterations are minimal.

not likely to be deserted (Lange and Rydberg 1972:430; Robbins 1973:212). However, expedient tools are more likely to be abandoned than more highly manufactured tools (Webb 1995:65, 1998). Furthermore, special purpose structures, such as kitchens, may have a higher likelihood of remaining intact than more general purpose structures, such as houses (Figure 9.4), which may be dismantled (Deal 1985; Joyce and Johannessen 1993).

In cases of provisional abandonment, there is a greater likelihood that usable items will be left at an abandoned housesite (e.g., Tomka 1993). It has been suggested that an orderly ar-

FIGURE 9.4. Abandoned and scavenged structure, Tusayan Ranger District, Kaibab National Forest, northern Arizona. Wooden hogans, such as this, were built and used, often seasonally, by individual Navajo households.

rangement of useful materials may reflect anticipated return to a provisionally abandoned site (Baker 1975). Caching of whole and functional items also implies anticipated return (e.g., Gould 1980:10; Stevenson 1982:253). A Maya practice resembling provisional abandonment—that is, the orderly leaving of a dwelling after a death in the family (also see Palka 2005:165-167)—can be traced back to at least the early Colonial period (Wauchope 1938:152). In such cases, a dwelling may be left virtually intact, but materials would eventually be scavenged.

In cases of planned abandonment, refuse that would normally be removed from living and working areas might be allowed to accumulate (Stevenson 1982:246). Larger items also might be given to relatives or sold if the new site is at any distance away or if the move takes place during a rainy season.

Instances of rapid abandonment are relatively rare and are generally associated with cases of the immediate threat of attack, an epidemic, or an impending natural disaster (e.g.,

earthquake, fire, or volcanic activity). In cases of fire or earthquake, some inhabitants might expect to return and rebuild at the same location. Friede and Steel (1980) suggest that rapid abandonment due to the burning of huts accounts for most occupation floors excavated in prehistoric African settlements.

Total abandonment is often associated with the destruction or rapid entombment of a site, as exemplified by the Classic Maya site of Cerén, El Salvador, which was buried by volcanic activity (Sheets 1992). Such sites create an ideal situation for archaeological interpretation because artifacts are left in association with activity and storage areas, which themselves are less likely to be affected by post-abandonment processes. Further, as a result of rapid abandonment, more complete and valuable items, which are normally removed, may be left behind. The effects of the two rapid abandonment modes are similar except that temporary abandonment may result in the removal of some items with social or economic value.

TABLE 9.3. Predicted effects of differential abandonment on pre-abandonment material culture patterning at sites of varying permanency

PERMANENCY TYPES	PROVISIONAL ABANDONMENT	PLANNED ABANDONMENT	TEMPORARY ABANDONMENT	TOTAL ABANDONMENT
Single event site			Low	Low
Single season site	Low	Moderate/high	Low	Low
Several season site	Low	Moderate/high	Moderate	Moderate
Many season site	Moderate	Moderate	Low/moderate	Low/moderate
Single year site	Moderate	High	Low	Low
Several year site	Moderate	High	Low	Low/moderate
Many year site	High	Moderate/high	Low	Low/moderate

Note: Permanency types adapted from Chang 1972:18.

ABANDONMENT OF ENTIRE SETTLEMENTS

When we consider the abandonment of entire communities, the major factor affecting the nature of abandonment processes and material culture patterning is the relative permanency of the settlement itself. Obviously, the longer a location has been occupied, the more complex its abandonment patterning will be. Not only will each activity area and household be differentially affected by abandonment processes, but the entire settlement will be affected in aggregate. Even if a permanent settlement were rapidly abandoned because of the spread of an epidemic, for example, many activity areas and structures would already have been gradually abandoned and altered due to post-abandonment processes. In other words, examples of both rapid and gradual abandonment patterning should be discernable within the same settlement. Kent's (1993) ethnoarchaeological research in Kutse, Botswana, for instance, suggests that "anticipated mobility" (or length of time a group plans to stay at a location) has a significant influence on the number of abandoned objects. She concludes that "the more mobile a group, the less material culture they carry and/or abandon" (Kent 1993:68). Saidel (2001) also reports low archaeological visibility for nomadic Bedouin tent camps. Shahack-Gross et al. (2004) have effectively used an exper-

imental geo-ethnoarchaeological approach at abandoned Maasai settlements to evaluate the visibility of ephemeral features. They found that they could distinguish certain cultural features (i.e., hearths, trash pits, and livestock gates) on such sites (and potentially also on similar prehistoric sites) using micromorphology (Goldberg, this volume), mineralogy, and phytolith analysis.

Table 9.3 presents some predictions regarding how variation in settlement permanency affects material culture patterning. Variation in settlement permanency is adapted from a typology by K. C. Chang (1972:18), who identified seven basic settlement types based on seasonality and/or length of occupation and the number of depositional units (components). The least permanent type is the single event, which Chang equates with an overnight camp. This type of site is the least affected by abandonment processes because there would have been little time to alter the landscape, develop facilities, and create disposal areas.

The next level of permanency is the seasonal site, which represents a single season of occupation. These are often specialized activity camps/structures, such as resource extraction camps (e.g., hunting, fishing, mining) or distant farm holdings; they may have specialized facilities and cached implements. It is unlikely that such sites would have much material culture of high social or economic value.

One would expect that under planned abandonment, all useful materials would be removed.

Chang's third settlement type is a seasonal settlement that is used repeatedly for several years. This pattern of occupation would allow for the more extensive development of buildings and facilities. Because the location would be occupied and abandoned each year, it would have many similarities to a permanent occupation, except for the seasonal nature of the toolkit and facilities. Planned abandonment would be the normal mode for such sites, and caching of site-specific tools would be expected.

Chang's Settlement Type 4 is the multiseason site, which is basically a seasonal site that is visited several times a year for many years (and presumably for at least one generation). Such sites are more likely to have semipermanent structures devoted to ritual and may include cemeteries. Some functional items, such as heirlooms and religious artifacts, may become grave goods in mortuary assemblages (e.g., Webb 1995:65). For example, Frankel and Webb (2001:125) note that a significant number of usable ceramic vessels (i.e., about 8 to 12 vessels per adult burial) were moved from domestic contexts to tombs at the Bronze Age Cypriot site of Marki. Conversely, Walker (1995:78) points out that archaeologists have been slow to recognize that religious objects are also utilitarian and, consequently, have use-lives and distinctive disposal patterns (i.e., ceremonial trash).

The last three of Chang's settlement types pertain to perennial occupations. Type 5 is a one-year occupation where a full range of annual activities would be expected but with minimal development of facilities or activity and disposal areas. Settlement Type 6 represents the continuous occupation of a location for several years and is similar to Type 7, the permanent settlement, except that the latter would be more deeply stratified. Nonetheless, Webb (1995:65) notes the difficulty of distinguishing room functions in long-occupied, contiguous structures associated with Types 6 and 7 because of the gradual depletion of artifact assemblages. Rapid abandonment would primarily involve the removal of valuable items.

POST-ABANDONMENT OF DWELLINGS AND SETTLEMENTS

Much of the disturbance of cultural remains that occurs after a settlement is abandoned can be attributed to natural processes such as soil erosion and the deterioration of perishable ecofacts (Wood and Johnson 1978). However, as Ascher (1977:237) points out, "there are also contributing human factors in the first stages of smearing [disturbance] and at every stage in its progression." These factors include several activities associated with the "open lot" stage experienced by many housesites in ongoing communities. This stage is characteristic of housesites that are left open to general public traffic and are thus accessible for various activities comparable to those conducted in vacant housing lots in our own towns and cities (see Wilk and Schiffer 1979). By comparison, abandoned lots that are not readily accessible, such as those that are fenced, are referred to here as "closed." Both open and closed lots are, of course, exposed to the same kinds of post-abandonment activities; however, one would expect those activities to be conducted with considerably less intensity in closed lots (Figure 9.5).

The most important post-abandonment process is scavenging, or the acquisition of usable materials from abandoned sites (Binford 1979; Schiffer 1987:89–91). Scavenging activities are generally associated with the early post-abandonment stage. Under normal, gradual abandonment conditions, a housesite would already be devoid of reusable items before becoming a vacant lot. Therefore, the intensity of scavenging at a given abandoned housesite is directly dependent upon the kinds and quantities of materials left during the abandonment process. Logically, there will be "better pickings" at rapidly abandoned housesites. Scavenging is also affected by the population flux of the community. The shorter the period of time during which the entire community is being abandoned, the lower the intensity level of scavenging. For example, one would not expect a great deal of scavenging

FIGURE 9.5. Exposed floor area of abandoned structure, Aquacatenango, Chiapas. Under normal gradual abandonment conditions, usable items and building materials are quickly scavenged from abandoned structures in open lots.

to have occurred when the entire population abandoned an Arab village en masse after their water supply was shut off (Nissen 1968). Scavenging is more intense in communities that are growing, maintaining a constant population level, or gradually being abandoned.

Observations at abandoned Maya housesites indicate that shortcutting is another important post-abandonment process. Once an abandoned houselot is accessible to the entire community, the probability that original pathways will be preserved decreases dramatically (Deal 1998:132ff). The use and preservation of such pathways are also affected by the nearness of the site to the community center, where the bulk of human traffic converges. New pathways are formed if they provide a speedier transect of the lot. After a short time it may be difficult to distinguish new shortcuts from the original pathways. Abandoned housesites in ongoing settlements are also popular play areas for children, especially if there are partially standing structures and material fragments about to serve as play equipment (also see Hammond and Hammond 1981).

Decisions concerning where to throw refuse within a compound are made in relation to the location of in-use facilities and activity areas (Dodd 1987), whereas in abandoned lots, decisions are more closely associated with pathways, fences, and structures that provide depressions or concealment of trash. Post-abandonment dumping along pathways could cause considerable distortion of the refuse patterning associated with the original compound occupation (Wilk and Schiffer 1979).

DISCUSSION

Michael B. Schiffer recently suggested that abandonment studies have gone through three stages (2003:xi–xii). The earliest, or Fundamental, stage (post-1970) demonstrated that abandonment processes have a significant effect on assemblage variability at archaeological sites, and defined a number of distinct abandonment modes and proximate factors affecting abandonment. The second, or Expansionist, stage acknowledged that rituals surrounding abandonment might also affect assemblage variability, and researchers began to explore abandonment patterning associated with different scales of societal complexity.

Currently, we are said to be experiencing an Explanatory stage, in which researchers are striving to explain the various abandonment scenarios identified in archaeological contexts (e.g., Inomata and Webb 2003a). For example, Hardy-Smith and Edwards (2004) use abandonment theory and disposal patterning to investigate the transition from mobile to sedentary settlement patterns in the Middle East. They demonstrate that Natufian sites share a set of abandonment characteristics that appear to be transitional between earlier and later periods. Although the sites they discuss have Neolithic style architecture, they also disclose Epipaleolithic disposal patterning that resembles the short-term refuse of mobile hunter-gatherers (Hardy-Smith and Edwards 2004:279). Similarly, Nelson and Schachner (2002) conceptualize abandonment as "movement" associated with a group's settlement strategy. They identify a number of "push" factors in the homeland—such as degrading environmental conditions, declining population health, and conflict—and "pull" factors in destination locales, such as a more productive environment, religious developments, and strong defenses, that affect broadscale abandonment (Nelson and Schachner 2002:172–177). They note that there is only one documented case of whole village abandonment in the Southwest, and that a far more common scenario involves fission of a community and movement to new locations (Nelson and Schachner 2002:179).

Equifinality is the notion that "different systemic processes can produce similar archaeological phenomena" (Sullivan 1995:181). This phenomenon has a definite bearing on abandonment theory. For example, Schiffer (2003: xii) suggests that ritual termination deposits can easily be misidentified as the remains of household inventories. Similarly, Aimers (2003) suggests that termination rituals at Maya sites, as well as post-abandonment rituals, could be confused with rapid abandonment. Hodder (2003:27) originally interpreted abandonment characteristics at Çatalhöyük

(i.e., scouring out of storage bins, filling in of ovens, cleaning floors, dismantling timbers, and filling in rooms) as evidence of ritual closure and cleansing, yet his modern informants considered them to be merely the reuse of construction materials by later occupants. Kent's (1993) work implies that sites left by mobile hunter-gatherers may have material culture patterning similar to that produced by rapid abandonment. Although ethnoarchaeological studies may help us interpret archaeological phenomena by illustrating cross-cultural variability in material culture patterning, and possibly through establishing prior probabilities when considering different hypotheses (see Salmon 1982), equifinality ultimately constrains us from interpreting the cultural past directly from the archaeological record (Enloe, this volume). It should be accepted as a caveat of archaeological inquiry.

CONCLUSIONS

Any interpretation of prehistoric dwelling or settlement abandonment must take into account certain preconditioning factors, including disposal practices, structure reuse and renovation, and the relative permanency of occupation. Ethnoarchaeological observations suggest that artifact clustering at archaeological sites may represent variation in refuse disposal rather than primary activity areas (e.g., Binford 1978:356; Murray 1980: 498; Wilson 1994). Such clustering may be attributable to disposal practices related to maintenance activities, which raise the visibility of work areas by concentrating refuse around these areas. One archaeological consequence of activities that occur in open work spaces around structures is a general size-sorting of discarded items, with larger items being tossed to the outer limits of the toft area. This characteristic may be useful for delimiting compound refuse areas.

Pre-abandonment refuse disposal occurs primarily around housesites, whereas post-abandonment dumping results in concentrations of refuse along fences and pathways. Similarly, reusable items may be scavenged after housesites are abandoned; thus, the frequency and condition of such artifacts may be

FIGURE 9.6. Church façade (*center*) indicates the location of an abandoned settlement in southern Chiapas, now converted to agricultural land.

useful for interpreting the conditions of site (or community) abandonment in terms of the speed of abandonment and anticipated return. For most sites, the effects of post-abandonment processes will subside after a few years. For example, Gorecki's (1985) excavation of abandoned agriculturalist sites in Papua New Guinea determined that abandoned sites were more or less stable after 15 years.

Complicating matters further, at large settlements one might find housesites reflecting varying conditions of abandonment, from households abandoned rapidly (e.g., due to fire) with relatively little post-abandonment activity to gradually abandoned housesites with a high degree of post-abandonment activity. Thus, entire settlements are likely to reflect the cumulative effects of abandonment and post-abandonment processes. Generally, the last structures in use prior to abandonment of a given compound will be the ones most intact in the archaeological record. Housesites that have been converted to gardens may be so obliterated as to escape detection during surface surveys, except as refuse scatters, while others may have suffered little from post-abandonment activities (Figure 9.6). For example, Snodgrass and Bintliff (1991:88–91)

discuss the vertical movement and horizontal dispersion (artifact "halos") of artifacts at both rural and urban archaeological sites in Greece, which they attribute to centuries of cultivation and pedoturbation events.

Unless abandonment of a housesite or settlement is rapid, all except the least valuable items are likely to be taken from the site and either transported to the new site, sold, or given to neighbors and relatives. Whatever survives to the abandonment stage may become exposed to further cultural and natural processes. The frequent scavenging of reusable materials and the use of the site for refuse disposal by other households probably have the most devastating effects on the final artifact assemblage of a housesite. Although the overlapping of such disposal patterns makes the analysis of depositional behavior somewhat difficult, it does not preclude it, and is an essential consideration when attempting to infer aspects of the cultural past from buried surfaces and artifact assemblages that were abandoned under a variety of different circumstances.

Cameron (2003:204) gives the current goals of abandonment studies as (1) determining the causes of abandonment (and especially the identification of regional variation), (2) linking abandonment to regional chronologies, (3) drawing lessons from catastrophic cases of abandonment, and (4) identifying site abandonment processes. The current study falls primarily into the latter category because it draws upon a wide range of archaeological and ethnoarchaeological information to develop a general (cross-cultural) model for the abandonment of dwellings and settlements. Models, by definition, attempt to simplify very complex situations, such as abandonment. The model proposed here attempts to consolidate some of the diverse conceptual elements from earlier abandonment studies and to make predictions for the effects of differential abandonment conditions on material culture patterning for dwelling sites and settlements. Further studies are needed to test these predictions in both systemic and archaeological contexts, such as recently abandoned sites. For example, Shahack-Gross et al. (2004) have demonstrated the value of vari-

ous geo-ethnoarchaeological methods for the investigation of abandonment characteristics in certain archaeological contexts, thus moving beyond a reliance on artifacts alone.

Many things about settlement abandonment practices are still poorly understood. Palka (2005:164) points out that people from some cultures, such as the Lacandon Maya, abandon their sites in ways that do not necessarily conform to Western interpretations. Recent studies also indicate that the role of ritual in abandonment practices and post-abandonment site use requires more attention, as does the variability in abandonment practices exhibited by households of different social and economic status (e.g., Nelson 2003; Palka 2003). Ultimately, actualistic studies (i.e., ethnoarchaeology and experimental studies) may be our best hope for gaining a basic understanding of the variability in disposal and abandonment practices (also see Sanders 2003:201), and for developing interpretive models of abandonment behavior.

ACKNOWLEDGMENTS

The information presented here on Maya household and settlement abandonment was collected as part of the Coxoh Ethnoarchaeological Project (1977), under the direction of Brian Hayden (Simon Fraser University). The original paper was prepared as part of a conference sponsored by the University of Utah Press. I would like to thank Alan Sullivan (editor) and Jim Skibo (series editor) for inviting me to contribute to this volume. I am also grateful for the comments and suggestions provided by two anonymous reviewers on the original manuscript.

REFERENCES CITED

AGI (American Geological Institute)
1976 *Dictionary of Geological Terms*. Anchor Press, New York.

Aimers, James J.
2003 Abandonment and Nonabandonment at Baking Pot, Belize. In *Archaeology of Settlement Abandonment in Middle America*, edited by Takeshi Inomata and Ronald W. Webb, pp. 149–160. University of Utah Press, Salt Lake City.

Ascher, Robert
1977 Time's Arrow and the Archaeology of a Contemporary Community. In *Settlement Experimental Archaeology*, edited by Daniel Ingersoll, John E. Yellen, and William MacDonald, pp. 228–240. Columbia University Press, New York.

Baker, Charles M.
1975 Site Abandonment and the Archaeological Record: An Empirical Case for Anticipated Return. *Proceedings of the Arkansas Academy of Science* 29:10–11.

Binford, Lewis R.
1978 Dimensional Analysis of Behaviour and Site Structure: Learning from an Eskimo Hunting Stand. *American Antiquity* 43:330–361.
1979 Organization and Formation Processes: Looking at Curate Technologies. *Journal of Anthropological Research* 35:255–273.

Bonnichsen, Robson
1973 Millie's Camp: An Experiment in Archaeology. *World Archaeology* 4:277–291.

Bradley, Richard, and Michael Fulford
1980 Sherd Size in the Analysis of Occupational Debris. *University of London, Institute of Archaeology, Bulletin* 17:85–94.

Cameron, Catherine M.
1991 Structure Abandonment in Villages. *Ad-*

vances in Archaeological Method and Theory, Vol. 3, edited by Michael B. Schiffer. University of Arizona Press, Tucson.

2003   A Consideration of Abandonment from beyond Middle America. In *The Archaeology of Settlement Abandonment in Middle America*, edited by Takeshi Inomata and Ronald W. Webb, pp. 203–210. University of Utah Press, Salt Lake City.

Cameron, Catherine M., and Steve A. Tomka

1993   *Abandonment of Settlements and Regions: Ethnoarchaeological and Archaeological Approaches*. Cambridge University Press, Cambridge.

Chang, Kwang-Chih

1972   *Settlement Patterns in Archaeology*. Addison-Wesley, Reading, Massachusetts.

Clarke, David L.

1973   Archaeology: The Loss of Innocence. *Antiquity* XLVII:6–18.

David, Nicholas

1971   The Fulani Compound and the Archaeologist. *World Archaeology* 3:111–131.

Deal, Michael

1985   Household Pottery Disposal in the Maya Highlands: An Ethnoarchaeological Interpretation. *Journal of Anthropological Archaeology* 4:243–291.

1998   *Pottery Ethnoarchaeology in the Central Maya Highlands*. University of Utah Press, Salt Lake City.

2002   Aboriginal Land and Resource Use in New Brunswick during the Late Prehistoric and Early Historic Period. In *Northeast Subsistence-Settlement Change A.D. 700–1300*, edited by John P. Hart and Christina B. Rieth, pp. 321–344. New York State Museum Bulletin 496. Albany.

Deal, Michael, and Aaron Butt

2003   The Great Want: Current Research in Beothuk Paleoethnobotany. In *Hunter-Gatherer Archaeobotany: Perspective from the Northern Temperate Zone*, edited by S. L. Mason and J. G. Hather, pp. 15–27. Institute of Archaeology, University College of London, UK.

Deal, Michael, and Brian Hayden

1987   The Persistence of Pre-Columbian Lithic Technology in the Form of Glassworking. In *Lithic Studies among the Contemporary Highland Maya*, edited by Brian Hayden, pp. 235–331. University of Arizona Press, Tucson.

Dodd, Walter A.

1987   Factors Conditioning the Placement of Fire-

Related Facilities and Refuse. Paper presented at the 52nd Annual Meeting of the Society for American Archaeology, Toronto.

Fehon, Jacqueline R., and Sandra C. Scholtz

1978   A Conceptual Framework for the Study of Artifact Loss. *American Antiquity* 43:271–273.

Frankel, David, and Jennifer M. Webb

2001   Population, Households, and Ceramic Consumption in a Prehistoric Cypriot Village. *Journal of Field Archaeology* 28:115–129.

Friede, H. M., and R. H. Steel

1980   Experimental Burning of Traditional Nguni Huts. *African Studies* 39:175–181.

Gorecki, Pawel

1985   Ethnoarchaeology: The Need for a Postmortem Enquiry. *World Archaeology* 17:175–191.

Gould, Richard A.

1980   *Living Archaeology*. Cambridge University Press, New York.

Green, H. J. M.

1961a   An Analysis of Archaeological Rubbish Deposits: Part Two. *Archaeological Newsletter* 7:91–93, 95.

1961b   An Analysis of Archaeological Rubbish Deposits: Part One. *Archaeological Newsletter* 7:51–54.

Hammond, Gawain, and Norman Hammond

1981   Child's Play: A Distorting Factor in Archaeological Distribution. *American Antiquity* 46:634–636.

Hardy-Smith, Tania, and Philip C. Edwards

2004   The Garbage Crisis in Prehistory: Artifact Discard Patterns at the Early Natufian Site of Wadi Hammeh 27 and the Origins of Household Refuse Disposal Strategies. *Journal of Anthropological Archaeology* 23:253–289.

Hayden, Brian, and Aubrey Cannon

1983   Where the Garbage Goes: Refuse Disposal in the Maya Highlands. *Journal of Anthropological Archaeology* 2:117–163.

Heizer, Robert F.

1962   Village Shifts and Tribal Spreads in California Prehistory. *The Masterkey* 36:60–67.

Hildebrand, John A.

1978   Pathways Revisited: A Quantitative Model of Discard. *American Antiquity* 43:274–279.

Hodder, Ian

2003   *Archaeology beyond Dialogue*. University of Utah Press, Salt Lake City.

Hughes, Philip J., and Ronald J. Lampert

1977   Occupational Disturbance and Types of

Archaeological Deposit. *Journal of Archaeological Science* 4:135–140.

Hurst, John G.
1971 A Review of Archaeological Research (to 1968). In *Deserted Medieval Villages,* edited by Maurice W. Beresford and John G. Hurst, pp. 76–144. Lutterworth Press, London.

Inomata, Takeshi
2003 War, Destruction, and Abandonment: The Fall of the Classic Maya Center of Aguacateca, Guatemala. In *Archaeology of Settlement Abandonment in Middle America,* edited by Takeshi Inomata and Ronald W. Webb, pp. 43–60. University of Utah Press, Salt Lake City.

Inomata, Takeshi, and Ronald W. Webb (editors)
2003a *The Archaeology of Settlement Abandonment in Middle America.* University of Utah Press, Salt Lake City.
2003b Archaeological Studies of Abandonment in Middle America. In *Archaeology of Settlement Abandonment in Middle America,* edited by Takeshi Inomata and Ronald W. Webb, pp. 1–10. University of Utah Press, Salt Lake City.

Joyce, Arthur A., and Sissel Johannessen
1993 Abandonment and the Production of Archaeological Visibility at Domestic Sites. In *Abandonment of Settlements and Regions: Ethnoarchaeological and Archaeological Approaches,* edited by Catherine M. Cameron and Steve A. Tomka, pp. 138–153. Cambridge University Press, Cambridge.

Kent, Susan
1993 Models of Abandonment and Material Culture Frequencies. In *Abandonment of Settlements and Regions: Ethnoarchaeological and Archaeological Approaches,* edited by Catherine M. Cameron and Steve A. Tomka, pp. 54–73. Cambridge University Press, Cambridge.

Lange, Frederick W., and Charles R. Rydberg
1972 Abandonment and Post-abandonment Behaviour at a Rural Central American House Site. *American Antiquity* 37:419–432.

Levy, Jerrold E.
1992 *Orayvi Revisited: Social Stratification in an "Egalitarian" Society.* School of American Research Press, Santa Fe.

Lewis, Kenneth E.
1976 *Camden: A Frontier Town.* University of South Carolina, Institute of Archaeology and Anthropology, Anthropological Series, No. 2. Columbia, South Carolina.

Lindahl, Anders, and Edward Matenga
1995 *Present and Past: Ceramics and Homesteads. An Ethnoarchaeological Project in the Buhera District, Zimbabwe.* Studies in African Archaeology 11. Department of Archaeology, Uppsala University, Uppsala.

Longacre, William A., and James E. Ayres
1968 Archaeological Lessons from an Apache Wickiup. In *New Perspectives in Archaeology,* edited by Sally R. Binford and Lewis R. Binford, pp. 151–159. Aldine, Chicago.

Markman, Sidney D.
1972 Pueblos de Espanoles and Pueblos de Indios in Colonial Central America. *International Congress of Americanists, Stuttgart-Munchen, 1968,* 4:189–199.

Martin, Louise, and Nerissa Russell
2000 Trashing Rubbish. In *Towards Reflexive Method in Archaeology: An Example at Çatalhöyük,* edited by Ian Hodder, pp. 57–69. British Institute of Archaeology at Ankara Monograph 28. McDonald Institute Monographs, Cambridge.

McIntosh, Roderick J.
1974 Archaeology and Mud Wall Decay in a West African Village. *World Archaeology* 6:154–171.
1977 The Excavation of Mud Structures: An Experiment from West Africa. *World Archaeology* 9:185–199.

McKee, Brian R., and Payson Sheets
2003 Volcanic Activity and Abandonment Processes: Ceren and the Zapotitan Valley of El Salvador. In *Settlement Abandonment in Middle America,* edited by Takeshi Inomata and Ronald W. Webb, pp. 61–74. University of Utah Press, Salt Lake City.

Murray, Priscilla
1980 Discard Locations: The Ethnographic Data. *American Antiquity* 45:490–502.

Nelson, Ben A.
2003 A Place of Continued Importance: The Abandonment of Epiclassic La Quemada. In *Settlement Abandonment in Middle America,* edited by Takeshi Inomata and Ronald W. Webb, pp. 77–90. University of Utah Press, Salt Lake City.

Nelson, Margaret C., and Gregson Schachner
2002 Understanding Abandonment in the North American Southwest. *Journal of Archaeological Research* 10:167–206.

Nielsen, Axel E.
1991 Trampling the Archaeological Record: An Experimental Study. *American Antiquity* 56:483–503.

Nissen, Hans J.
1968   Survey of an Abandoned Modern Village in Southern Iraq. *Sumer* 24:107–117.

Palka, Joel W.
2003   Social Status and Differential Abandonment Processes at the Classic Maya Center of Dos Pilas, Peten, Guatemala. In *Archaeology of Settlement Abandonment in Middle America*, edited by Takeshi Inomata and Ronald W. Webb, pp. 121–134. University of Utah Press, Salt Lake City.

2005   *Unconquered Lacandon Maya: Ethnohistory and Archaeology of Indigenous Culture Change*. University Press of Florida, Gainesville.

Reina, Ruben E., and Robert M. Hill II
1978   *The Traditional Pottery of Guatemala*. University of Texas Press, Austin.

Robbins, Lawrence H.
1973   Turkana Material Culture Viewed from an Archaeological Perspective. *World Archaeology* 5:209–214.

Sabloff, Jeremy A., Lewis R. Binford, and Patricia A. McAnany
1987   Understanding the Archaeological Record. *Antiquity* 61:203–209.

Saidel, Benjamin A.
2001   Abandoned Tent Camps in Southern Jordan. *Near Eastern Archaeology* 64:150–157.

Salmon, Merrilee H.
1982   *Philosophy and Archaeology*. Academic Press, New York.

Sanders, William T.
2003   Collapse and Abandonment in Middle America. In *The Archaeology of Settlement Abandonment in Middle America*, edited by Takeshi Inomata and Ronald W. Webb, pp. 193–202. University of Utah Press, Salt Lake City.

Schiffer, Michael B.
1972   Archaeological Context and Systemic Context. *American Antiquity* 37:156–165.

1987   *Formation Processes of the Archaeological Record*. University of New Mexico Press, Albuquerque.

2003   Foreword. In *The Archaeology of Settlement Abandonment in Middle America*, edited by Takeshi Inomata and Ronald W. Webb, pp. xi–xiii. University of Utah Press, Salt Lake City.

Shahack-Gross, Ruth, Fiona Marshall, Kathleen Ryan, and Steve Weiner
2004   Reconstruction of Spatial Organization in Abandoned Maasai Settlements: Implications for Site Structure in the Pastoral Neolithic of East Africa. *Journal of Archaeological Science* 31:1395–1411.

Sheets, Payson D.
1992   *The Ceren Site: A Prehistoric Village Buried by Volcanic Ash in Central America*. Harcourt Brace Jovanovich, Forth Worth.

Snodgrass, Anthony M., and John L. Bintliff
1991   Surveying Ancient Cities. *Scientific American* 264:88–93.

Sommer, Ulrike
1990   Dirt Theory, or Archaeological Sites seen as Rubbish Heaps. *Journal of Theoretical Archaeology* 1:47–60.

South, Stanley
1979   Historic Site Content, Structure, and Function. *American Antiquity* 44:213–237.

Stanislawski, Michael B.
1973   Ethnoarchaeology and Settlement Archaeology. *Ethnohistory* 20:375–393.

Stevenson, Marc G.
1982   Toward an Understanding of Site Abandonment Behaviour: Evidence from Historical Mining Camps in the Southwest Yukon. *Journal of Anthropological Archaeology* 1:237–265.

Stockton, Eugene D.
1973   Shaw's Creek Shelter: Human Displacement of Artifacts and Its Significance. *Mankind* 9:112–117.

Sullivan, Alan P., III
1989   The Technology of Ceramic Reuse: Formation Processes and Archaeological Evidence. *World Archaeology* 21:101–114.

1995   Behavioral Archaeology and the Interpretation of Archaeological Variability. In *Expanding Archaeology*, edited by James M. Skibo, William H. Walker, and Axel E. Nielsen, pp. 178–186. University of Utah Press, Salt Lake City.

Tomka, Steve A.
1993   Site Abandonment Behavior among Transhumant Agro-pastoralists: The Effects of Delayed Curation on Assemblage Composition. In *Abandonment of Settlements and Regions: Ethnoarchaeological and Archaeological Approaches*, edited by Catherine M. Cameron and Steve A. Tomka, pp. 11–24. Cambridge University Press, Cambridge.

Walker, William H.
1995   Ceremonial Trash? In *Expanding Archaeology*, edited by James M. Skibo, William H. Walker, and Axel E. Nielsen, pp. 67–79. University of Utah Press, Salt Lake City.

Wauchope, Robert

1938   *Modern Maya Houses: A Study of Their Archaeological Significance.* Carnegie Institution of Washington, Publication No. 502. Washington, D.C.

Webb, Jennifer M.

1995   Abandonment Processes and Curate/Discard Strategies at Marki-Alonia, Cyprus. *The Artifact* 18:64–70.

1998   Lithic Technology and Discard at Marki, Cyprus: Consumer Behavior and Site Formation in the Prehistoric Bronze Age. *Antiquity* 72:796–805.

Weigand, Phil C.

1969   *Modern Huichol Ceramics.* University Museum Mesoamerican Studies No. 3. Southern Illinois University, Carbondale.

Wendt, Carl J.

2005a Excavations at El Remoline: Household Archaeology in the San Lorenzo Olmec Region. *Journal of Field Archaeology* 30:163–180.

2005b Using Refuse Disposal Patterns to Infer Olmec Site Structure in the San Lorenzo Region, Veracruz, Mexico. *Latin American Antiquity* 16:449–466.

Wilk, Richard R., and Michael B. Schiffer

1979   The Archaeology of Vacant Lots in Tucson, Arizona. *American Antiquity* 44:530–536.

Wilson, Douglas C.

1994   Identification and Assessment of Secondary Refuse Aggregates. *Journal of Archaeological Method and Theory* 1:41–68.

Wood, W. Raymond, and Donald L. Johnson

1978   A Survey of Disturbance Processes in Archaeological Site Formation. In *Advances in Archaeological Method and Theory*, Vol. 1, edited by Michael B. Schiffer, pp. 315–381. Academic Press, New York.

List of Contributors

MICHAEL DEAL is a professor of anthropology and archaeology at the Memorial University of Newfoundland.

HAROLD L. DIBBLE is a professor of anthropology at the University of Pennsylvania and curator in the University Museum.

JAMES G. ENLOE is associate professor of anthropology at the University of Iowa.

PAUL GOLDBERG is a geologist and a professor in the Department of Archaeology at Boston University.

DAVID KILLICK is associate professor of anthropology, adjunct professor of materials science and engineering, and coordinator of the NSF/University of Arizona IGERT Program in Archaeological Sciences at the University of Arizona.

KENNETH L. KVAMME is a professor of anthropology and director of the ArcheoImaging Lab at the University of Arkansas.

JULIE K. STEIN is the director of the Burke Museum of Natural History and Culture, and a professor of anthropology at the University of Washington.

ALAN P. SULLIVAN III is a professor of anthropology at the University of Cincinnati.

Index

Page numbers in italics refer to figures or tables.

abandonment: goals of studies of, 152–53; and interpretation of preconditioning factors, 151–52; and pre-abandonment of dwelling sites, 142–45; and post-abandonment of dwellings and settlements, 149–50; role of in development of archaeological record, 141; and settlement patterns in Upper Basin of Grand Canyon, 11, 15, 17–18n3; stages in studies of, 150–51; and studies of dwelling sites, 145–47; and studies of entire settlements, 148–49; views of as process or event, 142

accelerator mass spectrometry (AMS), 42

Aché (Paraguay), 128

active technologies, in remote sensing, 65

actualistic experiments, in flintknapping, 92

additive deposits, and remote sensing, 76–77

aeolian processes, and damage to lithic artifacts, 96, 97

aerial remote sensing, 67

Aggregates Levy Sustainability Fund, 52

Aimers, James J., 151

Albert, Rosa-Maria, 29

Alexander, J., 113

Allison, John, 3

Alonso, Ana Maria, 62n8

altered deposits, and remote sensing, 76

American Antiquity (journal), 109–11

American Geological Institute, 142

Anghor Wat (Cambodia), 68

anomaly identification, and remote sensing, 66, 75

Anowitz, Lawrence M., 57

Antevs, Ernst, 55

anthropology: and comparison of archaeological science in Britain and U.S., 54–55; and future of archaeology, 58–60; and lithic studies, 85, 87, 101; and review of archaeological epistemology, 1–2; theory and methodology in archaeology and, 125–27. See also cultural anthropology; paleoanthropology; physical anthropology; social anthropology

Aquacatenango (Chiapas), 150

archaeological context, and systemic context, 8

archaeological horizons, and stratigraphic units, 28

Archaeological Institute of America, 58

archaeological phenomena: and concept of trace, 10, 16; and remote sensing, 76

archaeological sites, and remote sensing, 76

archaeology: comparison of state of archaeological science in U.S. and Britain, 40–62; and concepts for investigating cultural past, 2–3; and development of internal view of archaeological record, 7–17; and geoscientific data in interpretation of archaeological record, 24–36; historical foundations and interpretive potential of provenience in, 108–20; influence of anthropology on epistemology of, 1–2; and interpretation of lithic assemblages by non-anthropological approaches, 85–101; and remote sensing, 65–82; and settlement abandonment in archaeological record, 141–53; theory and method of in study of occupation surfaces, 125–37. See also behavioral archaeology; culture resource management; historic archaeology; marine archaeology; New Archaeology; Paleo-Indian archaeology; Paleolithic archaeology; processual archaeology

archaeomagnetic dating, 44–45

archaeometallurgy, 45

archaeometry, and use of term archaeological science, 62n1

Archaeometry (journal), 61

argon-argon dating, 45

Army City (Kansas), 69, 71

art history, and provenience, 108–109, 120n1

artifact(s), and remote sensing, 76, 79, 81. See also lithic studies

artifact orientation, and lithic analysis, 98–99, 100

Arts and Humanities Research Council (AHRC), 50, 51

Ascher, Robert, 7–8, 149

Ashmore, Wendy, 112, 114, 120

Aspinall, Arnold, 53

association, and pattern recognition, 73, 74, 75

INDEX

Sommer, Ulrike, 144
space, organization of as reflection of social organization, 128
Spaulding, Albert C., 88
spring polish, and lithic artifacts, 97
Stanford University, 62n11
Statistical Research, Inc., 56
Steel, R. H., 147
Stein, Julie K., 3, 121n2
Stern, Nicola, 116
Stevenson, Marc G., 141, 145
Steward, Julian H., 126
Stiner, Mary C., 116
Stockton, Eugene D., 145
storage, and pre-abandonment of dwelling sites, 142, 144. *See also* food storage
Stratigraphica Archaeologica (journal), 120n2
stratigraphy: and provenience, 114–15; and use of geological data in interpretation of archaeological record, 25, 28, 31. *See also* microstratigraphy
Strong, William D., 2
strontium isotopes, 42
Stuiver, Minze, 53
Sullivan, Alan P., III, 3, 151
surveying, and archaeological training, 31. *See also* remote sensing
Sylvester Manor (New York), 69, 71
synchronic acquisition, and food sharing practices, 128
systematics, and lithic typology, 88
systemic context, and archaeological context, 8
systemic repetition, and pattern recognition, 69, 71

Tainter, Joseph A., 10, 36
taphonomy, and lithic analysis, 95–96
Tautavel Cave (France), 129
taxonomy, and lithic typology, 88
Taylor, Walter W., 108, 113, 114
"technological organization," and lithic studies, 85
temporary abandonment, 145, *146*, *148*
tephrochronology, 43
terra rosa soil, 25, 29, *30*
textual model, of archaeological record, 8–9
theory: and archaeological interpretation of occupational surfaces, 127–28, 137; and methodology in archaeology, 126
thermoremanent magnetism, 78
Thomas, David Hurst, *112*
Thomas, Julian, 15
Tite, Michael, 53
Todd, Lawrence C., 129
toft, and refuse disposal, 144
total abandonment, 145, *146*, 147, *148*

trace, concept of in interpretation of archaeological record, 10, 16
trampling, and abandonment, 144–45
Turekian, Karl, 53
Tuross, Noreen, 55
Tylecote, Ronald, 54
Type II errors, 9
typological analysis, of lithic artifacts, 86, 87–89, 97

uniformitarianism, 9
United States, and state of archaeological science in Britain, 40–62
universities, and future of archaeology and anthropology in U.S., 60–61. *See also* institutions
University of Arizona, 44, 49, 51, 52, 55–56, 57, 62n7
University of Bradford, 40, 43, 53, 54
University of Bristol, 43
University of California, Berkeley, 46, 50
University of Missouri Research Reactor (MURR), 45, 49
University of Oxford, 40, 43, 53
University of Pennsylvania, 53–54, 56
University of Southampton, 51, 53
University of South Florida, 56
University of Wisconsin, Madison, 46, 49
Upper Basin Archaeological Research Project (UBARP), *12*
uranium-series dating, 45
urban archaeology, and provenience, 116–17, 120n2
use-wear, and lithic analysis, 90

van der Merwe, Nikolaas, 53, 55
VanPool, Christine S. and Todd L., 2
variability, trace-production contexts and degree of archaeological, 10
vertical orientation, of lithic artifacts, 98–99, *100*
Villa, Paola, 129
vulcanology, 43

Walker, William H., 149
water flow, and damage to lithic artifacts, 96–97, 99
weak-acid extraction, and ceramic provenance analysis, 46
Webb, Jennifer M., 142, 149
Webster, David, *112*
Weiner, Joseph, 53
Wenke, Robert J., *112*
Wendt, Carl J., 144
Wheeler, Mortimer, *113*, 116, 117
Whistling Elk Village (South Dakota), 68, *70*, *72*, *73*, *74*, *75*